BROTHERS & SISTERS:

How They Shape Our Lives

Also by Jane Mersky Leder

Dead Serious

BROTHERS & SISTERS:

How They Shape Our Lives

JANE MERSKY LEDER

St. Martin's Press   New York

Design by J. Dannecker

Library of Congress Cataloging-in-Publication Data

Leder, Jane Mersky.
   Brothers and sisters: how they shape our lives / Jane Mersky
Leder.
     p. cm.
   ISBN 0-312-06312-1
   1. Brothers and sisters. I. Title.
BF723.S43L43 1991
155.9′24—dc20   91-20035
                                       CIP

First Edition: December 1991

10 9 8 7 6 5 4 3 2 1

For Robin, John, Liz, and Mom and Dad

CONTENTS

ACKNOWLEDGMENTS

I am indebted to the handful of researchers who have made the stuff of sibling relationships their life's work, many of whom patiently and expertly answered my questions and encouraged me to carry on. I thank my agent, Berenice Hoffmann, for her wisdom and perseverance. And I thank Maureen Baron, my editor at St. Martin's, for knowing when to push me even further and when to say "It's great."

To the many brothers and sisters who trusted me enough to listen to their stories and to retell them, I am deeply grateful. You made me laugh and cry and stand in awe of the power of the sibling connection and how it shapes our lives across the life span.

And to my own siblings, Robin, John, and Liz. You are constants in my life: you are family.

FOREWORD

Starting with the jolt of her opening sentences, Jane Leder takes us on an eye-opening tour of the rich, confusing, and often painful world of siblings. Because sibling relationships are rarely talked about in any depth, most of us grope for words to describe our emotions; about brothers and sisters we are strangely inarticulate. I have never met a person who would not want to improve a stale or hurtful or confusing relationship with a sibling. This book repeatedly tells you that it's never too late to learn about ourselves or to close the gap between our brothers, sisters, and ourselves.

Jane Leder speaks with wisdom gleaned from her own attempts to better her relationships within her family, yet her voice is disciplined and informed by the best available knowledge and speculation of social scientists and clinicians. The result is a rich tapestry, allowing many possibilities for the reader to see his/her own life's sibling through a clearer lens.

As adults we are continually trying to understand why we are, how we are, and the way we are. Our siblings are important mirrors for identity, and Jane Leder has written in a way that provides such a mirror for anyone who wants to connect with personal experience. In this sense, I hope that this will do for the reader what Gail Sheehy's *Passages* did for our ability to understand ourselves at midlife.

Sibling relationships are life's longest-lasting family relationships. The sibling bond can be both mysterious and unconscious. *Brothers and Sisters* unveils the mystery and brings to awareness the feelings and forces that can help to make us more human, less ashamed, and more able to take advantage of the possibilities of being a brother or a sister.

Stephen P. Bank, Ph.D., A.B.P.P.
Adjunct Professor, Wesleyan University
Coauthor, *The Sibling Bond*
Codirector, Bank and Hiebel Family
and Child Associates

INTRODUCTION

I t was a hectic afternoon as I struggled to learn the ins and outs of my new job as writer/producer of educational filmstrips. Somewhere in the back of my mind, I remembered it was my brother Robin's thirtieth birthday. I'd call, I told myself, but later. My new job—the one that had monopolized three harried and nervous months—took priority over birthdays and everything else. My brother would understand.

I never had a chance to wish Robin a happy thirtieth. Sometime during the afternoon, while I worked and reworked a script on how to write expository paragraphs, Robin bought a hunting rifle, stuck the rifle in his mouth, and pulled the trigger. He died instantly.

And just as instantly, my world changed. There were suddenly just three siblings instead of four. Robin had been my closest sibling in age and in kindred spirit. His death left me with a sister six years younger and a brother four years younger, and sharing intimate feelings and experiences with them did not come easily, if at all. The pain of my brother's death did not bring the three of us closer together then, even in the face of our own mortality. Our childhood minds—the ones that reminded us of all the hurts, humiliations, and missed connections—kept interfering with our adult minds that longed to connect. Robin's casket was closed like the lines of communication between us.

It wasn't that we didn't want to console one another; we simply didn't know how. And with relatives and friends understandably focused on the grief of our parents, there was no one there to teach us. Unaccustomed to going to each other for solace and support, we each dealt with our grief independently, outside the family. I wrote a book about suicide, using the stories of complete strangers as a means to my own recovery. My sister turned inward and grappled with the nightmares and apparitions alone. And my brother pushed the family even further away, substituting instead a group of politically like-minded people who focused not on the ills of the individual but upon the ills of society at large. It would be years before we three surviving siblings would be able to talk with each other about Robin's death and how it had altered us forever.

I've never been one for loose ends. Maybe that's why I fooled myself into believing that with the publication of my book about suicide I'd put my brother's death (and all the other sibling stuff) behind me. The persistent dull ache of missing Robin—that was to be expected. But the gnawing need eleven years after his suicide to reopen the wound and look at the brother/sister bond across the life span, a bond that, until recently, has been ignored or relegated to a place of minor importance—now, that took me by surprise.

It's difficult to find anyone today who can't rattle off the issues with their parents—how their parents raised them, what they did right, what they did wrong, and the effect all this parenting (or lack of it) had on them. But talking about how brothers and sisters may have shaped our lives is, for many, new and sometimes unsettling territory. The ambiguity, ambivalence, and contradiction with which the sibling bond is hedged make it difficult to understand. This complexity and the emphasis our society has traditionally placed on hierarchical versus peer relationships are in part responsible for the sibling relationship having been put on the back burner. Yet eighty percent of Americans (and Europeans) have at least one sibling with whom they often spend more time during the formative childhood years than with their parents. The sibling relationship is potentially the longest lasting of any human relationship, outlasting those with our parents by twenty to thirty years. Even when we are old, seventy-nine percent of us have living brothers and sisters. Siblings are part of the daily life experience for most of us through adolescence and a continuing part of our world throughout life. How ironic, then, that laypeople more than family experts acknowledge the importance of such connections and that artists more than researchers have succeeded in capturing its essence.[1]

Ever since Freud and other psychotherapists labeled and focused on sibling rivalry, Western culture has tended to view the relationship as little more than one of struggle and controversy. We have no rituals that make, break, or celebrate the sibling bond. Yet we say that a close friend is "like a brother" or "like a sister." In religious organizations, fraternal orders, and the military, the titles "brother" and "sister" are used to connote solidarity and equality. When singing "America the Beautiful," we "crown our good in brotherhood." And when feminists rally, they chant: "Sisterhood is powerful." It's curious, if not downright confounding, that despite all these expressions of sister/brother relationships as being emotionally closer, more meaningful, and more enduring than other personal relationships, family experts have underemphasized them, instead concentrating their energies on parents and children and husbands and wives. It wasn't until 1955 that the modern field of psychotherapy began to acknowledge the full impact of the family on the development of the individual, although references to family influence were always present in the psychoanalytic literature. Once family therapy began to catch on, it was nearly another thirty years until the publication of *The Sibling Bond* (1982), a book that more fully explored the importance of the sibling relationship across the life span.[2] And only since 1982 have a handful of professionals begun to explore what one sociologist has called "the last unexplained adult relationship."[3]

When Stephen Bank and Michael Kahn, authors of *The Sibling Bond,* began their study of the emotional connections between brothers and sisters, they wrote that they felt as if they were "in a foreign country without a map." They had been taught and they believed that the sibling influence is fleeting, that parents principally determine our identity, and that, once we leave home, our spouses, children, and careers influence us more than any other factors until our death.[4] What they and other researchers have found, however, is profoundly different. Throughout our lives, siblings can be the only intimate connection that seems to last. Friends and neighbors may move away, former coworkers are often forgotten, marriages break up, but our brothers and sisters remain our brothers and sisters. As constants in our lives, siblings provide a reference against which to judge and measure ourselves. They knew us in a unique way during childhood and share a history that can bring understanding and a sense of perspective in adulthood. As we age, brothers and sisters serve as links to our past, helping us retrieve memories and validate our experiences. For many, the sibling bond, often diminished in importance after we are out of the house and involved in our own lives, gradually becomes more meaningful as we approach middle and late adulthood. Often, it is a crisis like the illness or death of a parent that brings brothers and sisters together again. And once reunited, many siblings choose to remain close, putting aside competition and other baggage from the past, rediscovering the values and strengths of family.

This is not to say, however, that all siblings cross bridges back into each others' lives. Those brothers and sisters who never bonded, who never needed one another in the first place, may not grow closer as they age. They may remain as distant and apart as members of a different family. The amount of accessibility during the formative years usually determines more than any other factor how close siblings are growing up and how close they remain or become during childhood. Siblings who are born many years apart, stepsiblings raised under very different emotional circumstances, and brothers and sisters whose parents were detached, even disdainful, may dismiss the sibling relationship as quite meaningless.[5]

Neat, tidy theories about birth order, gender, and age difference as predictors of how close siblings will be are usually no more accurate than the daily horoscope. Rather, these theories, as well as many others, must be considered collectively. There seems to be little doubt that brothers and sisters are "major players on the stage of human development."[6] The key is to determine when and how.

The alternate feelings of intimacy and distance—the spectrum of rivalry, ambivalence, and loyalty—make for the drama of the sibling relationship that has lured artists since the beginning of history. The popular interest in brothers and sisters has been the meat of biblical accounts, fables, fairy tales, plays, and novels. From Cain and Abel to Hansel and Gretel, the importance of the sibling relationship has captivated writers and their readers as they charted and explored the "grandest and meanest of human emotions."[7]

It is precisely this complexity that can confound and confuse. Unlike the parent/child bond or the relationship between spouses, there are no givens that help to predict the influence brothers and sisters have on one another. Because the "normal" sibling relationship is fluid, because each of us brings a unique genetic and environmental makeup to its configuration, professionals and the rest of us must fight the urge to find easy answers to all the questions about our own siblings and our children's—not an easy task for people constantly in search of just the right self-help book or movement to tell them all they'll ever need to know.

In a world of stress, insecurity, strife, and rapid change, the endurance of the sibling relationship can serve as an essential means of support and comfort. With more mothers working, many marriages ending in divorce, and most families shrinking in size, the sibling bond may be of even greater importance to baby boomers and subsequent generations. The traditional view that holds children responsible for taking care of elderly parents may be revamped to hold siblings more intimately involved in the care of one another as they grow old. Brothers and sisters may have to return to the siblings with whom they grew up for both emotional and practical support.

Everyone has a sibling story, even only children who covet a brother or sister or are tremendously curious about what it would be like to have one. Some of the stories strike a chord, while others read like science fiction. Yet against this backdrop of many colors and hues lies a human connection that when acknowledged, analyzed, and assimilated gives us a better understanding of ourselves and the choices we make in friendship, career, and love.

PROLOGUE

Brothers and sisters were a mystery to her.
There were Grace and Vera, speaking like
two mouths out of the same head, and
Wilfred and Albert without a thread of
connection between them.
          Alice Munro, "Visitors"

My brother Robin, the second born of four, was in
many ways our thread of connection. When he
died, the roles we three surviving siblings had
known and accepted were changed forever.

I had been Robin's loving, comforting, protective caretaker—his older sister/mommy. I had basked in the power,
influence, and adoration the mother mantle provided and
had grudgingly accepted my brother's developing independence. His suicide at age thirty, the end of his tentative
stabs at life, left me feeling sad, angry, guilty, and terribly
alone. I had lost a brother, a good friend, an ally, and my
sense of balance, no matter how precarious, within the
sibling constellation. I was still the oldest but no longer
needed in the same ways. I could not step back into my
role as caretaker because I'd never comfortably fulfilled
that role with either of my surviving siblings. And to carve
out a new, more meaningful niche in the midst of grieving

seemed a herculean task for which I was totally unequipped. Feeling adrift within a family that had temporarily lost its way, I swore off my older-sister duties as mother/trailblazer/ exemplar of perfect behavior and swore off my surviving brother and sister as well.

But I couldn't shake them, no matter how hard I tried. As siblings we were inextricably bound, even though our connections were loose and frayed. Times of celebration— marriages, birthdays, anniversaries—and times of crisis— illness and death—drew us back together again despite our discomfort. And each time we met, we discovered to our surprise and dismay how quickly the intensity of childhood feelings reappeared. Our former selves and old expectations still had the power to entrap us. No matter how old we got or how often we tried to show another face, reality was filtered through yesterday's memories.

Connections with my brother John were strained and uncomfortable. Although I had been able to recreate Robin in my own image (at least for a time), John had never accepted my attempts to mother and mold him. Perhaps I didn't go about my caretaking duties with the same enthusiasm the second time around. John's birth, only a year and six days after Robin's, changed the dynamics within my family before I'd fully accepted the fact that I was no longer an only child at the center of my parents' universe. My mother yearned for a large family, but she hadn't planned on getting pregnant with her third child while still nursing her second.

I hadn't planned on another sibling, let alone a brother who didn't fit into what could have been my burgeoning troupe of followers. His refusal to fall into line and his eventual march in an opposite direction deflated my sense of power and authority. John marched to a unique drummer, a voice from within that early on spoke up for his vision of fairness and equality in the family, in the family's interaction with others, and, ultimately, within society at large. I found myself, my friends, my goals always on the wrong side of his line of demarcation, a rigid line that separated good and bad, right and wrong. John's silent rejection successfully ousted me from my lofty position as confident and respected leader and created wounds that still fester from time to time. Friends who met me as a young adult were always surprised to learn that I had another brother.

Everyone knew I had a sister. Though six years separated us and diminished the number of friends and experiences we shared, Liz was my *only* sister, the other most like me of anyone in the world. One of our favorite pastimes had been to stand in front of a full-length mirror, naked, and to compare our bodies. Seeing that her hips were wider but my calves were bigger and that her waist was thicker but my behind was rounder established a sense of genetic justice and, at the same time, encouraged our separateness. Because self-definition often seems to proceed by deidentification, our preceived differences were exaggerated, our similiarities underplayed, and our parents divided between us. She was Daddy's girl; I was Mother's. She was the unconventional one; I followed a more well-traveled path. She was fair with blue eyes and blond hair like her daddy; I was darker with brown hair and brown eyes like my mother. My sister was both what I most wanted to be and what I was most happy *not* to be. I envied the warm, openly affectionate bond she shared with my father, a connection that to my way of thinking painfully underscored the fact that she was his favorite and that he loved her more. (That my sister secretly longed for the perceived closeness between my mother and me never crossed my mind.) Yet I never coveted my sister's position as the youngest. To stand at the end of the line behind three older siblings seemed even worse than to experience the distance between my father and me.

When I was twelve and on the brink of adolescence, my

sister was six. She wanted in on my life; I wanted her out. Our bedrooms were too close for comfort, across a very narrow hallway, and I expended a lot of energy slamming the door in her face. At a time when my main developmental task was to separate from my parents and siblings, my sister needed me to maintain the status quo. But I couldn't be bothered caring for a baby sister when more pressing issues like boyfriends, makeup, and hormones had to be reckoned with. Liz had a hard time accepting my attempts at self-sufficiency and the subsequent changes taking place in the family structure. She continued to push herself into my life, as I struggled to make it my own, and my frustration and her hurt forced us apart.

Over the years, we settled into a cordial but relatively superficial relationship. Sadly, neither of us had the emotional distance or the tools necessary to see and admit all that was complementary about us. In a very real sense, she grew up without me. I left for college when she was twelve and missed most of her important successes and failures. I became more like a cousin who visited from time to time. My sister and I grew up and we grew apart, not because we had so little to share but because we didn't take the time to find out all that connected us.

For their forty-fourth wedding anniversary, not quite eight years after Robin's suicide, my parents decided to take my brother, my sister, my husband, my son, and me (I am the only child who married) on a trip whose destination was to be a surprise. My mother was doing her best to bring her children together. She had already lost a son, and the possibility that her three surviving children would not be close was too much to bear. She and her two brothers had resolved their major differences as adults and continued to maintain a tight connection despite geographical distance. It was my mother's intention to encourage our coming together, and the mystery trip had become her vehicle.

Liz was the first to put my mother's clever clues together and guess that we were headed to the Galápagos Islands off the coast of Ecuador. We were all headed, that is, except for my brother John, who hadn't been feeling well for quite some time and who used his poor health and his professional commitments to avoid spending two concentrated weeks with the family. His unwillingness to join us didn't surprise me; in fact, I had serious reservations as well. I worried about my then eleven-year-old son spending two weeks with adults only. I worried about my husband spending two weeks with my family. But most of all, I dreaded having to confront the distance between my sister and me, even though I longed for the chance to build some meaningful connections between us.

And so began the awkward process of coming together, a process I bumbled through. There were no books to help explain the benefits of reestablishing a bond with my sister and how I might proceed. The journey would have to succeed or fail on intuition, guts, and the yet unexplored willingness of my sister to come along. Yet amid all the uncertainty lay one truth: I would have to take the risk of exploring our connection, with its joy and pain, protectiveness and bossiness, admiration and fear, because to have a sister again would reinforce my bond to family and restore a part of myself.

The family trip provided the obvious motivation for reconnecting with my sister. But underneath lay several other factors that would have led me on to admit the need sooner or later—the general mellowing with time and age, my approaching fortieth birthday, and the eight years since my brother's suicide. As I stood ready to start the second half of my life and to confront my own mortality, it was important to have my sister there to help me understand the past and prepare for the future. Since she knew me in special ways that no one else had, she could serve as both mirror and sounding board. The conflicts we had growing up—vying for parental attention and grappling with emerging needs that did not often coincide—no longer loomed as huge barriers to our understanding and mutual support. And in the years since my brother's death, my need for family and my desire to talk about what had happened and why overshadowed any feelings of blame or guilt. I felt sure that my relationship with my sister was elastic enough to make room for our differences and absorbent enough to take in and cherish our similarities.

I felt confident until the moment I got in the car and headed for my sister's farmhouse in another state. Liz had sounded open to my visit as we planned the weekend over the phone, but it would mark the first time we had been alone in years. Suddenly, I was racked with doubts. Would we have anything in common? Would we be able to talk freely about our feelings? Would we like each other as the women we had become? We were, on the surface, very different. I had a child from my first marriage and a "new" husband of three years; she had never married. I lived in the middle of a large city; she lived seven miles outside a tiny town. She craved solitude and space; I enjoyed the constant company of family and friends. *It will be worth it,* I muttered to myself as I crossed the state line.

I stopped the car in front of the locked gate that led up the dirt road to my sister's stone farmhouse. The latch was a maze of metal pieces crisscrossing in figure eights. I pushed, pulled, twisted, and yanked. Finally, the latch clicked.

My sister's house sat proudly overlooking a large vegetable and flower garden. I could see why she'd fallen in love with the place. I would tell her how much I liked it. Her yellow labrador ran to greet me. My sister was close behind, her jeans hugging a slim body.

"Let me see you," I said, turning her around. "You look wonderful."

"You don't look so bad yourself," she said as she picked up my bag and led me into the house.

If she was as nervous as I was, she didn't show it.

We went into the living room, where a huge wood-burning fireplace still smoked from the night before. The room was filled with country antiques and several pieces of furniture that looked familiar. I recognized a desk and a chair that had belonged to my grandmother.

"Weren't those Grandma's?" I asked.

"Right," she said. "From her house in Detroit."

"And I thought *I* was the traditional one."

"You are," she said with that girlish giggle of hers.

I couldn't help myself. I started laughing with her.

I had come to see whether my sister and I could be friends. We had never not liked one another; we just were not close. But we had grown up together under the same roof, and that had to count for something.

What helped Liz and me begin to establish a friendship was the fact that, as adults, we had each achieved a level of success and self-esteem. We felt good about ourselves as individuals outside the family, and that confidence allowed us to march back through the experiences of our past.

Don't get me wrong: Childhood insecurities continued to creep back into our relationship. I found myself comparing her body to mine and secretly not wanting her to lose another pound. And I held my breath when she talked about my dad. I will always believe that he loved her more and that I got shortchanged. However, from our reunion that weekend came the understanding that we were not responsible for how our parents treated us or for genetic differences. It wasn't my sister's fault that my dad was able to love her more. And it wasn't her fault that her legs were thinner than mine.

I also discovered that a sense of humor goes a long way

as adult brothers and sisters try to work things out between them. They can either take great offense at each other's accomplishments (particularly when these successes touch sensitive nerves) or they can see the pettiness in such jealousies and laugh at themselves. As Liz gave me a tour of her farmhouse, pointing out the ceilings she'd pulled, the fireplaces she'd opened, and the plaster walls she'd repaired, I kept thinking about how the prospect of doing anything to my house other than clean sent me into a tizzy. Here was my sister, Handywoman of the Year; I would rather pay someone to scrape paint or cut a board than do it myself. I could have resented my sister's obvious upper hand in this matter. Instead, I joked and invited her to visit me, suggesting that I could keep her real busy with a million repairs.

My sister lives in the middle of nowhere. Going to a restaurant in a shopping mall thirty minutes away is considered a hot time on a Saturday night. And that is what she had planned. The locale notwithstanding, I still had to put on some makeup.

"Why do you use that stuff?" she asked as I brushed dark brown mascara on my eyelashes.

"I like the way it makes me look."

"But you look just fine without it."

I didn't want to fight. Not after things had gone so well. "Thanks," I said.

"So why bother?"

I wanted to tell her she could use a little mascara herself. "It's not a bother."

"Okay," Liz said. "You have a right to wear the stuff. l just think it's a waste of time."

I finished with the mascara and stuffed it back into my cosmetic bag. I didn't bother with the lipstick.

Compromise, a sense of humor, and a strong sense of self are important tools to help brothers and sisters reconnect.

Years later, when researching this book, I discovered that I had done many things right as I crossed back into my sister's life. I met her on her own turf, far removed from parental influences, memories, and childhood roles so easily assumed when we go home. (Today, family therapists often suggest meeting on neutral territory.) I allowed my adult mind to take precedence over my child mind and the baggage it carried from the past. I also intuitively empowered my sister with respect for her way of life and, in so doing, put us on equal footing. The roles of firstborn and last born, of big sister and baby sister, were no longer meaningful. We were two adults who shared the extra blessing of being sisters.

The void I had only recently acknowledged filled with a joyful awareness that, as sisters, we were twice related—both within and outside the family. My sister was still Daddy's girl, comfortable with unbridled displays of affection. I was still Mother's daughter in my emotional reserve and my organizational and linguistic skills. But now, as adults, these legacies we carried with us from childhood complemented one another. The differences seemed a wondrous tool for learning and growth. We would compare notes, acknowledge our different paths, and enjoy the present. My sister is not just like me; she is *another* who started me on the journey to myself.[1] I see some traits in her that I want to claim as my own and some that I accept as different and distinctly hers. We are both flawed and cannot answer all of one another's needs. Yet the comfort of knowing that our relationship will survive despite the differences and imperfections—that our connection as sisters provides a more accurate picture of ourselves and a greater sense of worth—establishes a model for intimacy that guides us in all our close connections.

1

CLOSE ENCOUNTERS OF A
SPECIAL KIND

Thanksgiving one year taught me a lot about the strange things that can happen when adult brothers and sisters get together in the house where they grew up. The house was up for sale, and that made the holiday scene even crazier. My brother, my sister, and I were charged not only with readjusting to one another but also with helping my parents divide up the spoils of their nearly fifty years together—an unsettling task. "You don't know when you'll be back here," my mother said. "And I want to get this out of the way."

When my mother is on a mission, there is no stopping her. And there was no stopping Liz, John, and me from sliding back into our childhood roles as easily as successful dieters fit back into their old clothes.

The time had come to divide up my grandmother's china and the silverware with the pearl handles.

"I'm in the process of simplifying my life," my sister said.

"I don't need any of this. Besides, when would I ever use it?"

My mother glared at her.

I'd have to do something fast. Anything to keep the peace. "I'll take this set," I said, sliding spoons, knives, and forks over in front of me.

"Well, wait a minute," Liz said. "I might want those."

I wanted to punch her. "Just make up your mind. It really doesn't matter to me."

Where the hell was John? "Isn't John a part of this?" I asked.

"He's resting," my mother said.

"How convenient," I mumbled. Nothing had changed. John had bailed out like he always did, leaving us to juggle a ticklish situation.

Liz picked up two spoons. She was acting like a petulant little girl. Why couldn't she just choose the damn silverware and make things easier for all of us?

I stared out the floor-to-ceiling windows at the bare trees. They looked vulnerable, caught unprotected in the blustery November wind.

"I guess I'll take these," Liz said, picking a simple pattern.

"It's about time," I said, relieved.

The quickness with which all the "stuff" from childhood can reduce adult siblings to kids again underscores the strong and complex connections between brothers and sisters. We can enter a family gathering as confident adults and exit feeling as unsettled as we did during childhood. Our siblings push buttons that cast us in roles we felt sure we had let go of long ago—the baby, the peacekeeper, the caretaker, the avoider . . . It doesn't seem to matter how much time has elapsed or how far we've traveled. Our brothers and sisters bring us face to face with our former selves and remind us how intricately bound up we are in each other's lives.

Given the importance of the relationship between brothers and sisters—particularly adult siblings—why has it not been thoroughly studied? Has Freud's myopic version of the family drama, which minimized the significance of siblings, so blinded those in the mental health field that they could not consider the diversity of roles siblings play? Has personality development theory handcuffed us to the belief that our personalities are set in stone by the age of eighteen or twenty? Has the fact that until recently males have dominated the field of sibling research had an impact on methodology and theory? Bent on finding some answers, I questioned researchers, educators, and clinicians about why they felt the powerful connections between siblings have been underemphasized in a culture that presumably places great importance on family.

Some felt the answer lies in the overemphasis our society has placed on the parent/child relationship. Parents and children have different power sources, different areas of authority, different kinds of responses within the family. The relationship between siblings, on the other hand, is much more egalitarian; it is considered a relationship between peers. As such, scientists haven't seen as much differentiation between siblings as between parent and child and have consequently assumed the sibling relationship needn't be studied as fully or taken as seriously. "We've underemphasized peer relationships," said Stephen Bank, coauthor of *The Sibling Bond,* "and sibling relationships are part of that. Siblings are viewed as minor actors on the stage of humand development. If there were an opera, they would be there in the chorus, not as key players."[1]

Bank sees this lack of interest in brothers and sisters as a bias of both researchers (most of whom are firstborns or only children[2]) and of our culture, a culture that is very hard on parents. "We attribute a great deal to parental influence," he said in a phone interview. "There is a certain level of blame that occurs, since parents are seen as the originators of all good things in this culture and all bad things."

For Bank and others, such as Douglas Breunlin, Director of Training at the Institute for Juvenile Research in Chicago, most family therapy theory is based on the belief that things go wrong either because one generation has passed "crazy things" down to another generation or because parents aren't doing what they should to raise their children properly.

"The family," said Breunlin, "is usually centered on the pathology of the parents, the style of the parents, or the way the child is being caught up in marital conflict. Therapists often don't know how to involve siblings because they don't have a theory that says siblings are essential."[3]

We are not a society that pays much attention to siblings. As I mentioned in the introduction, there are no rituals to cement or sever the sibling bond. Although writers and artists have used the drama of sibling relations in their works from the Bible on, the typical American family raises its children to be individuals, who often compete for the spoils their parents have to offer. "We call that sibling rivalry," said Breunlin, "but I'm not sure that sibling rivalry would be nearly as bad if we didn't have the social structure that reduces the importance of siblings."

Other societies place a much higher value on brothers and sisters and the attachment between them. A study of child care in 186 societies has shown that forty percent of the infants were looked after by people other than their mothers, often by their siblings.[4] There are African societies in which the brother kinship is more important than parental kinship and where it is the brothers who make decisions about the family. "There exists a sense of loyalty between siblings in other societies," said Breunlin, "and a

4

determination to resolve differences . . . elements often missing among brothers and sisters in the United States."

Contemporary American society emphasizes individual achievement, not collaborative accomplishments. Children have their own bedrooms, their own television sets, their own telephones. When Breunlin suggested that, for the most part, parents are raising families that consist of a group of only children, I was intrigued. I hadn't considered how this emphasis on individualism gave brothers and sisters very few good reasons to interact. Yet as I thought about all the families I've observed, I realized how little time is spent by parents orchestrating activities in which their children work together. What ever happened to all those lemonade stands with siblings at the helm? Much more common is Johnny going off to soccer or karate practice and his sister being shuttled off to ballet or gymnastic lessons. There is, of course, the annual family vacation in which everyone piles into the station wagon or boards a plane. Despite good intentions, these once-a-year affairs too often deteriorate into Excedrin Plus headaches, with the kids at each other's throats and the parents at their wits' end. It's no wonder that this most sacred of American family traditions turns nightmarish. Kids aren't encouraged to spend long hours together in a spirit of cooperation and purpose during the rest of the year, so why should they be expected to do so this time?

If the interconnectedness between family members, siblings in particular, needs redefining, it can be argued that the women's rights movement has begun to help us to do just that. When I spoke with Karen Lewis, a counseling psychologist and coeditor of *Siblings in Therapy,* she pointed out that up until the publication of *Siblings: Love, Envy, and Understanding* by Judy Dunn and Carol Kendrick in 1982, males had dominated the field of sibling research.[5] And when most of these men studied brothers and sisters, they observed them in school or at a playground, not in the context of the home. "What information they got," said Lewis, "was often limited and lopsided."[6] I agreed, adding that this male perspective, colored by the more distant, competitive dynamics that mark the relationships between many brothers, distorted some of the "scientific" theories concerning siblings.

Sigmund Freud's theory of sibling rivalry is a case in point. A firstborn male, Freud produced a concept of brothers and sisters vying for parental attention that minimized the significance of the sibling experience and completely ignored the relationship between sisters. Subsequent theories were developed based on Freud, and very few people expanded the framework he established. The professional training and personal therapy of those in the mental health field were based on the same idea. "We started out with a half-open eye," said Lewis, "ignoring the role brothers and sisters play, and this limited view has been passed down over the generations. It's easier to ignore what we don't understand."

No doubt the complexity of the sibling relationship makes it difficult for both researchers and siblings to understand. A child may take many roles in interactions with siblings: friend, model, teacher, pest, caretaker, rival, and more. And it is likely that through the years a child will play a number of these roles, some of them simultaneously.

Not only are the dynamics of sibling interaction complex; so are the demands of sibling research design. A researcher must use adequate controls to determine which differences between siblings are due to their interaction and which are due to such variables as gender, birth order, age spacing, access, and a family's ethnic background.

Deborah Gold, assistant professor of medical sociology and Senior Fellow in the Center for Aging and Human Development at Duke University, knows only too well the complexity of such research. As she began her work with siblings in their old age, she talked with several researchers who had written one paper about siblings and quit. "They all said, 'You'll see why when you get into it.' I quickly learned that by the time you take into account the number of sibs, the gender of those sibs, the birth order of those sibs, the relationships of those sibs with their parents, you're controlling for so much that it makes it very difficult to analyze data. There is never going to be a Dr. Spock book for the sibling relationship."[7]

For Gold and other researchers interested in the sibling relationship across the life span the dominant literature on personality development has been of little help. "The studies," said psychologist Joel Milgram, "all theorized that major influences on development, changes, or modifications in one's personality occur between birth and late adolescence. Once you are an adult, you are an adult. The idea that something can happen to dramatically change a person later in life was almost unheard of until the 1960s, when a whole group of studies on men and women as adults appeared."[8]

Gail Sheehy's landmark best-seller *Passages* (first published in 1976) did for adults what Gesell and Spock had done for children. It detailed inner changes we all experience on the way to full adulthood. While not a book about siblings per se, *Passages* validated the now more readily accepted theory that things do happen to dramatically change a person's life after the age of eighteen or twenty. If we buy this concept of human development, we acknowledge the roles brothers and sisters continue to play throughout life, and we can more readily predict certain stages at which their influence may be stronger than at others.

The decade between ages thirty-five and forty-five, for example, provides us with the chance to rework the identities we defined for ourselves in the first half of life. This, says Sheehy, can create a "full-out authenticity crisis." But somewhere in the mid-forties, if we have confronted ourselves in the mid-life passage, a new level of stability is reached. This may result in forgiving our parents for their "sins," and reconnecting with brothers and sisters whose influence may have diminished or been downplayed over the years.

Still another understanding that can grow out of the "mid-life crisis" is that marriage cannot carry the burden of all our needs and wants. We start to understand the real benefits to be gained by developing rich relationships with other adults, including our siblings. Siblings share a common history yet a unique experience within the family. To find out what each sibling remembers and to put all the pieces together helps each of us know ourselves better and expands our understanding and appreciation for the brothers and sisters with whom we shared our childhood.

Divorce, shrinking family size, longer life spans, geographic mobility, employment of mothers, and various forms of parental insufficiency are placing brothers and sisters in a position of greater accessibility to one another and may be giving the sibling relationship even greater relevance.[9] "With increases in abandonment by parents, child abuse, divorce, and families being fragmented," said Michael Kahn in a phone interview, "kids are less likely to be able to know intrinsically and implicitly that they can always count on their parents. They can't. But human beings, needing to count on somebody or something, turn to whatever is close at hand. Very often, the sibling group is what's available. I think that is primarily why the sibling relationship is coming into focus now."[10]

Getting the sibling relationship into focus is no easy task. Professionals are being asked to dive into new territory, to put aside operative theories that have dominated their training and work and to consider different ways of looking at the family and the roles each member plays. Sisters and brothers are being asked to consider influences of relationships that have been traditionally underplayed or just plain ignored. We're more adept at talking about peers outside the family than about our peers within. Yet our quest for intimacy in an unsure world pulls us back to the family; the call of kin offers the promise of support and continuity. What we do along the way to keep those connections alive and meaningful or distant and painful will surely help us to understand and have an effect on who we are as individuals, partners, parents, and peers.

INTIMATE BONDS

Janis G. was born the third of six children and the first girl. The arrangement of two boys, then two girls, then two boys established three distinct sibling subgroups within her family: the "big boys," the "girls," and the "little boys." While each group had its own rules, history, and hierarchy, the close contact Janis and her siblings had every day as they waited for a turn in the bathroom, tried to get to the dinner table on time, and vied for parental attention shaped not only Janis as a young girl but Janis as the woman she's become.

"I really feel that I come from a very blessed situation," Janis told me as we sat in her museum office. "My mother and father tried to create a very strong sense of unity with their children that has marked each of us in different ways. Certainly where you come in the family means that you have a different experience and a different view of the family unit. But all of us share a very strong sense of family that is central to our worldview."

At the first girl, Janis's views and experience were unique and sometimes frustrating. "Being the first girl is tough. The standard is different. My father had very strict ideas about what girls could or could not do." Janis's brothers—the "big" boys—were allowed more freedom. They could stay out later and didn't have to battle to wear stockings and makeup or the rest of the "girl kinds of things." Such

9

hard-won rights came later for Janis than they did for many of her friends.

Did the double standard create animosity between Janis and her brothers? "I came to understand and accept that it was my father and his old-fashioned attitudes, not my brothers, who set the different rules. My brothers were empowered because of my father, and I eventually understood that."

Besides, the advantages of having two older brothers outweighed the disadvantages. The "big boys" provided Janis with a "wonderful feeling of being protected" and a group of male friends who were "really very interesting." "I loved to make these guys sandwiches. Whatever they wanted, I would do." And when she was old enough to travel in the same social set, Janis was always surprised to see her brothers taking on a protective air toward her. She'll never forget the times when fights broke out at parties and a brother "hightailed it in there to yank her out."

That "protective air" shaped Janis's expectations of the opposite gender. While she described herself as "very liberal in her thinking and independent in her approach," she admitted to falling back in a minute on looking for that kind of champion in her relationships with other men. "I still like for men to open doors and do things for me, and I know that comes from the values my father instilled in my brothers that was passed on to me."

Not surprisingly, the ideal of taking care of one's kin, a pattern passed down on both sides of Janis's family, prepared Janis to assume a caretaking role with her sister Samantha, not quite two years younger. Though they were known collectively as the "girls," the two sisters were very different from one another: Janis was the public one, much more social; Samantha was the private one, conservative, naive, and accident prone. "She was called 'Calamity Sam' at one point because she was always falling down or messing up something. I felt that I needed to take care of her. I was definitely the big sister. Even when she was in high school, I looked after her, checking out the guys who were checking her out, helping her put her outfits together." Janis tossed her head and chuckled. "God knows her color schemes were always different."

Sam didn't always take a backseat. Her musical talent blossomed early on. Janis described a wonderful two-month period when there were two baby grand pianos in the house. She and Sam played duets, each sister with her own baby grand. But then Sam passed Janis in skill, and Janis lost interest. "Her artistic talent was one of the things that I envied. And her intelligence. She was a much better student than I was. I know it was hard for her to be 'Janis's sister,' that she resented being compared to me, but fortunately she excelled in many areas of her own. Her resentment at being known as the sister of somebody else never drove a wedge between us. There were times when we each went our own way. But that was important. Sam could carve out her own space."

As an adult, each sister has carved a space that complements the other. The director of education at a large, metropolitan museum, Janis, who has not married, remains in the public eye; Sam is married and has four children. Janis recalled a four-hour phone conversation she and Sam had recently in which each sister yearned for the other's life.

Here she was wishing that she had my life because I have privacy and do things on my own without the responsibility of kids. And there I was miserable because she has four children and a husband and a nice little house. And at that moment, we wanted to change lives. I coveted those wonderful faces that wake you up and say "I love you, Mom," and she wanted my life because she could work and sleep and do whatever she wanted. I listened to her frustrations at trying to be an artist and a mother. And she listened to my disappointment at not having a family. Ours is a very

11

equitable, supportive relationship . . . a real source of comfort.

The adult relationships between Janis and her two older brothers, though not as close as Samantha and her, provided her with models of successful marriages and examples of how to cope with whatever life has to offer. Her oldest brother, though somewhat of a "loner" and "very private," has been happily married for many years. "His wife was very good for him, and that's all we can ask for, that he is happy in that relationship." Janis's number-two brother, a very "opinionated lawyer who tells everyone what to do," is married to a woman who can harness his energy and "help us know how he's feeling or why he's feeling a certain way and how to deal with it. None of us likes discord in the family. If there is discord between any two of us, it affects us all. It's important to find a way to connect."

The connection between Janis and the "little boys"—six and eight years younger—is, in many ways, an extension of their childhood relationships. Growing up, Janis was a caretaker for the boys, getting them dressed, taking them to school, and babysitting for them when she was older. "I felt a sense of responsibility, but I also thought they were real cute." Jasper, the older of the two, is an architect who has "done a lot of searching." "I play a supportive role, an encouraging role, a 'bring-him-up-on-the-stuff-he-should-have-done-better' role. But as adults, we share the same taste in music, art, and intellectual endeavors, which puts us at an equal place at the table." Like his older two brothers, Jasper is married, but his wife is, according to Janis, "the problem of the family." "His marriage hasn't diminished our relationship," said Janis, "but there's a frustration, a need for him to resolve that marriage because of the tension in the family. It makes me upset with him, but it hasn't changed the dynamics of our connection."

The very special connection Janis has with her "baby"

brother Stephen developed during childhood and has been strengthened as adults. "He was always special to me, even as a child. He was the one whose hair I really liked to brush, the one I really liked to get dressed. I watched for him as he grew up. It's not more love than I feel for my other brothers; it's just special." As the two "unmarrieds" in the family, Janis feels even more camaraderie with Stephen, who looks out for her in a certain way because he understands life as a single person. "As the youngest of four boys," said Janis, "he had a lot of inherited expectations. That was hard for him. But I think he came through it very well. He's been finding his own place and feeling very comfortable about that. He has become the anchor for my parents, taking care of their home and other properties. That position has given him a new respectability as the youngest son. He's a special person."

Janis's sibling experiences serve as good examples of how gender and closeness in age can affect the connections between brothers and sisters. As the first girl, she faced a different standard that caused its share of problems and forced her to work harder at getting what she wanted. Janis is convinced that the struggle as a child shaped the perseverance that has served her so well in the outside world. Her father's old-fashioned expectations of what a girl should or shouldn't do were fortunately balanced by love and a set of values that, in the long run, created unity, not dissension, among Janis and her siblings.

Growing up with two older brothers shaped Janis's expectations vis à vis men. Their protective and gentlemanly manner provided a sense of security and comfort that she has come to expect. Janis let all of her boyfriends know that she had two older brothers and claims that she was never mistreated because her brothers would have "killed any guy who tried to get away with something." Janis's brothers taught her what to expect from the opposite sex and their feelings about females. And while these expectations don't necessarily jibe with her self-described feminist views, she admits to easily falling back into the being-taken-care-of mode.

As reflected in myths and faily tales like "Snow White and Rose Red" (the tale of two sisters who are devoted to one another) and supported by scientific research, the gender of siblings may also affect the emotional bond between them. Relationships between sisters seem to be more intense and emotionally intimate than those between brothers or between brothers and sisters. Janis's close connection with her sister, deeper and more intense than the relationships with her brothers, reflects the influence of gender as well as the high number of life experiences they have shared.

Only twenty months apart, Janis and Samantha shared the same bedroom, attended the same schools at the same time, and had many friends in common. Such closeness between the two sisters increased the influence each had on the other. But as Janis recognized, this close contact had its disadvantages. Samantha often felt as if she were standing in her older sister's shadow, while Janis couldn't help comparing herself to her sister and feeling that she came up on the short end of the stick artistically and academically. Over the long haul, though, the differences between the two sisters gave them a sense of wholeness and helped them recognize the infinite possibilities in their own lives.

As Janis clearly pointed out, the role her parents played in "fostering a strong sense of unity" between her and her siblings helped mold the positive emotional bonds that have carried into adulthood. Not surprisingly, a majority of the siblings I interviewed, whether in their twenties or in their eighties, talked about their parents' role in either fostering cooperation and a sense of specialness among their children or in perpetuating hurtful comparisons and ineptitude when it came to solving problems and settling arguments. While Janis acknowleged the tough task her parents faced raising six children and keeping a balance between them, she gave them high marks for "making us all feel that we were loved and that there were no favorites." Working to change some of the dynamics within their own sibling groups and between them and their parents, Janis's mother and father "consciously tried to correct the problems of their childhoods." Janis's mother, who came from a family of thirteen children, remembered a lot of tension between her and her siblings, tension that she wanted her own six children to avoid. "My mother and my father helped each of us look at what were our good qualities," said Janis. "It was never a comparison, never a 'You should be more like so and so.'"

The significance of parents treating their children differently and the effects such treatment has on the siblings themselves are issues that are discussed again and again in the current literature on siblings. The value of equal treatment of siblings within the family, of nonintervention in sibling conflict, and of parents "distancing" themselves from the siblings' relationships have been shown to enhance the growth of positive sibling bonds and feelings of healthy cooperation within the family as a whole. When Janis said she'd been blessed, coming from such parents, she gave thanks for their unqualified love and astute parenting.

Adult siblings who were not blessed with such thoughtful parents will have to work harder at understanding that their childhood rivalries are left over from a struggle that was most likely not their fault. If they can see that, it will help them stop feeling guilty or blaming each other the way they did when they were children. Of course, talking to one another about such revelations is crucial. It is often wondrous how a few kind words ("I'm beginning to see that Mom's favoritism wasn't your fault," or "It must have been horrible to have the rest of us picking on you all the time") can go a long way in restoring positive feelings. If we adult siblings want to improve our relationships, parental blunders need to be discussed, forgiven, and put to rest.

BROKEN CONNECTIONS

The disturbing interview with seventy-one-year-old Estelle serves as a good example of how some siblings get stuck in old rifts and cannot "get together again."

Estelle W. and her seventy-three-year-old brother Robert live fifteen minutes apart, enjoy good health, and haven't seen or spoken to one another in over four years.

Their mother, a widow for many years, was an extremely capable woman who "ran everything for everyone." She was bright, active, and loved music and theater. In her late eighties, this martriarch of the family began to fail mentally. She started calling the police three or four times a week, convinced that someone was trying to break into her apartment. The police found nothing; her doctor diagnosed Alzheimer's disease. Robert refused to accept the diagnosis, certain that his mother was just a "little confused." Rather than put her in a home, he wanted Estelle to hire around-the-clock nursing care for her. Estelle said that was an impossibility. Her mother would have to live in a retirement home that provided medical supervision and care.

The retirement home Estelle found was three minutes from her house and not far from Robert's. But there were problems from the start. Their mother, who hated sick people and had never been ill a day in her life, became incontinent and physically abusive, bodily throwing people out of her room. Eventually, the director of the retirement home said she would have to leave, forcing Estelle to find another facility. Robert still felt that his mother should go back to her apartment. "My brother," said Estelle, "was the apple of my mother's eye. He was tall, slim, handsome, well-dressed—immaculate in every way. My mother was crazy about him. But he was very weak. He married a domineering, aggressive woman who continues to this day to control his life. Rose—that's his wife—claims that Robert didn't want to visit Mother in the retirement home because it was very unpleasant, and Robert couldn't take the unpleasantness." Estelle put her mother into a second home, this one attached to a hospital "in case anything happened," and Robert stopped calling. He and Estelle did not talk again until their mother died two-and-a-half years later.

"I called him up and begged him to meet me to help pick out the casket," Estelle said as she touched her well-coiffed hair.

I had never done anything like that. It was a horror to me. But he couldn't do it; it was too much for him to face. "Anything you do is fine with me," he said. "You do it on your own." We had the funeral, and he never came. A year later, we had the unveiling, and I called him again. He said, "Mother wasn't religious. If you want to do those things, you can do them on your own." And that was it. And there isn't a day that goes by that I don't think of him and ask, "How is he?" And I always think that tomorrow he'll say to hell with Rose and knock on my door and say, "Whether she likes it or not, I'm here to see you."

"His wife is jealous and envious, though economically well-off. She's so difficult to take and has driven everyone out of her life except my brother." I asked Estelle if her resentment was directed toward Rose or toward her brother.

Toward her . . . Robert and I had the chance to see a lot of each other before I put Mother in a home. We would meet for lunch and he would say, "Whatever you do, don't stop seeing me. I don't think I can live without you. I love

17

being with you whenever we can get together." I felt the same way. Whenever I would see him, it was as if we had never not been together. It was never difficult to get on a footing of closeness.

My brother's been unhappy all his married life. I know because he told me one time that the day after he got married he knew he'd made a mistake. And he said to me that he's been living with it all his life. He has come to me over the years and asked how he could get out of his marriage, if my husband knew a good lawyer. My older son even offered to have him live with him until he got things straightened out. But Rose holds the purse strings. And every time he has threatened to leave her, she puts something else in his name. He is weak and doesn't have the strength to leave her.

"At this point," Estelle said with tears streaming down her face, "I think too much has gone on for us to get together again. I think I would feel worse if I were rebuffed, if he told me to 'forget it.' And seeing a professional wouldn't help because of the tremendous influence his wife has over him. My only hope is that she'll fall out of the picture before it's too late.

"I think about him dying or getting sick all the time. We live in a senior citizens' complex where we had nine deaths this summer. And I say to my kids, 'Is Robert there? How's he doing?' I guess I would hear if anything happened."

Marker events, or concrete happenings in our lives, like the illness or death of a parent, often push brothers and sisters together to make important decisions about a parent's well-being and to confront emotion-laden issues such as wills, property, and one's own mortality. The way in which siblings respond in these charged times can cement a meaningful connection or rip them apart.

If the relationship between the siblings prior to a parent's illness or death has been close or compatible, chances are that the foundation of cooperation and support will help them as they face the difficult decisions together. If, on the other hand, the siblings have been distant or estranged, even the illness or death of a parent may not be compelling enough to pull them together. They may be unwilling to forget old rivalries and past problems or be unequipped to know how to reconnect.

The sad rift between Estelle and Robert that prevented them from supporting each other during their mother's illness and after her death appears to have had its roots in Robert's marriage to Rose many years before. It is not uncommon for a brother's or sister's marriage to significantly alter the dynamics between siblings. Early adulthood, the time in which many marriages occur, represents a rite of passage from the inner turmoils of late adolescence to the tasks of preparing for a lifework and forming intimate relationships outside of the family. Doing what we "should"—largely defined by family models, culture, and the prejudices of our peers—often instructs us to get married and settle down, to start our own family.[11] For some siblings, these moves toward independence dictate a move away from the close connections with brothers and sisters. For others, the insecurity and/or jealously of a sibling's spouse forces a wedge between them.

Apparently, such was the case with Robert's marriage to Rose. Envious of the intimate relationship between her husband and Estelle, Rose successfully controlled Robert's life, influencing him to sever most of his outside relationships. It might be argued that in marrying Rose, Robert substituted a controlling wife for a dominating mother.

Perhaps even sadder than the rift between Robert and Estelle is Estelle's inability to see any hope for them to "get together again." Fearful of being rebuffed by her brother and convinced that not even a therapist could break the influence Rose holds over Robert, Estelle's only hope for reconnecting is for Rose to die before her brother. The

19

job of maturity is to quiet old hurts and humiliations with the understanding that people can change. Yet Estelle, like a number of siblings, is frozen with anger, stuck in the past with no optimism for the future. Despite the daily pain of not having her brother in her life, she chooses to do nothing and to wait, hoping against hope that one of her children won't call with the news of Robert's illness or death.

For Estelle and Robert, there may never come a time when they will bury the hatchet and become friends again. For other adult siblings, however, there are things they can do to reestablish supportive lines of communication.

Karen S. and her younger sister, Sarah, are a good example. They had grown apart after each married and started a family. Even though they lived in the same city, they spent little time together. Then, for some reason—maybe it had to do with getting older and watching her children grow up; maybe it was her mother's bout with cancer—Karen wrote Sarah a letter. She tried to explain why she thought they had drifted apart, beginning with some childhood hurts. "You must have felt like a second fiddle," she wrote. "Mom, Dad, and I were so close and settled, and then you came along. Looking back, it couldn't have been easy for you." Karen wrote that she was anxious to see whether she and Sarah could rebuild their friendship. She admitted that putting their relationship together might not be easy but that she was more than willing to try. Finally, Karen invited her sister to meet her for a picnic lunch on a stretch of beach where they would be alone, unencumbered by the outside world.

Sometimes it takes one sibling reaching out to begin to break through what appeared to be a brick wall. Karen and Sarah are still in the process of getting unstuck. What has helped immensely has been both sisters' willingness to talk openly about their feelings and to try to see the other's perspective. "Now that some of our defenses are down," said Karen, "I'm beginning to enjoy my sister. In some ways, what we're doing must be like an estranged husband and wife trying to get back together. But with us, there's a history that goes all the way back. She is family; she's my sister."

SIBLINGS UNDER STRESS

David S., twenty-nine, is the middle child of three, sandwiched between a sister three years older and a sister three years younger. His older sister Jean has suffered from "some kind of mental illness" for the last fifteen years.

> Jean was in her senior year in high school and would come home and be very sad. Or having been disturbed at school, she would start crying and go to her room and remain there. She'd separate herself from the family, but in the evening she'd start blaming her lot in life on my parents. Normal teenagers rebel, but with her it would go to the extreme. It got to the point where she would become uncontrollably physical—yelling, kicking, screaming, biting, and clawing. Fights, hysterical tantrums, things like that. She was taken away to a state institution and hospitalized for two weeks, a month, six months. But she would always get better, or they couldn't keep her any longer, or they'd say there was nothing wrong with her. So she'd come back home, and things would start all over again and escalate until it became another crisis. She saw several doctors over the years, and the diagnosis was anything from paranoia to schizophrenia to behavior problems. We've never really known what is wrong with her, and that is very frustrating.

David described his family as "very close-knit" and his relationship with Jean was no exception. "As a child, she was always quiet and shy, with no friends. She was sort of the underdog, and I guess I was always sympathetic and sensitive to that. Jean could somehow sense that in me, and that's why our relationship had been close." When Jean became ill, David took control of the situation. He was the family "rescuer," the "savior," intent on maintaining some semblance of normalcy. "If something my mother loved was broken, I'd be the one to glue it back together. 'Let's cover up and pretend it didn't happen.' That was the message in my family."

David said the role of rescuer was so ingrained that he just took it in stride. "Ever since I was a child, I have been put into that role—rescuer, perfect child, the one who would make everything right. And all the time while this craziness was going on in my family, I was trying to maintain my grade point average to go on to college and become a doctor."

After two years in premed, David switched to theater. "I think that switch helped me open up more than the other members of my family." David completed both undergraduate and graduate degrees in theater, moving around the South doing small acting jobs, and ended up in Chicago to "start a serious acting career." But just about the time he moved to Chicago, he started going downhill emotionally. Acting began to frighten him, and he lost his confidence. "So my life has been on hold. And there's a strong message from my family that I've let them down, that I shouldn't have a life of my own but should stay home and take care of them. I'm always worried about what is going to happen to Jean and who's going to take care of her when my parents can't."

I really don't know what's going to happen. I don't know if Jean can hold a job to support herself. She's not incapacitated by the illness. She's been able to go through a vocational/technical program and get a degree in word processing. But she's very backward socially and doesn't know how to get along with people. She's very demanding and will throw a tantrum if things don't go her way. I hope that she will be able to do something to support herself. Maybe all she needs is some counseling. My parents are ignoring the issue, denying a potential problem. I have no idea what they plan to do in terms of finances. I know they don't have a lot of money. So when they go, I don't know if there will be a trust or something. I worry about what's going to happen.

How has Jean's illness affected David's relationship with his younger sister Susan? "I think we've grown closer." For the first time in years, David and Susan sat down and talked about themselves and their family. Susan now knows what's going on in David's life and the discoveries he's made since he joined the Sibling and Adult Children's Network, a part of the Alliance for the Mentally Ill. "It's ironic that as a nurse, Susan reaches out and helps others but finds it hard to help herself. She's had a hard stuggle with diabetes and feels that the family has ignored her, which it has. Things have revolved around Jean for so long. I told Susan that she has a right to attention and a right to make her own decisions, to lead her own life. My parents just gave her a ton of guilt when she told them she was taking a six-month nursing job in Hawaii. My dad told her, 'It's going to kill your mother.' I told Susan to be direct and say, 'I'm not doing this to hurt you. This is something I want to do for myself.' It was good for her to hear that from me, but I think it was hard to believe that it was true."

Jean's illness has had a "devastating" effect on David's social relationships. He described his social life, like his professional life, as "almost in a holding pattern." "I'm only beginning to realize that the message has been, 'You don't get married, you don't leave. You stay here and take care of the family.'" How does that tie in with his sister's illness? "Guilt—feeling terribly guilty that I'm going on with my life and she can't."

Amid the guilt of getting on with his life is the fear that, he, too, might become ill.

> That's part of the stigma of having an illness in your family. Only last week I went through a therapy session where I felt so ashamed. I felt that my family was the worst family in the world. And I was given an exercise by the therapist to go around the room and say, "I come from a crazy, mixed-up family, but I'm not crazy. I will not judge myself. I will take care of myself." It was a painful, painful experience for me.
>
> Right now, it's as if I don't have plans for the future. Partly it might be because Jean doesn't either. I guess at some point we all had dreams. I used to have very distinct dreams and goals about an acting career. But right now I'm not strong enough to make a decision and go after something. I'm still too tied in with what's going on at home to break the cycle and reclaim my life. I guess Jean and I are in the same boat.

Each year, millions of families like David's confront the emotional, physical, and financial upheavals caused by divorce, alcoholism, and a host of physical and mental disabilities. Most of these embroiled families include brothers and sisters, yet the relationships between the siblings—whether children still at home or adults living on their own—have been overlooked by mental health professionals and family members. The ramifications of having a disabled or ill sibling reverberate far beyond the confines of the parental home. As David's story so clearly illustrates, the "well" sibling is often forced to become the "rescuer" in the eyes of the parents (and her- or himself) and to somehow compensate for the "ill" sibling and the disruptions he or she causes. At the same time, the "ill" sibling also assumes a distinct identity, often an unhappy one. Such role assignments can follow siblings throughout their lives, unless they are fortunate enough to get professional help.

The part parents play in assigning and perpetuating contrasting roles among their children in both embroiled and "normal" families can amplify differences. In David's case, quite possibly because he was the only male, the parents labeled him the responsible caretaker. His older sister became the "crazy" child, and his younger sister the "martyr" who was supposed to suffer in silence. As is often the case with siblings who face a special set of stresses in their family lives, the stresses don't seem to manifest themselves in negative feelings or behavior toward one another. Instead their reactions seem to be more internalized. David talked of feeling a special closeness to both of his sisters but also of feeling anxious, fearful, and completely unfocused at this stage in his life.

A portion of David's anxiety (and the anxiety of many people with a disabled sibling) stems from the ever-looming possibility of having to take care of his sister once his parents are no longer able. As he approaches his thirtieth birthday, David feels restricted and out of sync with the choices he made in his twenties. Important inner aspects that were left out in his career and personal choices are begging to be taken into account. Although such issues become a rite of passage for most men and women in this age group, the stresses David feels are compounded by the problems of having a sister who is mentally ill. The work ahead of David involves great change, turmoil, and crisis as he tears up the life he spent most of his twenties putting together.

Reclaiming his own life will involve breaking some very strong patterns that have operated for generations in David's family. For a third-generation American of Italian ancestry, the emphasis on close family relationships and the importance of maintaining a veneer of closeness, even in the throes of disunity and his sister's illness, remain a persistent factor in David's family's expectations and behavior patterns.

In our family, there exists this way of being, a denial of the truth. For years, I've thought that that's the way things are with all families. Now I'm beginning to see that that isn't true. Both of my parents came from large families—nine children in one and eleven in the other. There was always this big family group. And there was a strong message that you don't go outside the family for anything. You stay inside, you keep family secrets, you don't seek outside help from anyone. I'm the first one in this family to seek therapy and I've had to go through a lot of shame and guilt about doing that.

The tricky part here is how to move away from this strong pattern of not going outside the family without completely disconnecting from parents and other relatives. Some siblings like David find it necessary to live far away from their parents and to visit only when they feel up to it. David has cut his Christmas visit down to only a week this year because he knows staying any longer will put pressures on him to fall back into the "old ways." "I'm worried about going there. Having worked through all the things I've worked through, it's going to be very hard for me to perpetuate the denial that exists there. I'll just take it moment by moment, and if the opportunity arises, I might have to say something."

Learning how to give clear statements about emotional issues without blaming or judging takes great skill. It takes practice and planning to be able to tell a family member how you *really* feel, particularly when you know your position will upset them. Clear "I" statements ("I feel burdened when I'm asked to take care of everything" or "It makes me feel guilty when you ask me not to leave") can break the silence and begin to clarify how you are feeling. If a parent (or other relative) begins to argue, it is wise not to get drawn back into the same old fights. Listen respectfully, and then make it clear that while your intention is not to hurt anyone, you have needs, too. Predictably, such an approach will cause anxiety, but the important thing is to stay on track and to not get drawn back into the familiar fray. You may find that you have to repeat yourself like a broken record, but your ability to say how you really feel in a noncombative manner will eventually pay off.

SIBLING LOSS

Harry was his sister Jenny L.'s hero. When the neighborhood boys tied her to her tricycle, Harry came home from school and rescued her. She always had the sense that he'd protect her, even in the face of things that "scared him to death." There are pictures in the family album of Harry trying to get between Jenny and a deer, despite the fact that Jenny had told her brother countless times that she loved animals and wasn't afraid.

"We were best buddies," said Jenny L., "all the way to the end." At age eight, Harry was diagnosed wtih leukemia. Despite nine months of remission halfway through his illness, he died two years and seven months later. Jenny was nine.

> I remember one day when he was feeling good just like old times, and we were roughhousing around and Harry said, "You know I'm going to die." And I said, "Don't be silly. Kids don't die." But as I said that, I knew it wasn't true. Nothing like that was ever said again, but I tucked it away in my mind. I don't remember thinking about it a lot until the end. My brother collapsed outside of church. My father put him in the car and took him to the hospital. That was the last time I saw my brother alive. My parents basically spent the next week in the hospital, leaving us with neighbors and relatives. I hated it! It wasn't normal. And on a Thursday night I can remember saying, "I'm sick of it! I'm just sick of it!" I prayed and asked God to take my brother.

When Jenny came home from school the next afternoon, her mother was there with tears in her eyes. "She put her arms around me and said, 'You're my oldest now.' I had a friend with me, and we just went on with our play. I didn't know how to talk about death, and nobody gave me any tools." Jenny's sudden "promotion" to oldest child was something she resented. She'd been given the job, she said, without the privileges and special, undivided attention the first child gets. "I am the eldest *living* child of my parents, but I never had those two years he had. I never had that undivided attention."

Jenny's confusing and sudden "promotion" was coupled with a complete lack of sympathy from others for her loss. Her parents, concerned with their own loss, basically put her and her two younger siblings in front of the television set. Her mother did walk around crying for a time, saying things like "We have to get on with it now" and "Oh, dear, I'm setting an extra plate at the table." Otherwise, life for Jenny and her family was very matter-of-fact.

Death wasn't something to be talked about. And nobody seemed to recognize the fact that I'd lost a brother. Everybody recognized the fact that my parents had lost a son, but nobody came to me and said, "I know you're hurting because your brother is gone. I'm so sorry." When I returned to school two days after the funeral with a note explaining my absence, I handed my teacher the note and she said, "I don't need that. I know what's happened." She never said another word to me. And I didn't discuss it with my two younger siblings. My sister was too young, and my brother who was five didn't want to talk. I guess I got the feeling that it was a taboo subject.

The feeling that she couldn't talk about Harry's death taught Jenny to suppress any sad, unhappy emotions and to always be in control. "I don't cry in front of other people," she said. "People think I don't get emotional, but they don't see what goes on behind closed doors."

Jenny described herself as a "bossy" and "aggressive" adolescent. She had a hard time getting along with anyone and pushed people around verbally and physically.

> I look back and wonder if I had this sense that I couldn't trust people to be there for me. My brother had been very important to me, and he was gone. Nobody recognized that I began having great difficulty maintaining friendships with my girlfriends around that time. The safest thing was to keep people at arm's length, never let them get close, never open up completely. And I still find myself thinking that way at age thirty-three. I have to constantly remind myself that it's okay. It's not going to cost me.

The high cost of not being allowed to grieve for her brother, of having to hide all the sadness and pain and anger and guilt, continues to take its toll. "I've discovered so much anger and guilt deep down inside me that's been there for all these years. I believed that I'd caused my brother's death by wishing him dead, and that guilt hampered me from grieving for a long time. And I've operated on the idea that nobody likes you if you're sad or unhappy. So I just pushed those emotions inside. Sitting on those kinds of feelings is exhausting."

The death of a brother or a sister will set off a host of feelings, many of them conflicting, some of them seemingly inappropriate, no matter if the survivor is six or sixty-six. The pain of surviving siblings speaks of the intense connections between siblings and the many ways in which they shape each other's lives. Yet despite the intensity of feelings, what is striking is the degree to which grieving siblings fail to share their reactions with others. This may be due, in part, to our culture's discomfort in talking about death and, in part, to the general view that the death of a sibling can't compare to the death of a child. It is expected that children outlive their parents. When they do not, it is understandable that parents are devastated. Also understandable, but only recently acknowledged, is that siblings are often devastated too.

The failure of families to talk together about death is not unusual. An unfortunate result of this lack of communication is to further a sibling's sense of isolation and to underscore the message that surviving siblings have not experienced a significant loss. Almost twenty-five years after her brother's death, Jenny is still learning what to do with the feelings she sat on for so long. The process is a slow one. "I'm learning how to let go," she said, "but it's new for me. No one taught me that I don't have to close doors in order to be myself."

When a sibling dies, part of our connection to family, to the past and to the future is changed, sometimes dramatically. We need to talk about these changes. We need to educate family, friends, and therapists about the importance of recognizing our grief and of giving us permission to mourn for as long as we need. And, if it might be helpful, surviving siblings ought to find a group that addresses the special issues related to the death of a brother or a sister. The alternative to not taking these measures is to condemn many adults to lives plagued by guilt, sadness, and overwhelming loneliness.

2

FROM SIBLING RIVALRY
TO SIBLING GENETICS:
THEORIES THEN AND NOW

iecing together the dynamics of human relationships
and personalities demands that we take a look at a
long list of factors and how each one affects the others. The way sisters and brothers interconnect is no exception. To say that siblings are close simply because they don't
fight would be as nearsighted as concluding that the oldest
child will automatically be responsible and the youngest a
follower. Such simplistic assumptions obscure the complexity of human bonding and the interplay between heredity and environment. Nonetheless, narrow theories like
Freud's theory of sibling rivalry and Toman's birth order
"portraits" continue to dog both professional and popular
literature as the two most compelling factors in determining
how siblings develop.

A CASE IN POINT

The enormous success of the book *Siblings Without Rivalry* (Faber and Mazlish, 1987), a guide for parents on helping children live together, underscores how many of today's parents believe in the concept of sibling rivalry and how inept they feel handling it.

> The more we talked to parents about what went on between their chidren, the more we were reminded of the dynamics that produced such high levels of stress in their homes. Take two kids in competition for their parents' love and attention. Add to that the envy that one child feels for the accomplishments of the other, the resentment each child feels for the privileges of the other, the personal frustrations that they don't dare let out on anyone else *but* a brother or a sister, and it's not hard to understand why in families across the land, the sibling relationship contains enough emotional dynamite to set off rounds of daily explosions.[1]

It would seem, then, that "daily explosions" between brothers and sisters threaten the sanity, safety, and well-being of American families "across the land." Are there no siblings left who spend more time being happy together than not? Has our obsession to be perfect parents who raise perfect children colored our ability to see what's good and "right" about the children living under our roofs? All young mammals have their differences. Young chimps and wolf cubs, for example, scratch, pull, poke, and roll around. Are they vying for parental attention or trying to get a reaction from one another? Aggression toward one another (not toward their parents) is common among young chimps and wolf cubs, and it is common among young children. To label this behavior sibling rivalry is to demean the role parents play in raising their children, to ignore genetically based differences between the children, and to deny the numerous other influences that mold each sibling and the connections between them.

WHO SAID SIBLING RIVALRY IS INEVITABLE, ANYWAY?

Sigmund Freud, of course. Freud was the oldest sibling, and he understood only too well how it felt suddenly to share what had been his mother's undivided love. His "dethronement," as it were, and the emotional distance between him and his sisters fueled his later detailing of the sibling relationship as hurtful, competitive, and often defined by underlying rage. In addition to the five younger sisters, and his brother Alexander, who was ten years younger, there had been an older and a younger brother, both of whom died in infancy.

In fact, according to Freud, his rage was initially directed toward the younger brother, Julius. Freud, who was only ten months old when Julius was born, viewed this baby brother as an unwanted intruder who stirred up all kinds of "murderous" thoughts. Then Julius's death only nine months later, Freud felt, aroused in him a tendency toward self-reproach that plagued him throughout his life.[2]

To add insult to injury, Sigmund was in the throes of what he later determined was a dominating, tyrannical siblike relationship with the son of his older half-brother, John. A year older than Sigmund, John's "very bad" treatment of Sigmund helped determine his later feelings "in intercourse with persons his own age." So there was Sigmund having to deal with both the tyranny of this siblike nephew and the sudden death of his brother Julius, a death for which he felt somehow responsible.

Then along came five sisters: Anna, Rosa, Marie, Adolfini, and Paula. In her memoir, "My Brother Sigmund Freud," Anna described her brother Sigmund as favored

33

by their parents and removed from his sisters. "No matter how crowded our quarters," Anna wrote, "Sigmund always had a room to himself. . . .When I was eight years old, my mother, who was musical, wanted me to study the piano and I began practicing by the hour. Though Sigmund's room was not near the piano, the sound disturbed him. He appealed to my mother to remove the piano if she did not wish him to leave the home altogether. The piano disappeared and with it all opportunities for his sisters to become musicians."[3]

As the firstborn male and a genius to boot, Sigmund was treated with respect and deference. His sisters learned very early to look up to him and to stay out of his way. From all accounts, Sigmund dominated his sisters, seeing himself as better and separate—feelings abetted by a weak father and a mother who adored him.

Despite the emotional distance between Freud and his five sisters, his relationship with his brother Alexander was, by all accounts, a close but unequal one. Ten years younger than Freud, Alexander idolized his older brother. Because Alexander posed "no real challenges to [Sigmund's] authority" and was willing to follow orders without question, the alliance between the two lasted throughout their lives.

Jealous rivalry for parental love and attention dominated Freud's evaluation of the sibling relationship. He emphasized intensity and ruthlessness of the child's hostility to his siblings. And though Freud saw this emnity possibly overshadowed by a more affectionate attitude as siblings matured, he believed the rivalry persisted, revealing its continuation in dreams.[4] Freud postulated that children can much more easily allow themselves to hate a sibling than hate a parent on whom they are completely dependent. He saw that expressing negative feelings toward one's siblings was treated matter-of-factly by most parents and thus concluded that children make little attempt to hide or disguise the hostility that dominates their relationships with their brothers and sisters.[5]

Created from a male perspective and filtered through the lens of a favored firstborn, Freud's concept of sibling rivalry minimized the significance of the sibling experience and completely ignored the relationship between sisters. Freud never tried to understand the relationship among his five sisters, between his wife and her sister, or among his own three daughters.[6]

It's no secret that Freud's sibling experience influenced not only his theory of sibling rivalry but the way he dealt with peers outside the family. According to Ernest Jones, Freud's biographer, Freud had to dominate any relationship with those who were intellectually his equal. His struggles with fellow psychoanalysts Adler and Jung, his domination of Victor Tausk, and his refusal to compromise intellectually or socially in his role as leader of the psychoanalytic movement "make more sense as sibling dynamics than as the simple result of his relationship with his parents."[7] That Freud's psychological development was so obviously colored by his sibling experience forces us to question the soundness of his theory that diminishes the influence of siblings and considers the influence of parents on the development of their children as all-pervasive.

BIRTH ORDER

How many times have you commented about a personal problem or a personality trait and had someone ask, "Are you the oldest child? The middle child? Or the youngest?" The assumption that our birth order molds our emotions and personality both in our family of origin and with our future spouse and children has become as acceptable as the assumption that only children are spoiled, precocious, and social loners. An oldest child is expected to be overresponsible, conscientious, and parental, while the youngest child is more likely to be childlike and carefree, accustomed to having others take care of his/her needs. Middle children frequently have to struggle for a role in the family, caught between the trailblazer and the baby.

Birth order, contend its supporters, also predicts our "best" marriage partners. Those who marry someone in the same sibling position (an oldest marrying an oldest, for example) are predicted to have more trouble adjusting to marriage, while couples who come from complementary sibling positions (an oldest marrying a youngest, perhaps) will have an easier time, all things being equal. As the birth order theory goes, when two oldest children marry each other, they will compete for power in the relationship. And if two youngest children marry each other, they will both want to be taken care of.

Viennese-born Walter Toman first published his birth order theories in a book titled *Family Constellations: Its Effects on Personality and Social Behavior* (1961). Since then, the controversy over whether birth order, more than any other factor, influences our personality and shapes the course of our relationships outside the family has raged among researchers and practitioners alike.

Based on the assumption that a person's family represents the most influential context of his or her life and exerts "its influence more regularly, more exclusively, and earlier . . . than do any other life contexts," Toman postulates that sibling position is basic in determining a person's social behavior, preferences, interests, and attitudes.[8] These behavior characteristics and preferences, writes Toman, may not appear on the surface or may even be a mystery to the individual. But others recognize them and respond to them instinctively and often unconsciously.

In presenting his "portraits" of siblings based on birth order and gender, Toman details eight basic positions: old-

36

est brother of brothers, youngest brother of brothers, oldest brother of sisters, youngest brother of sisters, oldest sister of sisters, youngest sister of sisters, oldest sister of brothers, and youngest sister of brothers. In addition, Toman devises a "portrait" of the male only child and of the female only child. The members of any sibling group of three or more, Toman suggests, should use all of the "portraits" that describe his/her position to better understand one's behavior and attitudes. Toman also writes that of several sibling roles one may hold, "the one that will be stronger is the one he holds vis à vis the sibling closest in age to himself. If a younger brother has a sister two years older and a brother four years older . . ., his role of youngest brother of a sister should be stronger." Obviously, the permutations are too numerous and the focus too narrow for Toman's theories to be helpful except as another way of exploring our attitudes.

Just as many popular assumptions about only children have been scientifically disproved, so have most studies failed to show that the order in which we're born affects our behavior and psychological makeup.[9] (One exception is a study by historical scientist Frank J. Sulloway, who found that most of the major innovators in science over the last four hundred years were preceded in birth by a least one other sibling.[10]) Nonetheless, many of the siblings I interviewed insisted that their order of birth has left an indelible mark on them as adults. My own feeling is that their limited—though certainly understandable—knowledge of the sibling bond and all of its complexities pushes them to explain their attitudes and behaviors in terms of the few theories with which they are familiar. The concept of birth order is as much a part of most siblings' vocabulary as is sibling rivalry. Few of us have been encouraged to look elsewhere as we try to unravel the sibling connection. Often when I asked siblings to consider other concepts, their eyes lit up as if seeing something for the first time.

37

"I've never thought about that," they would say. "But I think you're on to something!"

It would be unwise to completely discount the possible effects birth order might have on our personality and on our relationships outside the family. The point is to realize that birth order is only one of many factors that shapes visions of ourselves and our family ties.

GENDER

If we accept the idea that siblings are often the first partners in life, the first "marriages," where the issues of intimacy can be learned, then we accept the premise that it is from siblings that many people discover some of the basics about who they are—or dare not to be.[11] Growing up with all sisters or all brothers, for example, creates "marriages" in which the partners learn a lot about dealing with one gender but not the other. Conversely, growing up with at least one brother and one sister close in age creates "marriages" in which partners have the chance to learn a lot about getting along with both genders.

The observations of Janis G. in Chapter One, the thirty-five-year-old who grew up with four brothers and a sister, reinforces this point. "I believe very strongly that my brothers are very different men because of their two sisters and that my sister and I are different women because we grew up with four dynamic, strong brothers."

Janis feels she learned about her role as a female from her brothers and that, in turn, her brothers discovered and developed their attitudes toward the opposite sex by living with two sisters.

Sisters and brothers growing up together can not only learn about the opposite sex but also develop a more concrete sense of themselves. One seventy-one-year-old mother of four daughters spoke in glowing terms about the role of her brother, fourteen months her junior, played in the development of her positive self-image: "I received a great deal of male support growing up. My brother thought I was darn cute. He always said that I had better-looking legs than my older sister. Why, he was the one who taught me how to dance. And to this day, I credit him with helping me like myself and with feeling good in the company of other men."

A psychiatric social worker, the second oldest of four children, and two and a half years older than her only brother, talked about the importance of having a male sibling: "I think I would be a different kind of woman if I hadn't had a brother who taught me about being female. Some of the lessons were easier than others. There was a fair amount of teasing and putdowns that cost me a bit. But I think his assistance was very important in my development as a woman."

Therapists Clark Falconer and Colin Ross labeled families with all boys or all girls "tilted" families. Their research suggests that members of these families may face some unique problems, including a confusion about "masculine" and "feminine" roles, difficulty making autonomous, independent choices, problems with behavior control, and a greater sense of loss because there are not children of both sexes.[12]

Children of "tilted" families can certainly grow up without the potential problems cited by Falconer and Ross. When I interviewed three sisters, each talked very fondly about their childhood together and their continuing friendships as adults. The middle sister, who is a professor of education, discussed the advantages of having all sisters.

> I can say things to them that I wouldn't say to anyone else . . . certainly not to a brother. Even though none of us lives in the same city, hardly a week goes by that I don't talk to both of them by phone. I consider them a tremen-

dous support network. My sisters help keep my perspective. I've attained a certain amount of esteem professionally, and it's easy to take yourself a little too seriously. But they know my failings intimately; they've seen me wrestle with them. They can tell me the truth, and I can accept it from them.

When I asked an eleven-year-old youngest of three brothers what is good about having only brothers, he barely skipped a beat before answering. "I think I'd be like an only child if I had two sisters because I wouldn't do anything with them that would be appealing to me."

The gender of siblings may also affect the emotional bond between them. In a study of sibling relationships of people over sixty (Cicirelli, 1979), both men and women tended to name sisters as the ones to whom they felt the closest. Over and over again in the interviews I conducted, sisters were singled out as the ones who kept family ties alive and who had earned the love and respect of their siblings. Sam, seventy-three and the oldest of a sister and a brother, said: "My sister is constantly helping others. Hers is a sterling spirit with the gift of caring. She took care of our mother who was ill for eight years until her death. She did something I never could have done."

From what I've observed, I tend to agree with Christine Downing, author of *Psyche's Sisters,* when she writes that relationships between sisters seem to be more intense and emotionally intimate than between brothers. She points out that myths and fairy tales show brothers as "engaging together in the outer world, whereas sisters share feelings and inner experiences." The tales about sister-brother relationships, Downing continues, suggest the "deep meaning this bond has in the inner lives of men; 'sister' seems to signify that which connects them to the realm of feeling, to their own inner depths, their soul."[13]

The intimacy sisters bring to the sibling relationship is

verified by scientific research as well. In their work with siblings in middle adulthood and old age, researchers have found that the closest, most long-standing relationship is between sisters, the next closest between sisters and brothers, and the least close between brothers. When I asked Deborah Gold why she thought sisters make such a difference in the connection between siblings, she said, "There is something about having the presence of a woman, a traditional kin keeper, that makes sisters have a real commitment to keeping the relationship going."[14] In general, females are given the role of maintaining kin ties, no doubt because it's part of the traditional sex role expectation, which says that women are more adept at expressing themselves on a personal level.

Relationships between siblings are also influenced by the parents' attitudes and beliefs about gender roles. Families in most cultures have traditionally shown a preference for sons. Often that has meant that an older brother who has a younger sister will be favored more than an older sister who has a younger brother. While a recent study indicates that this preference for sons is diminishing (Entwisle and Doering, 1981), there is still a greater likelihood that a family with only female children will continue to try for another child, while families with only sons will stop with fewer children (Broverman et al., 1972).

The words of a forty-eight-year-old second of four sisters painfully underscore her sense of loss of parental affection because she was born a girl: "My older sister was the first child and the first grandchild. I remember my mother saying at one point that if I had been a boy, she would not have had another child. I think I spent a lot of time trying to be the son my parents never had. If I had only been a boy, it would have been much better for everyone."

Gender, of course, is not the whole ball of wax. It is one of many components that shapes the intricate connections between siblings. Yet without question, the gender com-

41

position of the sibling group affects our sense of ourselves, of the opposite sex, and of the threads between us and our siblings. We don't need scientific studies to prove that the way we act with a brother, if we have one, is different from the way we act with a sister. And we don't have to read fairy tales or myths to feel that the level of intimacy between us and our various sibling may have something to do with their sex and ours. Being female or being male carries a host of internal and external differences that first get played out within the family as a whole and within the sibling subsystem in particular. Our first marriage partners teach us all about love and hate and self-esteem and who we are as males and females.

AGE SPACING

The generally accepted rule of thumb is that the closer siblings are in age, the more life experiences they share. Most experts say that siblings born more than eight years apart are apt to be more like only children than siblings, since they go through each developmental phase separately.

A twenty-five-year-old journalist whose brother is just a year older described their adult relationship as "unbelievably warm and fuzzy" and remembered how the closeness in age affected her need to stick up for her brother in trouble, even when *he* was the one who started an argument or provoked other problems. "We would be angry at each other until it came time to be disciplined, and then I would stick up for him. After all, he was my peer. We were close. He was my brother and he was so close in age. He was more like me than my parents were, and I just felt I shouldn't turn him in."

Siblings close in age like this brother and sister can share much, but sharing is double edged: They develop a special closeness but also collide and struggle with one another more frequently.

Jim M. and his brother Kent were only a year apart. Despite the closeness in age and their sharing the same bedroom for most of their childhood, the brothers were not emotionally close. Jim talked about how startled he was looking through a high-school yearbook and seeing pictures of him and Kent together on the same sports teams. "I never remembered him playing on the same team," Jim said. "So it started me thinking that there was probably a lot of competition between us in all sorts of things."

Jim was jealous of Kent's "greater intelligence" and remembered that he needed only four or five hours of sleep each night. "He never really had to work hard at school like I did, yet he did pretty well. I was perceived as the good student, but he held his own without even trying."

Even though Jim and Kent shared some of the same friends and always attended the same school at the same time, Jim never felt particularly close to his brother. "We never confided in each other or discussed our inner thoughts. We never even talked that much about girls. That's a bit strange." For Jim, his relationship with Kent was often an uneasy truce that sometimes broke into obvious dislike and, at other times, settled into a calmer but distant connection.

For Jim and Kent, the closeness in age proved to be a negative component in their relationship. They had trouble avoiding one another in every arena; it was difficult for each to have "room" of his own. Jim found himself going outside the family for friendship, support, and a separate identity. And as the two brothers grew into manhood, the distance between them remained.

There is evidence to support both the claim that closely spaced siblings develop special emotional bonds and the opposite notion that a larger age gap fosters closeness. To draw simple conclusions about the importance of the age gap without looking at the whole picture is risky business.

SIBLING ACCESS

When they studied the factors that influence the emotional impact siblings have on one another, Bank and Kahn determined that age *and* gender are two of the most powerful components. They called these components (and other influences) "access." "High access" siblings are usually close in age and the same sex. They spend a good deal of time together during childhood, often sharing friends and experiences. On the other hand, "low access" siblings are neither close in age nor the same sex. In many ways, they grow up as members of a different generation, sharing few relationships and activities.

The higher the access between siblings, the greater the emotional impact (positive and negative) they have upon one another. And the more intense the relationship will be when it is stressed by separation, social comparison, and death. The bond between Jenny L. and her brother Harry is a good example. They were "high access" siblings who were "best buddies" both in and out of the family. When Harry died not long before his eleventh birthday, Jenny was devastated. She had lost a brother and a friend. Adjusting to his death has been a long and arduous process— a process complicated by other people's lack of understanding of what they shared.

Most of the siblings whose stories are told in this book are "high access" brothers and sisters. They spent a good deal of time together during childhood and influenced each other's lives in many ways. How that influence gets played out as adults is what makes unraveling the sibling bond such a challenging and fascinating affair.

FROM GENERATION TO GENERATION

Since family patterns can be handed down from one generation to the next, siblings and their parents are, in part, products of their ancestors and *their* patterns of behavior. This legacy shapes the ways people become intimate with each other. The sibling legacy is no different. Most parents are siblings and marry someone who is a sibling. Children grow up knowing their aunts and uncles and seeing and hearing all about how they got along. One woman I interviewed discussed the model her father and his siblings established for her and her siblings.

> I come from an immigrant family. When they came to this country, my father and his three siblings went into business together and worked every day of their lives, providing this kind of umbrella over the family. When I was growing up, I observed this very tight sibling group. They watched over each other and took care of each other and the rest of the family. When my parents began ailing, I noticed how strong *my* sibling group became and how much we began turning to each other to be guardians of our children and that sort of thing. It became apparent to me how significant my siblings had been in my own development and how important they were at this stage of my life. And I also appreciated how important the elder generation sibling group had been.

Another woman, older than her three brothers, talked about watching the change in relationship between her mother and her aunt.

> My aunt is sixteen years older than my mother. She's eighty-five, and my mother is almost seventy. I've watched as their relationship has improved so much in quality as time has gone by, but sixteen years must have been a lifetime when they were children. But now that they've both

matured and are facing, in essence, the same crises, there is a bond there that has become very, very strong.

There is a strong need for parents to either replicate their sibling experiences with their own children or to avoid them. Bank and Kahn use the example of a father who was always brutalized by his older brother. Now that he has two sons of his own, he has vowed that they will be able to hold their own against each other. He has sent both boys for karate lessons. Bank and Kahn also describe a mother who always got along with her two siblings in a home where conflict was avoided and who is now very confused whenever her own children quarrel.

In addition, parents tend to project their unresolved feelings, ideals, wishes, and hopes on their children. Such parents may hope that one child will become a professional athlete or a respected physician, forcing the other siblings to move in different directions. This cultivation of a specific direction for one child may limit the possibilities for the others. And if parents seem to like one child more than another because he/she either reminds them of themselves or is quite different, the apparent favoritism can easily fuel resentment between the siblings and create feelings of one-upmanship or jealousy.

A seventy-four-year-old photographer angrily recalled how her parents' nagging about being skinny like her younger sister affected her self-image throughout her life: "My sister was a bad eater, and I had to fight not to eat too much. My parents were always stuffing her and telling me not to eat. I fought my weight problem successfully, but that doesn't mean that I don't feel it or didn't feel it then. As a matter of fact, I look at old pictures and my first thought is that I wasn't fat at all!"

And a seventeen-year-old oldest of three boys told me how his parents' expectations could be "very burdensome."

In the eyes of my parents, I was always known as the "smart" one for years. My middle brother was the "athletic" one, and my youngest brother was the "crazy" one. I was always expected to be a role model . . . to do the right thing in school. I was expected to set a good example and get good grades, to always be involved, a model person, student, and brother. It was very burdensome. And I think the expectations are much lighter for my brothers.

The recognition of family patterns—whether they are unequal parental treatment or maladaptive ways of dealing with problems—offers the possibility of changing them. When counseling psychologist Karen Lewis discussed how she works with adults on issues ranging from marriage to self-esteem, she told me how useful it is to have her clients go back and look at their connections with their siblings. "This approach makes it much easier to trace back and undo some of the family myths and patterns that get in the way," Lewis said. "It opens up doors for people and often helps them see that they've been blaming their problems on the wrong person. Looking back at their own and their parents' sibling relationships allows them to see how those patterns got recreated, how the fantasies are passed down from one generation to the next."[15]

ETHNIC PATTERNS

All siblings are not created equal nor are they treated the same. Sometimes a family's ethnic background will dictate a preference for boys, dissuade family members from making autonomous decisions, or discourage the open display of emotions. Such patterns can be lifelong, influencing siblings during childhood and continuing to do so in adulthood.

Tradition informs us that boys, most often the oldest son, are favored in many cultures. The oldest son is expected to be a role model for his siblings and to have the last word. Younger siblings are expected to follow the guidance of the oldest son, not only as children but throughout their adult lives.[16]

In both Western and Eastern cultures, boys are valued more than girls, a prejudice that affects the roles and expectations of siblings. In West Indian families, for instance, a son is doted on regardless of his sibling position. In cultures where having a son is the wife's main source of prestige and validation, preference for male children carries additional importance. Boys are taught that they are superior to their sisters; girls are taught to accept their inferiority. This inequality can easily affect the brother's and sister's self-image, motivation, and life plans.

Whether a sibling is a first- or fifth-generation American, the ethnic component often remains a factor in the family's expectations and behavior patterns. We saw this very clearly in the story of David S. in Chapter One. The emphasis placed on close family relationships and the importance of maintaining a united front have handcuffed David and made it very difficult for him to assert his independence and get on with his life. In many families, independence and individual achievement are still not encouraged. The individual is expected to sacrifice in the name of the family. Separating from the family becomes very difficult; the process is rife with guilt feelings, and the children tend to remain physically and emotionally tied to their parents in unhealthy ways.

The degree to which expressing emotions is promoted within families also appears to run along ethnic lines. Mediterranean cultures tend to encourage the open display of feelings more than non-Mediterranean cultures. When family members are dissuaded from airing both positive and negative emotions, the end result is often indirect aggression toward one another and an inability to support and comfort each other.

Adult siblings are better equipped to tackle unresolved issues from childhood if they understand how ethnic expectations may have colored or strained their relationships. For example, it is not unusual for younger siblings to resent the preferential treatment bestowed upon the oldest son. Whether this parental favoritism continues into adulthood is not the point. What matters is that the younger siblings still resent their oldest brother for getting a lot more good stuff than they did. If, as adults, these younger siblings realize that ethnic expectations—not their brother—dictated his position of privilege, they can stop blaming him and put the blame where it belongs. And the oldest son, having felt some guilt all along for having enjoyed his status, can forgive himself. Once adult siblings stop blaming themselves and each other for what went on when they were kids, they stand a much better chance of becoming friends.

GENETICS VERSUS ENVIRONMENT

Underlying the debate as to why some siblings share a close emotional bond and others do not is the genetic (nature) versus environment (nurture) controversy. There are those who feel that what we become after birth is largely a result of environment and learning. And there are those who believe that the main course of human development is largely predetermined by our genetic makeup. Earlier in this century, there was a real interest in and emphasis on genetics and the biological basis of development. Psychologists agreed with the evolutionist viewpoint that the genetic transmission of both bodily and behavioral characteristics molded everything from personality to intelligence. That trend changed, however, when a number of psychologists rejected the biological basis of development and behavior in favor of a learning theory that emphasized the role of the environment.

Today leading researchers like Sandra Scarr, Commonwealth Professor of Psychology at the University of Virginia, are studying the interplay between heredity and environment. "I was very interested in why people differed from one another," said Scarr in a phone interview. "It seemed to me that our accounts of environments were incomplete and that people were also genetically different." Scarr set out to test her theory that we determine the kind of experiences we have by selectively exposing ourselves to one kind of environment or another, based on our talents, interests, and personality.[17]

One of the avenues taken to test this theory is the study of identical twins adopted separately soon after birth and reared apart. If identical twins, formed from the splitting of one fertilized egg and genetically identical, are raised in different communities and different homes yet share similar experiences, then, reasons Scarr, it can be said that people's genetically acquired characteristics are basic to their personalities.

Whether one is a twin or not, one's genetic predispostion is related to the way parents, peers, and others react to and treat us. An easygoing child with an even disposition may be favored over a less cooperative sibling. Parents and others may be less critical of the easygoing child, even when he or she deserves criticism. This is certainly one important way that children in the same family can have such different experiences. The more different siblings are genetically, the more different parental treatment is likely to be. And the less genetically related siblings are (it may be that some siblings share as little as 35 percent of their genes while others share as much as 65 percent), the fewer interests they're likely to share and the less time they will spend together. Conversely, the more genes in common, the closer their experiences will be and the more similar the treatment from others.

Our genetic backgrounds predispose us to different emotional and intellectual reactions to the world. These differences lead to different experiences. For example, one sibling may be devastated when his parents get a divorce. His sister, on the other hand, may be less upset and more easily able to adjust to the changes within the family. "That kind of difference in emotional response and ability to cope with changes and stress," said Scarr, "means that each sibling gives different meanings to changes in life."

Intelligence, too, affects the way siblings react to their environment. Siblings who are very bright can think of all kinds of alternatives to a particular event. They can intellectually examine many different options, rather than allow a situation to make them victims of circumstances. A sibling who can see a variety of possibilities will experience the environment in a more expansive and less stressful way than the sibling who sees no choices.

The same event, then, can have very different meanings for different siblings. It is not so much *what* happens but the *meaning* siblings attribute to the event that is important. What is stressful to one is not necessarily stressful to another.

If Scarr and other behavioral geneticists are correct—if siblings "make" their own environments according to genetically based talents, interests, and personality—how does a theory like Freud's (on sibling rivalry) stand up? It can be argued that genetically based differences in intelligence and personality—not vying for parental favor—may be, in part, responsible for the distance between some siblings.

Freud's evaluation of the sibling relationship rests on the intensity and ruthlessness of *every* child's hostility toward his or her siblings. This hostility, an assumed product of jealous rivalry for parental love and attention, ignores the possibility of siblings sharing anything but enmity for one another. Freud was blinded to the possibility of affection between siblings similar in talents, interests, and personality because he saw his own sisters and the deceased brother as enemies with whom he had absolutely nothing in common. He ignored the ways in which genetics could mold similarities as well as differences and the ways in which genetically based intelligence and personality could mold experiences as well as the ways in which parents parent. Could it have been that Freud's interests and temperament, apparently so different from those of his siblings, did as much to widen the gap between them as the vying for parental attention? One psychologist has suggested that although Freud had a superb intellect, he seems to have had a rather small heart. There were things he could not, or would not, understand.

For adult siblings trying to understand emotional ties (or lack of them), it is helpful to evaluate how both genetics and environment have shaped our personalities and the ways in which we approach the world. The recent swing toward emphasizing heredity should not blind us to the equal importance that environmental factors play. As we investigate how we are like our siblings and how we are different, we benefit from thinking about the traits we share and those we do not. How did the qualities we share evolve? How did our differences take shape? To answer these questions about ourselves is to better understand the interplay of heredity and environment and why some of us enjoy warm and supportive connections and others do not.

3

GROWING UP:
CHILDHOOD AND ADOLESCENCE

We know more about human development during childhood than during any other stage of life. Popular literature about periods of personality development (such as the "Terrible Twos" and the "Noisy Nines") discusses the birth of a sibling and the inevitable quarrels between the siblings over the next sixteen years or so. Many a parent has found solace in the fact that most siblings quarrel (not just their own) and that the initial trauma of a sibling's birth does subside and is often followed by signs of independence and maturity. However, most of the literature stops there. Questions about the differences between siblings, the close connection between parental treatment and sibling development, and the ways in which siblings influence one another have either been left unanswered or discussed in professional journals and books not addressed to the general public. It doesn't matter that many of us were baffled by how different we were from our sib-

lings or how our own children are like "night and day."
Our questions about how a mother's or father's favoritism
for one child over another child could wreak all sorts of
havoc have gone unanswered. And the many ways in which
siblings affect each other's lives are all but ignored. For all
the time spent carefully deciphering ages and stages, most
of us know next to nothing about brothers and sisters growing up.

THE BIRTH OF A SIBLING

When I talked to children and adults about the birth of a
sibling, the reactions ranged from utter joy to complete
devastation. These highly emotional responses appeared to
have had less to do with the age of the child at the time of
the sibling's birth than with how the parents prepared the
older child for the new baby and how they treated that child
following the birth.

One older sister described the birth of her baby sister
as the "most important event in my life." Maria B. explained:

> I consider the way it was handled enough to cause trauma
> to anybody. Nobody told me what it was to be pregnant. It
> was never mentioned that my mother *was* pregnant. I had
> a German nurse. When my sister was born, the nurse be-
> came *her* nurse. She was taken away from me without any
> preparation. For all these reasons, my sister's birth was a
> very traumatic experince. It took a long time for us to like
> each other. I always felt that it was warfare between us.

As we talked further, Maria stressed how difficult it was
as a four-year-old to have had her whole life turned upside
down: "The people I was close to just disappeared from

my life. Suddenly there was this little thing getting all the love and attention that used to be mine. I was very jealous and had to fight that feeling for many, many years. By the time I realized what a wonderful person my sister was, I was living here in the States and she was still in Germany."

If the basis of healthy relationships between siblings needs to be established in childhood, it's not surprising that Maria and her sister got off to a bad start. Changes in a child's daily routine are particularly upsetting following the birth of a sibling. When the level of play and attention drops drastically, the older child's confusion, anger, and jealously are heightened. Maria felt abandoned by her nurse. Little effort was made to enlist her help in the care of her baby sister. And neither her mother nor her father stepped in to offer special attention to offset some of the insecurities Maria felt so keenly. It's also quite possible that Maria was a particularly vulnerable child who had more difficulty than some children in accepting change. Such a predisposition, coupled with an apparent lack of care and attention from her parents, extended what should have been short-term stress into years of envy and insecurity. Even after the two sisters developed a warm but long-distance friendship, Maria sought a therapist's help to work through the trauma associated with her sister's birth. "I relive the jealousy and envy with each new friend I make."

Lisa. N., a forty-four-year-old media consultant, vividly recalled the arrival of her baby brother when she was five. Unlike the birth of her sister when she was two—an event she does not remember—the birth of Lisa's brother was the "first real recollection" she has of her childhood.

I remember my brother being brought home from the hospital and my mother walking in and saying to the housekeeper, "Here's your boy." And there was this adorable

redheaded kid. I was very happy. I liked him, and he was
so cute. I remember telling everyone that I had a little
brother. I don't ever remember feeling jealous. There are
pictures of me with him on my lap. There's one of him
peeing all over me. I didn't mind at all.

Lisa attributed her joyous acceptance of her brother to
her basically open and receptive personality. She had always wanted siblings, she said, and the fact that she and
her sister (an identical twin whose sister died in infancy)
were not close pushed Lisa to work even harder at establishing a tight bond with her brother. Unfortunately, her
parents didn't seize the opportunity to encourage Lisa in
her hope for a warm, supportive friendship, as we'll see
later in this chapter.

Most detailed accounts of how children react to the birth
of a sibling come from parents; fewer come from in-home
objective observers. No matter the source, the consensus
is the same: The birth of a sibling is an unsettling event,
marked by upset *and* great interest and often followed
sometime later by strides toward independence and maturity. Most children show signs of being upset soon after
a sibling's birth. They don't sleep well, they cry a lot, some
forget about toilet training, and they make parenting a real
challenge with their demanding, often downright "bad"
behavior. Yet these same trying children can just as easily
endear themselves to their parents (and to their sibling) as
they cuddle, entertain, and attempt to take care of the new
baby. Because periods of stress and apparent regression are
usually times of growth and progression, the negative reactions to the birth of a sibling are often complemented by
signs of positive development. The older child not only
begins to develop empathy for another person but can take
a great leap forward and start demonstrating his or her
newfound maturity in a number of ways.[1]

THOSE INEVITABLE QUARRELS

Most parents want more than one child, even in the face of the upset associated with the birth of a sibling and the inevitable quarreling that takes place between most brothers and sisters. Parents are convinced that the benefits of having siblings—learning to share, to negotiate, to empathize—far outweigh the usually manageable brush fires that erupt along the way. Yet when push comes to shove and the children are fighting over toys, screaming for control of the TV, vying for personal space, many parents find themselves embroiled in the fray. Losing sight of the reasons why they wanted more than one child, they try to mediate or actually solve the "hot" issues dividing their kids.

When I asked one seventeen-year-old how his mother had handled the arguing between his older brother and him, he described an intrusive approach that characterizes the way many parents react: "She'd always punish us and put us in corners or separate rooms. Even if we'd apologize to the other, she'd keep us there. She always said we were abnormal kids because we fought so much. She never tried to stay out of it and let us work things out for ourselves."

Letting siblings work things out for themselves (not as easy as it sounds) is the current recommendation for achieving ultimate peace in the house. While more research is needed to test this approach, initial findings have shown that the more parents intervene, the more siblings fight. And the bigger the role parents assume in settling arguments, the less chance siblings have to learn how to resolve conflicts for themselves. When parents send their children to separate rooms, the children don't learn how to make deals, to compromise. One clinical psychologist went so far as to say that the best scenario is for one sibling to be the "victim" half the time and the "perpetrator" the other half.

Problems occur, she suggested, when one sibling is always the saint, the other always the sinner. The process of arguing becomes fixed, usually because parents get involved, don't allow the children to quarrel, and take the side of whomever has been singled out as the "good" kid.[2] Labeling one sibling as "good" and another as "bad," instead of pointing out the *behavior* as acceptable or unacceptable, creates a split between the siblings and between the siblings and their parents.

The happiness Lisa N. felt after the birth of her baby brother did not last long. Her sister required so much of her mother's time that Lisa felt completely left out.

> She wasn't there for me, and I became a difficult child. Then my brother arrived. For a while, I felt better. But he demanded attention, too. There just wasn't enough left over for me . . . Later, my parents set the tone for the house. I was the black sheep, the difficult one. Their negative attitude toward me gave my brother and sister permission to not look up to me, to not show me any respect.

Because Lisa had been singled out as the "bad" one, her parents never took her protests seriously. She described a scene often repeated where her brother would get her in the corner of a room, clench his fists, and pretend that he was going to beat her up. Lisa would yell every time. She was "terrified." Her parents thought the scene was "funny." Her unhappiness and fear went unattended, her relationship with both siblings became strained, and the difficulty at home spilled over into the classroom. When she turned thirteen, Lisa was "sent off" to a psychiatrist because she had stopped working in school and had fallen from the top of her class to the bottom. "The only time I got attention was when grades arrived," she explained. "My dad would sit down with me for a long, one-on-one talk. I never worked hard in school again." And the strained relationships with her brother and sister have never been resolved. "We're as far apart as we've ever been."

Once Lisa was labeled the "bad" sibling by her parents, there was no turning back. Her parents created a fixed dynamic in which Lisa was always the "perpetrator." Whenever she turned to her parents for support, they refused to give it, convinced that she was the root of all the trouble. Unwittingly or not, they gave permission for the other two children to pick on her and usurped her potential as role model. Lisa's brother and sister could get away with everything, and that is what they did. Lisa became her brother's favorite "hobby" as he teased her incessantly; she became her sister's scapegoat for everything that went wrong. "If only my parents had acted like I was wonderful and all of us were wonderful. If only they had never given my siblings permission to tease and hurt me. *I* never felt permission to do that to them, even if I had wanted to."

RECENT INSIGHTS INTO
COMMON PROBLEMS

Okay. We know most siblings quarrel. It's normal and actually quite healthy, if parents stay out and let their kids learn how to resolve their own conflicts. And we can see how parental favoritism can split siblings and pit them against one another, upping the stakes and encouraging more fighting. What other factors cause some siblings to fight more than others? Recent research (Brody & Stoneman, 1987) shows that temperamental differences between siblings (differences that are more than likely genetic) can fuel fighting, particularly if at least one of the siblings is highly active or impulsive.

The oldest of four sisters explained the conflicted childhood relationship between her and her next oldest sister.

> Jamie was the rebel of the family from the day she was born. She wasn't close to the rest of us and acted out in all kinds of ways. I, on the other hand, was more of a caretaker type and a "good" child. I did well in school, helped at home, and had lots of friends. Jamie and I never got along. I'm sure she resented me and all the positive attention I got. That made her fight with me even more.

From the "day she was born," Jamie was an impulsive child who acted out her intense feelings. She behaved antagonistically toward her older sister, the "model" child, and initiated a good deal of the fights between them. Responding to Jamie's "rebellious" nature, her mother constantly compared her to her older sister. "Why can't you be more like her?" "She doesn't start fights. Why do you?" With good reason, Jamie translated her mother's constant comparisons and complaints into a clear message that her sister was loved more than she. Feeling less loved (and impulsive by nature), Jamie reacted by going against family rules and expectations. In reality, her mother liked her older sister's *behavior* more than Jamie's but was unable to make that distinction. Parents like Jamie's often have trouble differentiating between who their children *are* and how their children *behave*. Often it is the difference in temperament that is especially annoying or particularly appealing. Yet few parents can admit that they may like one child more than another at any given time. The thought is disquieting, as if it were a sure sign of their failure as parents. So they mask their true feelings and ignore ways to recognize and show respect for the differences between their children.

LIKE NIGHT AND DAY

"We're different . . . very different. When she's angry at someone, she can be angry at them for a long time. Me—I can't stay mad. We're so different that way."

"We are very different physically, mentally, and with our activities. I am underweight; she's overweight. I'm retiring; she's outgoing. She makes friends easily. I do not. We have different friends and completely different interests."

"He's last minute in everything. I'm not. His personality is a little more confined. I don't want to seem immodest, but I think I have a better personality than he does. I'm also more athletic, but he's more intelligent."

One of the most surprising discoveries about siblings is that they tend to see themselves as different from each other as though they were children from different families. Despite their shared genes and their shared home and community environments, brothers and sisters easily describe these differences but have a harder time recognizing the similarities.

What is the process by which siblings contrast themselves and what are some of the benefits? Clinical psychologist Frances Fuchs Schachter and others have called this phenomenon *sibling deidentification*. They see it as a pattern that diminishes competition and comparison between brothers and sisters. "I have my turf, and you have yours." Deidentification is viewed as a peace-keeping process whereby a person perceives that they can excel in one arena while a sibling can shine in another. ("I'm more athletic, but he's more intelligent.") Uncertain as to how deidentification evolves, researchers like Schachter think that parents play an important role by projecting their own ideas of what their children should be like. The projection can be conscious and aboveboard ("You explain things well and would be a great teacher") or subliminal and unconscious. The process by which siblings themselves negotiate who they will be is usually unconscious. However, Schachter told of an eight-year-old who wanted to be an artist like his mother and his ten-year-old sister who wanted to be a writer like her father. When the brother no longer wanted to be an artist, his sister said, "Good, now I can be the artist!" She moved right into the turf vacated by her brother and claimed it for her own.[3]

If we assume that awareness of differences mitigates sibling rivalry, it makes sense to also assume that the process begins with the first- and secondborn children in the family and is the most intense when they are the same sex. (First- and secondborns are likely to be the most rivalrous if comparison, competition, and conflict are "undiluted" by a thirdborn.)[4] By expressing themselves in different ways and on different turfs, siblings don't have to constantly defend their "land" from incursions from each other. They can each be the "king" or "queen" of their own domain.

WHERE IT BEGINS

During childhood the seeds are planted for what we know can be a relationship of immeasurable importance throughout life. Siblings are physically and emotionally closer during these early years than at any other time. What affects one usually affects the others, though not necessarily in the same way. And what affects the parents is usually passed on to the siblings, though, most likely, in different ways. And it all becomes a practice ground for future relationships. It is with our brothers and sisters that we learn to love, share, negotiate, start and end fights, hurt others, and save face. The basis of healthy (or unhealthy) connections in adulthood is cast during childhood.

Siblings are a separate group within the family. The "sibling underworld" has its own code of behavior, its own loyalty bonds, and its own history and hierarchy. Because much of what goes on between siblings takes place behind closed doors, what parents see is often form, not substance. Out of parental view, brothers and sisters may not be killing each other but exploring their identities, developing self-esteem, and practicing such important life skills as conflict resolution. The perception of themselves and the degree of maturity and understanding young siblings achieve might surprise many of us.

At times, the impact siblings have on one another is great; at others, it is insignificant, and middle childhood (ages six to nine) is generally the most uneventful period in the sibling connection. Siblings operate under the illusion that their bond (happy or unhappy) will never change. As siblings move into preadolescence, they usually talk about everything except what each really means to the other. They have neither the language nor a sense of separateness to see the other siblings realistically. But with the start of adolescence, the relationship between brothers and sisters is much more likely to change.[5]

ADOLESCENCE: A TIME OF CHANGE

We are children until we reach puberty. We are adolescents until we reach that point in our twenties when we take hold of a personal identity—an identity that is, to be sure, subject to change over the course of a lifetime. Testing our capabilities and seeking our own truth dominate the quintessential period for change called adolescence. And talk about change! Young people anticipate adolescence as the beginning of their emancipation from adults and rules; their lives are going to be, at long last, different. They begin taking risks in the way they dress and the things they do.

"Model," "conventional" preadolescents are altered before our very eyes, shedding their "old" skins in favor of new and different identities. They may pierce an ear, change their hairstyle, try smoking cigarettes, experiment with alcohol and/or drugs, drop old friends, alter study habits, withdraw from parents, and generally become strangers in their own homes. These marked changes affect the relationship not only between adolescents and their parents but between adolescents and their siblings. Brothers and sisters tend to experience a sense of loss with any marked change in a sibling. If the adolescent is suddenly "different," he and his siblings will no longer relate in the same ways. The greater the changes, the more likely the other siblings will resist.

Carrie P., the youngest of five sisters, discussed how the dynamics between her and her next oldest sister, Pam, changed when they started high school.

> My sister was pursuing straight things, and I was pursuing sex, drugs, and rock 'n' roll. The problems between us were caused by me. I'd come home "wasted," and my sister would take it upon herself to see that I'd get through the night. She hated it when I'd come home drunk, but she wouldn't leave me. She'd try to lecture me about staying out late and doing "bad" things . . . She was mad at me until just last year, and I'm turning thirty!

The changes in Carrie's behavior when she started high school made Pam uncomfortable and angry. Pam had a hard time accepting her sister's rebellion against her own code of behavior. But instead of ignoring her, Pam chose to be almost "motherly" as she nursed and lectured simultaneously. The cost of Carrie's dramatic changes during adolescence was high. It took almost fifteen years before Pam accepted Carrie as "more grounded." "She used to reject offhand anything I'd have to say because she thought I was coming from a warped perspective," said Carrie. "She was convinced she couldn't use anything that I had learned. It's just recently that she sees me as an equal. She doesn't think I'm crazy anymore."

Changes in the sibling relationship during adolescence don't have to be fraught with problems. One seventeen-year-old described how he and his older brother used to argue all the time, but as both boys matured, the quality of their relationship improved: "As we got older, most of the fighting stopped. We're closer now. I try to be like him. We both love skiing. And he influenced me in school. I try to work hard because he worked hard. We like the same things . . . music and stuff like that. I follow in his footsteps, doing what he did."

I asked the same seventeen-year-old to talk about the changes in his life now that his brother is a college freshman.

> We talk on the phone a lot. When he calls up each week, he'll talk to my parents for ten minutes and then I get on the phone and he tells me everything that's *really* happening. But the main thing is that he isn't around twenty-four hours a day. I can't go into his room and ask him to help me with my homework. He can't show me through a math problem or help me with Latin. But when he's home on vacation, he's a friend . . . someone to go to for advice, to get help from, to play a board game with. Now that we're older and more independent, we don't need our parents as much. We can go and do things and spend more time together outside the house.

Greg P., whose next oldest brother, Stephen, is just nineteen months younger, wasn't as positive about having another adolescent in the house.

> It's very difficult socially, especially now that we're both in high school. You have someone who is so close to you that knows the same things you do . . . all the gossip, all the relationships. It's very difficult to have secrets and to have

privacy. You don't want everyone to know everything about you and you want to be able to do certain things or be a certain way that your brother doesn't have to know. When he turns up at the same places, it's almost as if there's more responsibility than just for yourself—not so much caretaking but responsibility to act in a certain way. My brother is almost like a peer, but he lives in the same house and I never get away from him.

Greg feels his strides toward independence are being hampered by having a brother so close in age who shares many of the same friends and activities. It's difficult for him to experiment with new roles when Stephen is always looking over his shoulder. Yet Greg is very philosophical about the arrangement. "I don't mean to overplay it. It's nothing that's so terrible that I haven't learned to live with. As we get older, we are more alike."

As Greg entered adolescence, his youngest brother, Mike, who is five years younger, had difficult adjusting to the changes in Greg's personality. The "loss" of the brother he knew was confusing and quite upsetting. His teenage brother was "really different," and it took Mike "a while to get used to the changes."

He is going through a phase and is totally different from me and my other brother. He sorta . . . he has to prove that he's . . . I don't know how to say it. He used to be real calm, very different. But when he got into ninth grade, he left a group of friends and he is trying to get into another group. And he has to prove something to those kids.

Mike went on to describe a "big" party that Greg threw when their parents were out of town. "He wouldn't have done that before. It was really a dumb thing to do. He was really stupid. I think he did it to impress his new friends."

Dumb . . . stupid . . . words that Mike used to describe Greg, who in his experimentation with new friends and new behaviors, altered the sibling connection with which Mike had grown comfortable. Greg had changed; he wasn't the studious, well-behaved kid he used to be. He was "just different." As a result of the changes, Mike began to identify even more closely with Stephen, also an adolescent but not as changed as Greg. "We both love sports. We know how to talk with people. We are already in the popular group at school." When I asked Mike in what ways he and Stephen were different, he couldn't think of a thing!

Carol W., three years younger than her brother Josh, recalled how their relationship blossomed once Josh reached adolescence. Before that time, the two were not "buddy buddy," although Carol sensed that Josh was an ally in the family.

> It was when he was in high school that the connection between us grew. We used to hang out together in his room all the time. I was the little mascot. Even though I was three years younger, we had mutual friends. I was always crushed out on his boyfriends, and he had crushes on some of my girlfriends. We were like a little secret society. He led the way for me. I looked up to him and loved him a lot.

As Carol matured, she realized how philosophically and spiritually alike she and Josh were. "We were both sensitive and highly emotional, whereas the rest of the family was very studious and achievement oriented. We never bought into what our parents and the rest of culture felt was important." Josh was a rebel, and Carol first saw that independent spirit when he was an adolescent. Josh said what he felt and did what he wanted. That model gave Carol "permission" to be her own person and to resist pressures from her family and others to be a "certain kind of young girl." Because of the similarities in character and general outlook between her brother and her, Carol experienced

Josh's marked changes not as a loss but as a bridge that connected the two of them.

With the onset of adolescence, the sibling relationship is bound to change. Generally, the greater the changes, the more apt siblings are to resent and resist the differences. Adolescence often requires that siblings stop and reevaluate their relationship. The brother or sister they used to know (or used to be) is no longer the same. The differences may be subtle or glaring, welcomed or resented. Yet no matter the intensity, things *are* different. The loyalty bonds, history, and hierarchy of the sibling underworld are changing because the siblings themselves are changing, like it or not.

Whether changes in the sibling relationship during adolescence create long-term rifts that spill over into adulthood depends upon the ability of brothers and sisters to constantly redefine their connection. Siblings either learn to accept one another as independent individuals with their own sets of values and behaviors or cling to the shadow of the brother and sister they once knew. For those siblings like Carrie and Pam, giving the other permission to change did not come easily. Pam did not approve of the things Carrie did as an adolescent, and it was fifteen years before she began to see Carrie as anything other than a "warped" teenager. For Carol and Josh, adolescence enhanced their friendship. Carol respected the changes in Josh's behavior and was encouraged to follow in his footsteps. Adult siblings who do not get along may want to look back and consider how adolescence altered their relationship. Were they crippled by a sense of having lost their comfortably familiar brother or sister? Did the feelings of loss turn to hurt, anger, and resentment? Do these negative feelings continue to dog their views of one another? Adolescence is a time of change and regrouping. If you and a sibling got stuck, consider regrouping now. It is never too late.

4

YOUNG ADULTHOOD: PUSH AND PULL

In the years between adolescence and middle adulthood—our twenties, thirties, and early forties—we attempt to take our place in the adult world, first by doing what we think we *should* and eventually by doing what we *want*. The twenties, dubbed the "Trying Twenties" by author Gail Sheehy, challenge us to make our goals a reality, goals largely determined by our family, culture, and peers. During our twenties, we are convinced that whatever choices we make are irrevocable; we must make the "right" decisions that will set us up for the rest of our lives. Action, not introspection, characterizes this period. We attempt to bury any parts of our personality and our past that might prevent us from establishing our life pattern.[1]

As we work to carve a niche for ourselves in the world, we look for role models, or mentors, who can help show us the way. Depending upon our feelings toward our siblings, we can turn to them for support, pass them over, or consciously avoid them because of past hurts and humiliation. Chances are that if our parents have stoked the fires of competition between us, we will either see our siblings as better than we are or be convinced they can never measure up. Childhood memories are all too fresh; there is not yet enough objectivity between us. On the other hand, if we've reached our twenties with a healthy respect for our siblings, we may turn to each other as we grapple with the challenges of establishing a career and an identity outside of the family.

Kate R., the youngest of three sisters, is very clear about the role her next oldest sister Amanda played in helping her choose to become a librarian: "She has always encouraged me to do things I don't think I can do. She's never been pushy, just gently asks me to think about certain things and to try. She is my professional mentor, a professor of education, as well as my sister and friend."

For her part, Amanda credits Kate with "cementing" *her* choice of profession.

> I had always wanted to be a teacher but then I saw what happened to Kate when she was in first grade. She had a very cruel teacher, someone who was fired after that year. My sister went from being this happy, bright, energized child to having a stomach ulcer and being hospitalized. That was a real influence on me. It opened my eyes. That was it . . . I went into teaching with such a commitment. In fact, one of my teachers said that I had a real "Joan of Arc thing." And he was right!

Kate, now in her early thirties, and Amanda, pushing forty, both recognize how the other helped cement a career choice and encourage professional growth. In addition, Amanda understands how their oldest sister, Suzanne, influenced the way she approaches her work as a professor of education.

Suzanne used to make decisions for me, and I think, to this day, that I'm much better at coming up with the larger picture. In fact, one of my colleagues with whom I've written described me as a balloon and herself as the string. I have the grandiose ideas, and she brings me back to earth. It was like that with Suzanne, too. And when I choose graduate assistants, I look for the same kind of detail person who can do the things that I'm not comfortable doing.

When asked how growing up with four other siblings might have influenced her professional temperament, Ellen, the youngest of five sisters said, "I have a great tolerance for noise, and I mean emotional noise, household noise. I can concentrate in a lot of noise . . . I love the web. I loved that there was always someone with something going on. There were all these lives in a big bucket together, and they'd go swimming, bumping, and crashing. I loved that sense of community." How did that love for community and all of its "noise" affect her choice of profession? "I'm a television writer and producer, and growing up in a community as I did determined my career. I love nosing around in other people's business and getting them to tell me about themselves and their lives. And growing up in a house full of people taught me how to concentrate when I'm surrounded by the kinds of disturbances—the noise—of working in television."

For many of us, the idea that our siblings may have helped shape our choice of career is a new one. We may acknowledge how our parents' pressures and/or models pushed us in one direction or the other, but recognizing how competition with our siblings encouraged us to pursue a career different from theirs —or how the closeness propelled us to follow in their footsteps—does not come as easily. One sister I talked to always assumed her decision to become a teacher was based on her mother having taught. Only recently did she consider how being the oldest of three molded her love for helping and instructing others. "I'm not sure I would have been a teacher," she said, "if I'd been the youngest or an only child. But as the oldest, I helped my two siblings learn to count, to read, and, later on, to speak French. I loved working with them. And the positive feedback I got made me look for the same kind of rewards in my career." It is a useful exercise to clarify the ways being a sibling in your family shaped your visions of what you wanted to be when you grew up.

RESISTING OUR PAST

A great resistance arises during our twenties to being seen as "like our parents." We need to feel that we've chosen the one true course in life that is uniquely our own.[2] This drive to deny our link to our parents can influence the amount of emotional stock we put in and the actual time we spend with our brothers and sisters. One brother put it this way: "My older brother always represented family and dad, things I've had trouble with. When I was in my twenties, it wasn't very comfortable to be around him." Once we leave home, contact with our siblings is less obligatory; we can *choose* how much time to spend together. Many siblings in early adulthood are more "out" of each other's lives than "in."

Or are they? Young adulthood may be a time when siblings have less *overt* importance, but the residual effects of earlier experiences echo throughout adulthood. No matter how hard we may try to shake our brothers and sisters during our twenties, their influence can continue to affect us, even if our contact is limited. The decisions we make and the things we do are often a reflection of both positive aspects of the sibling relationship and unresolved issues.[3]

Psychologist Karen Lewis cites as examples a man who feels disloyal becoming close to nonfamily friends because he was not close to his siblings, and people who are underachievers at work because they are uncomfortable outperforming a peer (read sibling). Even though brothers and sisters often drift apart during early adulthood, their internalized siblings remain a constant.[4]

THE THIRTIES

As we approach our thirties, we are again challenged to alter our lives. It is the time of "wanting to be something more."[5] One woman remarked, "A lot of things happened to me when I turned thirty. I was trying to take care of myself, trying to straighten out some of my problems, trying to get my head clear about what *I* wanted." The "shoulds" that dictated our choices in our twenties no longer feel right. We are compelled to either change our commitments to career and to our relationships or to reaffirm and deepen them. The thirties are a time when some brothers and sisters feel a need to readjust their ties. If the connection has been loose, it may be the time to initiate a more meaningful friendship. A thirty-two-year-old said: "I noticed a difference in the way I felt about my sister. Sometimes we got along; sometimes we didn't. But I felt I could count on her to back me up. My sense of her . . . of family . . . changed."

Siblings reevaluate their ties to one another and they also take a long, hard look at the other important relationships (or lack of them) in their lives. There is a high number of divorces among people in their thirties, as there are more and more first marriages. The way in which siblings adjust to these changes in each other's lives affects the quality of their bond. Both marriage and divorce can put pressures on siblings as they struggle to accept a new member of the family or to accept the dissolution of a marriage (particularly if there are children or if the ex and a sibling were friends).

TYING THE KNOT: WHEN SIBLINGS MARRY

We are not unlike ex-husbands and ex-wives when it comes to the marriages of our siblings. They were our "first" marriage partners, and we have a tremendous amount of emotional stock invested in them. We are more than curious about those with whom they choose to "love, honor, and obey." Are they like us? Do they share the same values? Do they come from a similar background? Are they "good enough" to be accepted as one of the family? Apparently, many of them are not. You'll recall Estelle W., the sister in Chapter One whose "very close" relationship with her brother was completely stifled after he married. Estelle described her sister-in-law as a "domineering, aggressive woman" who, to this day, controls her brother's life. And since their mother's death four years ago, the two siblings have not spoken a word to one another.

While such a rift represents an extreme case, two-thirds of the siblings interviewed said (in one of the few studies of young- and middle-adult siblings) that the marriages of their brothers and sisters detracted from their relationship. They felt rejected by the newly married sibling. Or they felt their sibling had "married down." Or they simply didn't like a sibling's spouse or were not liked by them. In some cases, the rift lasted a lifetime; in others, marriages dissolved, giving the siblings another chance; in a few, adjustments were made.[6]

TWISTING THE KNOT

In the interviews I conducted for this book, stories of strained relationships between siblings following one or the other's marriage far outweighed the stories of marriages that enhanced the sibling connection. The following comments from two different sisters were typical:

> Don and I are probably as far apart as we've ever been, which is very painful to me. His wife is very difficult. She basically does not talk to anyone in my family. She had her own problems growing up—an alcoholic father and mother. Her parents got their marriage annulled after having three daughters. The mother is a very rigid, difficult person and so is my sister-in-law. Yet I have to play by her rules because she's the gatekeeper to my nieces and nephew.

> My brother married when he was twenty-four, and his wife was very protective of him. She kept us apart, though I don't know if he realized that. She would not let me come near him. She was cold and controlling . . . not like anybody else in our family. My brother and I weren't part of each other's lives. I felt very empty then, like I was floating in space.

In these two cases, the brother's spouse was described as someone who kept the siblings apart. And in both situations, the spouse was "not like anybody else in our family." Both sisters felt the strain of trying to get along with sisters-in-law who were of different religious and/or different personality types. For the first woman, her brother's marriage continues to be a problem. Yet she perseveres because the connection with her brother's children is too important to jeopardize. She has no children of her own, and her nieces and nephew count for a lot. The other woman got a reprieve when her brother divorced his wife, giving them a chance to reestablish their sibship. "I can tell by the way he is and the intensity with which he pursues our relationship now that he spotted the danger," she said. "I know he also felt empty without a connection between us and that he won't allow someone else to split us apart again."

David F., estranged from his older sister for fifteen years, talked with great sadness about the distance between them that only recently has been bridged. David's wife didn't like his sister Cheryl; in fact, she disliked everyone in her husband's family. She was convinced that David wasn't getting a fair shake in the business he ran with Cheryl's husband. Rather than encourage David to discuss the perceived inequities with his family in the hope of working things out, she made it more and more difficult for him to spend any social time with them. Things got so bad that when David and she decided to sell out and move to Europe, they planned to leave without saying good-bye. They finally agreed to visit Cheryl and her children but refused to visit when Cheryl's husband was home. The visit was "awful," and David and Cheryl saw and spoke to each other infrequently for the next ten years.

It took a personal tragedy to bring David and Cheryl together again. After David fought and won a battle with cancer, he felt a need for family and called his sister. Those first conversations and, eventually, first visits, were emotionally charged. David was smart enough to visit alone, which freed him from worrying about what might transpire between his wife and Cheryl. To this day, the two women tiptoe around each other. David, however, is strong enough now to stay clear of the fray. He can't change the past but has vowed never to let his wife (or anyone else) get in the way of his friendship with Cheryl.

UNTYING THE KNOT

When talking about how a brother's marriage affected their relationship, one woman struck a sensible "wait-and-see" pose. Her patience has paid off.

I am the oldest and only girl in the family. I have three younger brothers. The middle brother and I were always the closest. When he got married, there was a great change in the quality of our relationship. The focus went from me being the critical person in his life to his wife being the most important. I think I was sad. I don't think it was jealousy. It was sadness that a discrete life stage had come to an end. I wanted to know if other people had experienced that. I wanted to be reassured that it wasn't a permanent termination of our relationship.

And, in fact, it has not been. Her brother has been married for seven years and, as his relationship with his wife has become stronger and better, he has not had to put as much "psychic energy" into his marriage and has had more time for his sister. "I understood that my brother needed to go off and chase his own identity and make his own place in the world. His focus on his wife was absolutely appropriate. Now that he's more sure of himself, he has a greater need for me and the rest of the family."

"THE TRUTH"

When I asked Tina C., an executive director of a national not-for-profit organization, how her siblings' marriages had affected their relationships, she described a family "truth" that dictated how she and her two sisters and two brothers were to react to such an event.

> One of the things we all knew as "The Truth" was that when one of us got married, the rest of us were not allowed to have any judgmental thoughts or feelings. I don't know where that came from. It was just something we all knew; it was something that had to be. And, by and large, that has been the case. We have welcomed the new spouses into the family, although they have never been equal to the brothers and the sisters. They've always been brothers- or sisters-in-law.

In our interview, Tina had already detailed special childhood sibling connections that had been nurtured over the years. "We like each other a lot and would probably choose to spend time with each other over anyone else in the world." She described an almost idyllic childhood in which she and her brothers and sisters were "never allowed to fight." Her parents concentrated on "what each of us had to offer the world and focused our energies on that rather than the fact that so and so took my toy or did this to me."

Tina and her siblings always have a good laugh when they talk about the "French Fry Principle." "Whenever we had french fries for dinner, my mother would count them out, making sure that we each had exactly the same number. Things were always equal between us. Whatever it was, my parents bent over backward to make sure we were treated and appreciated in an equal way." Accordingly, Tina and her four siblings were never aware of their strengths and weaknesses being compared. There was a sense of equality and open acceptance that defined their relationships. And it must have been these attributes, so firmly entrenched from childhood on, that molded their nonjudgmental acceptance of each other's spouses.

MARKER EVENTS IN YOUNG AND MIDDLE ADULTHOOD

Until recently, there was little recognition of predictable marker events that adult siblings face as they navigate the uncharted waters of young and middle adulthood. There were no concepts to help siblings understand the potential difficulties of leaving the parental home or of accepting a brother or sister's spouse as "one of the family." These specific events, expected to occur when siblings are young adults, change the dynamics of the sibling connection and provide either opportunities for growth or pitfalls for hurt and humiliation.

In the Ross and Milgram (1982) study, the marker event mentioned most frequently as bringing about changes in the sibling relationship was a geographical move, usually a move out of the parental home. Whether the move was to the next town or across the country, siblings felt that the geographical distance diminished their emotional ties. While the reasons for moving varied, most siblings took the move in stride. They accepted the geographical and subsequent emotional distancing as a "normal" passage from adolescence to adulthood.[7]

Sometimes distancing from our brothers and sisters can be a good thing; it gives us the needed perspective to figure out just what went on between us. One sibling remembered that she and her sister were always angry at their brother because, as the first boy, he was "fussed over, beloved, and spoiled." It took these two sisters distance and time to figure out that their brother was a "nice, sweet guy who tried to get out from under that attention given the first son."

Another sister talked candidly about how the geographical distance between her brother and her had all but obliterated any real emotional connection between them.

His definition of a relationship is a ceremonial one—sending birthday cards, talking about our children and how wonderful they are. We avoid the subject of our parents because we have totally different experiences with them. For me, improving our relationship means having a real time relationship. Then you automatically remember to do the little things because they have real meaning. When you talk about real things, there's a shared sense of life, including looking at who we used to be because we're old enough to look back.

This sister went on to talk about an incident that occurred when she and her brother were preadolescents—an event that she feels was central to their relationship but that neither has discussed since.

We were home alone, and my brother was opening a can of soup when the contents shot to the ceiling. I thought it was very funny—all those red spots all over the ceiling. But my brother got violently angry and threw a butcher knife at me. I was terrified; so was he. The two of us began to cry. And that marked the end of anything bad happening between us. We entered neutral territory with a bit of positive connection here and there. I would like to have a better, more connected relationship with my brother now. Yet I don't feel I need it to be happy. But as I get older, it would be very nice to have because he's it. I have no other siblings and very few first cousins.

The geographical distance between these two siblings has made it difficult or impossible to work out the conflicts in their relationship. Seeing each other only briefly on occasional visits has not provided opportunities for resolution. Even though the sister said she'd like to improve the relationship, she hasn't taken any steps to reconnect. Her brother is apparently content with the "ceremonial" relationship they have, and the sister, though thinking it would be "very nice" to have a more meaningful connection, isn't unhappy enough with the present state of affairs to make the first move. Chances are that, with time, her need for family will propel her to strengthen the ties with her brother because "he's it."

KEEPING THE FAITH

Not all siblings in young adulthood allow the geographical distance between them to diminish their emotional ties. If siblings feel close to one another and, in general, if one is a female (females, as noted earlier, are usually given the role of maintaining kin connections), chances are good they will not allow their immediate responsibilities of career and "new" family to significantly alter their relationship. A solid foundation laid in childhood seems to be a crucial factor in maintaining closeness once siblings leave the parental home.

Though Susan K. and her older brother do not live in the same city, they go to "great lengths" to see each other. Possibly because Susan is married and her brother is not, it is he who makes more of an effort to travel and visit Susan and her husband. "I see more of my brother than I do of my parents," said Susan. "We are very close, and though it's been kind of unfair lately because he always comes here, we still love to do things together. We are completely candid with each other about everything. I'm able to tell him anything, and the same goes for him. He asks my advice a lot, and we spout off about jobs and relationships." For Susan and her brother, geographical distance has not meant psychological distance as well. They continue to play an important part in each other's lives and aim to keep it that way. "For me, the ideal scenario is for us to end up in the same city and raise our kids together, though neither of us has any yet. I think it would be fabulous."

If and when siblings move closer to one another during adulthood, the geographical proximity invariably results in more frequent contact and often generates increased feelings of closeness. However, the problem of accepting the fact that the sibling is now an adult and has a separate life is not always easy.

When Lori P.'s sister Irene relocated to the same town, Lori acted like the "good, responsible" older sister and tried to include Irene in all of her social plans. But Irene rejected all of it; she wanted to establish her own circle of friends and activities. The transition was tough for both sisters.

> At first, I tried to take over, to be the big sister—sort of mothering—trying to make sure that everything was going smoothly for my sister and her family. I'm sure she resented it a bit, thinking that I didn't have confidence in her ability to settle in and make a life for herself. But she managed to establish her own circle of friends and her own life. And our relationship has been much better. We see each other fairly frequently but not all the time. It is a much more healthy and satisfying relationship for both of us.

The "more healthy and satisfying relationship" Lori described did not develop without some conflict. Lori needed to work through her tendency to still "mother" her younger sister, and Irene had to work overtime to assert her independence. The process of shedding childhood roles did not happen overnight. Yet with time, and because of each sister's willingness and growing capacity to see things from the other's perspective, the geographical proximity translated into opportunities for an improved relationship. "Things are so much better now," said Lori.

These sisters, like many young adult siblings who try to reenter each other's lives, found that their expectations of one another were echoes of the past. They reverted to the childhood roles of older sister/younger sister but with a twist. Instead of Irene placing a good deal of import on her older sister's advice as she had as a young girl, the adult Irene resented Lori's attempts to orchestrate her life. It took some time, but Lori eventually understood. In fact, she was relieved; she no longer had to be the "responsible" older sister charged with caring for Irene. The freedom from childhood expectations that no longer fit empowered both sisters to continue to grow as adults, both within and outside of their relationship.

The thirties are years in which many of us select the qualities and experiences from our childhood that we want to retain and blend them with qualities that distinguish us as individuals. It may be a bit easier for us at this stage in our lives to assess what went right between us and our siblings and what went wrong. And while we still might not be able to share all of what we conclude, we begin the process of reestablishing a link to our past and to our family.

As Norman P. approached his thirtieth birthday and celebrated the birth of his second child, "something just happened."

> My younger sister, who had recently married, and I started confiding in each other. That was something we didn't do much of when she was much younger. We just had different interests, and I was so wrapped up in my young family. It was just the right time for us to connect. We became closer as we started to talk about our parents and the things we liked and didn't like. I think concern for family members brought us together.

Many of us put down roots in our thirties. We may buy a home, start a family, dive head first into a new career, or seriously commit to the one we chose earlier. Having roots becomes very important; they provide a sense of security in a life that we are beginning to realize is much more difficult and painful than we thought. Brothers and sisters can be an integral part of this root system. They can link us to the past and give us strength to move forward.

KEEPING UP THE SIBLING TIE

Keeping up the sibling tie during our twenties and thirties may take some special effort with our commitments to our professions and later on to our new families, but the rewards are many. A sibling who has already moved away from home and begun life as an independent person can pave the way for other siblings. She or he can not only provide practical information about finding an apartment and setting up house but can serve as a sounding board for any of the potential emotional upheavals young adults may feel as they strike out on their own. It is a great comfort to talk to someone who knows the unique pushes and pulls of your family—someone who has already weathered the separation from Mom and Dad.

Once we are on our own, siblings as friends offer us all kinds of reasons to spend time together. They can introduce us to their special activities and to their circle of friends. Several siblings who had recently left home talked about what fun it was to be together in neutral territory, away from their parents' home. There was a felling of being free to do and say what they wanted without the real or perceived judgment from parents. One twenty-three-year-old remarked: "I never realized how funny my sister is. I think my parents squashed her humor. They didn't appreciate it. But I do, and I'm seeing her in a whole new light." A twenty-six-year-old who had lived in Europe for several years talked about his reunion with a younger brother: "He is so grown up. I don't know what happened to the pest I knew, but he's gone. I really like the person he is now and enjoy spending time with him in his new apartment."

A close connection between siblings can be a real blessing when we start having children of our own. We become aunts and uncles with great potential influence on both our nieces and nephews and on each other. Aunts and uncles can babysit, pass along their parenting experiences, and be there for support and friendship. The celebration of holidays and other special occasions becomes a true family affair; rituals are observed with the extended family in attendance. One twenty-eight-year-old talked about the joy of having her two younger brothers close by following the birth of her son. "It's not one of those long-distance relationships that so many brothers and sisters seem to have these days. My brothers adore my son and are wonderful with him. If I'm in a pinch and need to go somewhere, one or the other is usually more than willing to babysit. It's almost as if my son is theirs. I love having my brothers so involved in our lives right now."

When I was growing up in the Detroit area, many of my relatives lived nearby. I enjoyed close ties with aunts, uncles, and cousins on both sides of the family. I visited with them after Sunday school, during vacations, and on holidays and other family events. Not until I had my own child in a different city where I had not one close relative did I realize how lucky I had been as a child. My son Josh grew up barely knowing my siblings, his aunt and uncles. (He has no first cousins on my side of the family.) They were strangers in Josh's life and in mine.

Making up for lost time has not been easy. Josh and his aunt and uncle don't have a base from which to operate. They missed sharing most of the important marker events that bring family together. And I missed having them there with me.

Childhood memories of *my* aunts and uncles and cousins help me put my life in perspective. I remember how special I felt as the flower girl at my Uncle Stan and Aunt Lennie's wedding, sharing the spotlight in what was such a joyous occasion. I remember the camping trip to Michigan's Upper Peninsula seven or so years later with the five first cousins on my mother's side, her two brothers (my uncles), their wives (my aunts), and my entire family. All fifteen of us piled into three station wagons and headed for the wilderness for a week of tenting and bickering and laughing in the woods. And I remember when my Aunt D divorced (not something aunts, or anyone else, did back then), when my Uncle Bill married a woman with a child from her first marriage (another shocker at the time), and when my Uncle Milt and Aunt Inez relocated to Texas. Who the hell ever moved to Texas? The point is that the memories create a family history. The history is something tangible that we can hold on to and use as a road map of ourselves. As brothers and sisters, aunts, uncles, and cousins, we can reminisce about camping trips, births, weddings, holiday get-togethers, divorces, anniversaries, deaths. . . . We can compare notes, laugh, cry, get upset all over again. We can appreciate the ways in which we have changed and the ways in which we've remained the same. Without family in our lives, we are handicapped; part of us is missing. With them, we are more grounded, more whole.

5

MIDDLE ADULTHOOD: CHANCE FOR RENEWAL

Some of us enter middle adulthood as early as thirty-five; others enter it sometime during our forties. Whenever middle age sets in, we can count on being awash with a host of questions, doubts, and fears. "What's life all about, anyway?" "Is this all there is?" "How can I possibly do all I need to do in the short time I have left?" "Will it even be worth it?" We alternately feel bereft of the wherewithal to rescue ourselves and enthusiastic about the promise of putting our lives back together again. We examine our attitudes about everything—money, death, career, family—and confront our feelings of success or failure. Suddenly, time seems to be running out. Either we take advantage of this "last chance" to get it right or settle for mediocrity, even self-loathing. The "mid-life crisis" turns us upside down, yanking up the roots we so carefully laid down in our thirties.

Where do brothers and sisters fit in? How can the mid-life crisis affect our relationships? If any period of upheaval or regression is followed by a period of progression, or growth, these mid-life crises can work in similar ways. We not only move on to a renewed and stronger sense of ourselves but also to a reaffirmation of the value of family. This renewal, often enjoyed by the age of fifty, allows us to forgive our siblings (and parents, too) for real or perceived wrongdoings. Accompanied by an approval of ourselves, this "wonderful time" can erase the scorecard we've been lugging around with us since childhood. One fifty-year-old whose connection with her older brother had been tenuous at best, explained it this way:

> As I've become more comfortable with who I am and what I do . . . increasingly less self-conscious . . . I am much more able to appreciate my brother and his differences. I don't need to harp so much about the ways in which I thought he was incompetent or on the ways I didn't measure up. It may be an aging or developmental process. Some people accomplish that earlier in their lives than I have, some wait even longer, and some don't accomplish it at all.

The marker events of middle adulthood test the strength and will of the sibling network and offer brothers and sisters the chance for renewal. During our late forties, fifties, and early sixties, most of us will experience the illness and/or death of our parents, the growth of our children and their leaving home, and the reevaluation of our marriages. The connection with our siblings will either help us meet these special challenges or continue to stress an already weak bond.

88

WHEN PARENTS ARE ILL OR DYING

The illness or death of a parent often pushes brothers and sisters together to make important decisions about a parent's care and to confront emotionally laden issues such as money, property, and one's own mortality. Rarely are the ties between siblings tested as strongly. As with other marker events, the quality of the sibling relationship prior to a parent's illness or death often determines how they will react under such stress. A foundation of cooperation and support will usually serve them well, whereas a history of distance and unresolved hurts will often exacerbate an already difficult situation.

Like many young adults, fraternal twins Angela and Ted had grown apart. It wasn't that they didn't like each other; it was rather a matter of different interests and life-styles. A self-described 1960s "hippie" who had stopped being the "good"' girl and the "good" student by her sophomore year in college, Angela had hooked up with a group of artists and musicians who encouraged her interest in art and approved her "antiestablishment" stance. Ted, on the other hand, was a science major who spent his free time either surfing or partying with his fraternity brothers. Angela and Ted were separated by their own growth and development; there was little to push them back together again.

Angela married first at age twenty, a week pregnant but unaware of her condition at the time. Her husband was the brooding type whose "romantic dark side" compensated at first for his silence. Ted was married five years later to a woman who was the opposite of his sister. She was, says Angela, "cold and controlling" and did everything in her power to keep Ted and Angela apart. Angela never got to know his brother's wife and doesn't remember why the marriage didn't last. And Ted never got to know his sister's son.

Things changed dramatically following their mother's surgery for ovarian cancer. While the operation was deemed a success, there were postsurgical complications. Ted was able to be at his mother's side (Angela lived in another city a day's drive away). As soon as he realized the gravity of his mother's condition, he called Angela and urged her to come. "I finally got down there," she said, "and my mother was curled up in her bed. She looked awful. And there was my brother doing the best he could. From then on, Ted and I were a team, and my mother knew it. I could just see her watching us, because she had been so sad that her only children were not close as young adults. It was one of the healings in her life to see that we were back together again."

It took time for Angela and Ted to reconnect the frayed emotional ties from early adulthood but no time at all to complement one another in the long and draining care of their mother. Ted was more competent and practiced in handling logistics; Angela was better equipped to "go to the heart" and talk about the tough issues of illness and death. They made a very thorough support team. "It was important to have Angela there," said Ted.

> She was someone else to help share the burden, to talk to about the practical and emotional difficulties. I discovered that my sister is very responsible and direct in responding to need—that she's very tough and emotionally sound, able to deal with heavy problems and still maintain her sense and perspective. Seeing that was a surprise. I hadn't had an opportunity to test or be aware of her reactions under such stress. We got to be very good at crisis control.

"As things got worse," said Angela, "we'd call and talk to each other. We saw how much we shared . . . feelings of anger and guilt and sadness. Our connection gave us both a basis, an understanding of the situation, rather than being lost in it. Let's face it. If you work together, two are much better than one. That's when we started saying 'I love you' again."

By the time their mother died, Angela and Ted were "intensely bonded again." Their shared experience in caring for their dying mother pushed them back into each other's lives after many years of distance. That their mother constantly rejoiced in their "coming together" was one of the "beauties" of her dying. And after she died, Angela and Ted's relationship continued to blossom. The process of "revealing" themselves to one another had its share of starts and stops, but today Ted describes his sister as the "single most important person in my life," and Angela says with a broad smile, "I'm more fully alive and happier and feel much safer now. Having my brother back in my life has healed a split that I felt for a long time. I don't even think of him as my best friend. He's more than that; he's my brother."

When a parent is frail or ill, the vast majority of primary caregivers are daughters or daughters-in-law (Brody, 1981). Sons are rarely placed in the position of being the provider of hands-on care. In families with several daughters, the daughter who lives closest to the parent will most often take on the responsibility.

Because Ted lived in the same city as his mother, was single, and had no children of his own, he assumed more of the day-to-day caretaking responsibilities than Angela. That Angela and Ted viewed the caring of their mother as a joint venture and shared the emotional issues, as well as many of the practical ones, speaks to their supportive relationship and the loyalty they shared.

UNFULFILLED EXPECTATIONS

Sometimes the illness or death of a parent can throw the sibling hierarchy up for grabs and create a host of unexpected challenges. You will recall Tina W. whose parents' expectations of the meaning of family guided her siblings and her in their unequivocal acceptance of one another, as well as of each other's spouses. Accustomed to such support from her brothers and sisters, Tina was thrown for a loop when her oldest brother, Daniel, did not respond to their father's illness as expected.

"I automatically looked to Daniel to take over the reins following my father's illness. But he didn't. He was not the one who in subsequent months made sure that every weekend someone was visiting my mother, keeping her company. He was not the one who arranged conference calls among us so we could share our sorrows, concerns, and frustrations. He just wasn't there for us, and we expected him to be."

As the oldest son, Daniel was expected to be the leader who would orchestrate his younger siblings' roles during the aftermath of his father's stroke. That he abdicated his "assigned" responsibilities and let his siblings down made Tina angry and distressed. Then a matter of months after her father's stroke, Tina's aunt, a "precious" member of the family who had lived with Tina's parents for years, died rather suddenly. With her father completely incapacitated and her mother tending to him, Tina and her siblings were left with the job of planning the funeral. Again Daniel did not step forward; the pecking order no longer existed. Everyone was forced to relate and to respond in a whole new way.

"When my father died," said Tina, "we'd almost been through a dress rehearsal with my aunt's funeral. So we each pitched in and organized my father's funeral service to be held in his hometown, where he would be buried.

Daniel and his family did travel across the country to be there, but when the rest of us flew to my father's home in another city, he returned home. I thought he was *supposed* to join us. It was expected of him."

As the only sibling with young children (he married late), Daniel was caught between the expectations of his siblings and the demands of his "new" family. Although he was in his late forties, he was, in a real sense, more like a man in his thirties, involved in the raising of children and the support of his family. Daniel didn't have the time, energy, or inclination to be "big brother" *and* family man. His father's illness and ultimate death came at a time when he was unable to assume the lead and carry his younger siblings through the emotional roller coaster ride and the practical caretaking duties.

Unlike many siblings whose expectations are unfulfilled when a parent dies, this story has a happy ending, because the others eventually understood the pressures in Daniel's life. "I can see more clearly," said Tina, "how the stresses in his life limit him from taking on the responsibilities of our family because he has his own family to take care of. He has to abide by his choices, not mine. He is still my brother, and I still love him."

BITTER ENDINGS

The Ross and Milgram study of adult sibling relationships showed that the on-time deaths of parents—deaths that occurred in the later years—brought siblings closer together. Shared grief and the recollection of happy experiences and family closeness was one theme. "Mom (Dad) is not there anymore to keep us together, so we have to do it ourselves," was another.[1] While many siblings enjoy a closer bond with each other following the death of a parent, there are those brothers and sisters who revert back to childhood rivalries and are unable to get beyond the bickering. For these siblings, the death of a parent drives them further apart, sometimes creating wounds that are never healed.

"My brother was always the favorite," began Gina B. as she talked about her mother's death. "My mother spoiled him and treated him as if he was her prized possession. I, on the other hand, could never do anything right. When my mother died, it was as if her legacy got even stronger. I felt as if I'd been left out for life, and that nothing could change my feelings of inadequacy." Since her mother's death, Gina and her brother have seen each other only once. And their phone conversations have been a series of arguments about the will and what to do with their parents' home. "Part of me feels terrible that my brother and I are so far apart. But there's this other part that feels so angry and hurt. I don't see us settling this thing."

As we've seen over and over again, parental favoritism is a significant factor in the rivalry between siblings. Another dynamic that can cause dissention occurs when a younger adult sibling continues to see an older sibling as mentor and that mentor does not appreciate the younger siblings' accomplishments.

Miriam T., fifty-five and the only daughter, looked up to her older brother as "the greatest person to walk this earth." "From the time I was a little girl," she said, "Brian was my idol. His approval meant more to me than my parents'." When her mother became ill, Miriam took charge. She was the one who visited her mother every day in the hospital, made important decisions about her care once she was home, and eventually handled all of the funeral arrangements. "Brian disagreed with everything I did. Yet when I asked him to step in and call the shots, he didn't have the time. I'd looked up to him all my life, and there he was knocking me down every chance he got. I don't know what got into him, and I'm no longer interested in finding out."

If only siblings could go into training long before the turmoil of a parent's illness or death. Making decisions about care and funerals and property is so emotionally powerful that it can send siblings into a tailspin. To construct some framework for how to proceed under such stress would help to eliminate or lessen many of the potential pitfalls. But, alas, there are no seminars that prepare siblings for the tough issues they will face when a parent dies. We are left to our own devices to either handle ourselves with grace or to fall apart under the strain. By and large, those adult brothers and sisters who established close emotional ties in childhood will weather the storm and feel even closer as their family begins to dwindle and they are forced to confront their own mortality. For others, their work is cut out for them. The more they can put childhood baggage aside and work together as a unit in the face of loss, the better their chances of forging closer ties to carry with them into their later years.

AS OUR CHILDREN GROW: FACING THE "EMPTY NEST"

My son, Josh, is about to go off to college. I can already taste the loneliness and anticipate how my role change from full-time mother to occasional mom will redirect much of my time and energy. There will be no more children for me. And while that decision is mine, the radiant face of a new mother gazing into her infant's eyes makes me cry. I don't covet what she has ahead of her; I mourn what is behind me. And that, it seems, is one of the hurdles of middle adulthood—the recognition that with half of our lives behind us there are precious roles, energies, and dreams we can no longer pursue. We must redefine our directions, keeping in mind the limitations that didn't exist before and the freedoms that now make dreams deferred a possibility.

For many women, whose job of serving others has consumed their lives, the challenge when children leave home is to cultivate undeveloped talents and to, at last, serve their own needs. When a woman loses her powers of procreation or decides that she will never have another child— at whatever age this happens—an intriguing phenomenon occurs. A new kind of creativity is released. And a woman pours more of herself into it than she ever did when the option of reproducing was still available.[2] To have a sibling at her side to support her in any new pursuit, particularly if her husband and family are less than enthusiastic about the change, makes the transition from caring for others to caring more for her own needs easier.

For many men, the challenge of facing children moving away physically and emotionally is often exacerbated by bad timing. Men who have been busy climbing the success ladder find themselves ready to slow down and spend more time with family just when their children are pulling away. How to be softer, more available, more vulnerable, even if their children are not responsive? And complicating this already difficult transition is a man's conditioning to keep his feelings to himself. That makes talking with brothers or sisters or anyone else about letting his children go a difficult leap of trust. As one forty-eight-year-old father put it: "I stuffed all the emotions about my son leaving home until I was ready to explode. My wife and I talked some. But we were going through our own share of readjustments. So at some point I was having lunch with my sister, and I just spilled the beans. It's not my style to let my emotions go like that, but it felt good. And it felt good to know that I could count on my sister to listen to me and not make me think I was nuts." Gail Sheehy points out that a man might feel a lot better if he knew that the confusion he feels about his children (and his wife and his job) is predictable, temporary, and necessary for the "period of easement" that follows.[3]

Several of the siblings I interviewed—all of them women—mentioned how sharing their feelings about their children leaving home made them feel closer and helped relieve some of the loneliness and confusion. One forty-five-year-old had this to say:

> My younger daughter looks so much like my sister that she could be her daughter. Their physical likeness seems to have cemented their relationship. When my daughter left for college, it was as if my sister's own daughter had gone. We both mourned the passing of an important life stage. And we dreamed together about the future and its possibilities. My sister has two children still at home. And I know that our talks will help her when they leave. It's wonderful to have a sister with whom I can share some difficult emotional stuff. My husband isn't always willing.

Another sister talked about how invested she is in her nieces and nephews:

> I share my sister's children's lives a great deal. I care deeply about them and their well-being. I can remember when the oldest boy moved out of the house. My sister was hysterical. It was as if she'd lost part of herself. I was there to listen and to help her see that her son would always be there. And I was able to suggest some of the ways her life would now be more her own. I married late, and my kids are still young. But I know what it is to be a parent and can feel for my sister's emotional ups and downs right now. And I know she'll be there for me when I face the same situation.

There is great comfort in being able to share our fears about our children striking out on their own with sisters

97

and brothers who know us (and our children) so well. They can remind us about past separations and how we came through them after all. They can recognize our insecurities about facing change with an objectivity we can rarely muster. Our siblings, often very involved in the lives of their nieces and nephews, recognize our feelings, acknowledge them, and encourage us to grow right along with our growing children.

MARRIAGE AFTER THE MID-LIFE CRISIS

Many couples who survive the mid-life crisis together begin to realize that their shared interests and need for privacy and outside relationships are not mutually exclusive. There is an understanding that our spouse cannot meet all of our needs and that we must go beyond the marriage and cultivate valuable friendships that enhance our lives as individuals and as marriage partners.

In our late forties and fifties our responsibilities to family and to career become less consuming, so we are freer to go beyond the confines of home and work to explore an expanded world. For many, the sibling relationship comes into clearer focus again. We are more in touch with the internalized siblings we've carried since childhood and more willing and able to reconcile our past with the present. We can look forward to pleasing ourselves and to feeling more secure and comfortable with our siblings. We are less and less interested in trying to change them to mirror our values and expectations. However they choose to lead their lives is fine with us, as long as they're happy and as long as they have stopped trying to convert us. "My brother doesn't have a dime in a savings account," commented one fifty-one-year-old. "I don't know how he can live that way. But I've given up trying to talk money with him, and he's stopped criticizing my capitalistic ways. We get along much better now."

And for the first time, many spouses accept their brothers- and sisters-in-law as valuable additions to the family. Spouses who may have been threatened by the close ties between their mate and a sibling feel more secure in their own marriage. They realize that an intimate sibling connection does not have to detract from the value of their marriage. As one sister put it: "There were times when I've called my sister and couldn't get past her husband to talk to her. Either I had to talk to him first or he'd put me off. More than once I had to tell him that I wanted to talk to my sister, not to him. But as we've gotten older, he doesn't do that anymore. He puts me right through when I call, and the relationship between us seems the better for it."

As we accept our essential aloneness, we become more loving and devoted to our spouse, our family, and our friends. The realization that our safety does not reside in anyone else encourages us to find safety in ourselves. And once our individuality is no longer endangered, we can be more magnanimous with another.[4]

MIDDLE ADULTHOOD: MAXIMUM INFLUENCE

Middle adulthood is the time of maximum influence in the work place and within our family. We are in our prime and possess the tools, experience, and self-esteem to make a difference. Our physical prowess may start to slide but not far enough to impair our big chance to leave our mark. Siblings can offer sensitivity and understanding as we confront the weighty emotional issues that befall each of us: mid-life crises, the illness and/or death of our parents, the empty nest and the subsequent reevaluation of our roles, and the changes in our marriages. We have the opportunity to move on to face the second half of our lives as stronger individuals, more in tune with our own needs, and also as eager partners within the sibling group. Older siblings who have already made the journey can show us how. Their example, whether we choose to follow it or not, serves as a reminder that we will survive and be better off for the struggles along the way.

6
SIBLINGS IN LATER LIFE: COMING TOGETHER

In our youth-oriented culture, with its emphasis on staying fit and getting ahead, it's no wonder that the emotional connections of people sixty-five and older have been ignored. They no longer cling to the "shoulds" and "musts" that so often dictate the goals of young and middle adults. Instead, many older adults have come to understand what Gail Sheehy calls the concept of enough. Good enough. Successful enough. Rich enough. Socially responsible enough.[1] They have learned to like and approve of themselves. Quite independent of other people's standards and agenda, this older generation focuses more on their inner lives than on the outer trappings of professional and monetary success. They have fought their share of battles and struggled with the discomforts of change. For those who move through the mid-life crisis and find a renewal of purpose, the later years herald a time in which they can give a blessing to their own lives and to the people close to them.

Almost half of the people over sixty-five see at least one of their siblings every week, and ninety-seven percent of older brothers and sisters value their connection sufficiently to keep it going by mail, phone, and personal contact.[2] While young and middle adult siblings are adjusting to the various mid-life crises, siblings in later life are striving to find solace and peace with one another. They have come full circle.

FULL CIRCLE

Sisters Irene and Diane, seventy-nine and seventy-seven, live across the hall from one another in what has been hailed as a state-of-the-art retirement complex in the heart of Chicago. Their front doors are always open, and the two sisters walk back and forth day and night. "I don't think I could live without her," said Irene. "We are very close now."

Irene and Diane, each other's only sibling, were not always so close. Though they shared the same bedroom growing up and are only eighteen months apart, the emotional bond between them was distant at best. "She went her way," said Diane, "and I went mine. We just didn't have much in common." Irene was a dancer; Diane didn't like to dance. Irene finished high school and went on to college; Diane took a two-year secretarial course and then stopped. And though the sisters married within a short time of one another, Diane had two children right away, while Irene adopted two children many years later. "Our time schedules were different, and we saw very little of one another as young and middle adults," said Irene. "She was busy raising children, and I had to go back to work. By the time I had my two babies, her boys were in high school. We didn't even see each other on holidays. She was with her husband's family, and I was with mine."

Irene can pinpoint the moment she and Diane realized and acknowledged their connection as sisters. Their mother lay in bed, where she had died during the night. Without anyone else to advise them, the two sisters bathed and dressed her. "We became closer and closer," said Irene. "She's my sister," said Diane, "the only one I have. It's ironic, isn't it? My mother had to die before we began to realize what we meant to one another."

After their mother's death, the sisters saw each other frequently until Irene's husband took an early retirement and they moved to Arkansas. "We made trips to Chicago as often as possible," said Irene. "I came up at least two times a year to be with my sister." Eleven years after their move to Arkansas, Irene's husband died. "I was perfectly happy to stay where I was," she said, "but I began to realize that I needed to be closer to my sister and the rest of my family. I had many friends in Arkansas, but I needed to be with family."

After some soul searching, Irene packed her things and moved into the recently completed retirement complex in Chicago. She and Diane found themselves walking back and forth between their respective buildings or on the phone "every ten or fifteen minutes." "Irene suggested that I move into her building," said Diane, "but I was certain I couldn't afford it. Then I counted my pennies and found that I could. So now we live across the hall from each other. We tell each other wherever we're going and what we're doing and everything else. I guess it is advanced age and subconsciously thinking that one of us will probably be alone. I haven't thought about expressing it, but that must be there."

"We share our present lives and memories of the past," said Irene. "We're still different, but we just know that we'll take care of one another. We're very, very close."

early eighty percent of seniors have at least one
__ing, brothers and sisters can counteract the threat
of isolation and offer a source of social integration as members of a family group. Siblings can provide psychological
help by boosting morale, providing companionship, serving
as confidants, giving advice, and aiding in decision making.
They can also provide instrumental help by homemaking,
shopping, transporting, and caring for one another. Older
siblings stand ready to help one another in times of need,
even if not called upon very often. They appear to function
like an insurance policy: there is comfort and satisfaction
in just knowing that a sibling is there.[3]

If you ask siblings in young adulthood to name their
closest relatives, they'll list their spouse, their children, and
possibly a parent. Siblings often end up fourth on the list.
When you ask the same question of older adults, they say
they feel closer to siblings than to any other relatives except
their own children.[4] The fact that brothers and sisters feel
closer as they age has been supported by the work of key
researchers like Victor Cicirelli and Deborah Gold. Cicirelli
(1979), investigating sibling relationships of adults over
sixty years of age, found that eighty-three percent reported
feeling "extremely close" or "close." In a 1986 study, Gold
discovered that forty-five percent of siblings in old age had
a relationship that could be labeled "intimate" or "con-
genial," and another thirty-five percent had a relationship
that was labeled "loyal."[5] Gold used the same men and
women in a follow-up study two years later to further explore sibling relationships in the later years. While these
siblings did not report feeling any closer or having any more
contact than two years before, they did report thinking
about their brothers and sisters more often and experiencing deeper feelings of acceptance and approval. The shared

memories of a lifetime appeared to be more important than direct interaction. As one brother wrote, "Just knowing she's there means more than anything."

Gold's follow-up study also found that older brothers and sisters may be able to "forgive and forget." Very few of the older siblings discussed feelings of resentment, envy, or rivalry. They gave less attention to hostility and jealousy in later life than they may have earlier in adulthood. Even though Gold's sample reported that older siblings give less practical support over time, these late-life siblings continued to provide strong emotional support. The combination of being the same age *and* a family member creates a psychological bond that is difficult to equal[6]

THE SUNSET OF OUR LIVES

"It's hard to admit," said Sam, a sixty-seven-year-old retired military man and businessman. "The older generation is gone. We're the older generation now. We're the patriarchs and matriarchs of the family as we move into the sunset of *our* lives. Maybe that's why we have gotten closer."

Sam seemed to surprise himself as he spoke. He hadn't really given the issue of brothers and sisters much thought; he just knew that his sister, three years younger, and his brother, six years younger, provide him with a sense of belonging, security, and comfort that he values as a "great asset" at this stage in his life.

> I used to think my brother was a pain in the neck. We didn't do much together as we were growing up because he was so much younger. Today he's a well-known and respected historian. I'm very proud of him and think he's a wonderful guy.
> I always liked my sister. And I like her more now. Why,

105

I saw her just last week. She lives a thousand miles away, but we talk by phone at least twice a month, as is attested by the size of our phone bill. We keep in constant touch.

For Sam, the strong emotional ties to his siblings are based not so much on seeing them often but on the emotional support they provide and the memories they share. "When we talk, we frequently reminisce. We swap stories about our childhood and about our parents. My brother and sister are people I can rely on and trust. I appreciate our closeness, and I only wish that *our* children will someday have the same strong connections."

Though their age difference kept them apart during childhood and early adulthood, Sam and Harry have developed similar interests in history and books. As mature adults, they were able to parlay those shared enthusiasms into a viable relationship that has grown in importance. Sam and Harry have forged a mutual admiration society. "We're very close now," said Sam. "We can talk about anything. I rejoice at his successes!"

Having a sister, Sam feels, has given him greater emotional security. His sister provides a sense of happiness and stability. "When our mother got sick, she took care of her. She did something I couldn't have done. I love her very much." Like a majority of elder brothers, Sam realizes that his sister has had a great influence on his feelings and concerns. His life would be significantly emptier without her.

SISTER LOVE

The role sisters play in keeping siblings together is most pronounced in later life. Possibly for the first time, brothers recognize and give credit for all the things a sister has done and continues to do to foster a close and supportive relationship.

Frank, seventy-five and the middle child with an older sister and a younger brother, had this to say about his sister:

> I credit my sister with teaching me a lot about the opposite sex, about caring for other people, and about developing certain tricks of the trade that led to my successful career in sales. My sister and I are alike in many ways. We both like people. She likes to play golf, and I like golf, too. And we enjoy friends and relations and keep in touch with them. We have a very good relationship.

The fact that Frank's sister and his wife have always gotten along well adds another bond. While they weren't as involved in each other's lives when they were busy with their own families and jobs, aging has brought them in closer emotional contact. The importance of shared memories is not lost on either of them. "My sister and her second husband live several hours' drive away. We make an effort to get together at least a couple times each year."

SISTERS AS CARETAKERS

Joel always liked his sister, but the eight years difference in age seemed enormous. "I had eight years as an only child," said Joel. "I don't remember feeling jealous when my sister, Susan, then my brother, Rob, were born. My mother made sure we all felt loved. But we were really almost two separate generations."

Susan's health was an issue of concern growing up. She was frail and underweight, and she could not keep up with her brothers or other children her age. Although she attended a special school, she made friends easily and became a fine pianist. Rob, on the other hand, was a "pest." Though the boys shared a bedroom, the ten-year difference in age kept them apart. Joel tried to be the good, older brother and taught Rob how to play ball when he was old enough. "That," said Joel, "was a lot of fun." But unlike Sam and his younger brother, Harry, Joel, and Rob did not grow closer as they matured. Rob didn't finish college, and "that's been a handicap to him all these years." Not once but twice Rob got involved in bad business deals, and both times Joel tried to bail him out. "I finally told my lawyer not to loan him another cent. I learned the hard way not to get involved with my brother's business. It made me too angry." Despite his frustrations, Joel describes his relationship with Rob today as "occasional . . . but not detached . . . more than fraternal." He calls Rob on the average of once a month and sees him three to four times a year. "He doesn't need my support," said Joel, "like my sister does."

Susan has no children of her own. Just as she was getting ready to adopt, her husband died of a heart attack. Somehow she managed to carry on. "I'm very proud of her," Joel said. "She's an active, busy woman who is constantly helping others." That caretaking role was never more pronounced than when her mother, at age eighty-three, had an accident that rendered her completely dependent. Susan left her job, moved out of her brand new condo, and moved into her mother's home, where she spent the next eight years. "I owe my sister a great deal. She did something I couldn't do. I've never seen her spirits down." Though Rob lived close by and took care of emergencies, he didn't handle the day-to-day responsibilities. Those fell on Susan. And while Joel provided financial assistance and visited four to five times a year from another state, his obligation to his own family and to his work prevented him from spending more time relieving his sister.

"I tried to give Susan a weekend off during my mother's illness. It was the worst weekend of my life! My mother was so demanding; she wanted everything 'Now!' I quickly understood the emotional reversal of a parent being treated like a child. She was so dependent. The experience was terrible for me, and it just increased my appreciation for my sister."

Dealing with a parent's estate can be a traumatic experience for some siblings. That was not the case with Joel, Rob, and Susan. The estate was split three ways, though each sibling initially said they didn't need the money. Joel wanted it all to go to Susan because she'd given up a job and eight years to care for her mother. Rob wanted the money split between Susan and Joel because he'd borrowed money from his mother that he'd never repaid. Susan wanted the estate divided equally three ways. Her brothers acquiesced without a fight.

At age seventy-three, Joel cherishes all that he and Susan share. "We both have a love for music. We grew up in the Big Band Era and still exchange records and sheet music. And, of course, she can sit down at the piano and play all of it." Rob stays pretty much to himself, but Joel and Susan are "joiners." They both like people and are involved in various clubs and organizations. "My sister created a cottage industry for herself. She is a broker of quilts. She will take orders and then have the women in the Amish community make the quilts for her. She's got a license plate that says QUILTS, and she calls herself the 'Quilt Lady.' She's built this business for herself! Plus she's active in community groups, she's taking dancing lessons . . . She does all these things on her own. My sister is quite a woman!"

Joel also described a "great" relationship between Susan and his children. "They're her family. She constantly sends them notes and presents. When my daughter had a knee operation, my sister went all the way to Texas to take care of her. She'll go anywhere, anytime to help anybody."

When Joel talks about his sister, his whole demeanor changes. His gravelly, monotone delivery becomes animated, and his eyes sparkle; his hands, normally quiet on the table in front of him, gesticulate like an orchestra conductor's. The mere mention of his sister brings Joel great happiness, as if a warm light has been turned on at his very core. Susan, with her abundance of love and willingness to care for "anybody, anywhere, anytime," is the traditional kin connector, working hard to keep all the members of the family together. She remembers birthdays and anniversaries and gives unselfishly of her time and of herself. Joel's wife thinks so much of her that she turns over her Social Security check every month to be included in the money Joel sends her. "Susan doesn't know," said Joel. "But my wife is ever grateful for the kind of sparkling spirit my sister exudes. We are all very lucky."

Even when sisters don't feel particularly close to a sibling, they may feel compelled to help out in a jam if other siblings are unwilling to step in. Such is the case with Jackie, eighty-eight, and her seventy-eight-year-old sister, Sara. The two sisters moved in together because none of the other siblings would take Sara. "She can't get along by herself," said Jackie.

> So what am I supposed to do? We have absolutely different ideas about everything, but I feel morally responsible for her care. It's been very difficult, partially because of Sara's health and partially because she's never helped me take care of our apartment. I don't believe in divorce, but I do believe in murder. Sara is killing me. I'm older by ten years, and I'll probably die first. But what choice do I have? I wouldn't feel right putting her in a home, so I do the best I can.

While Sara and Jackie fight every inch of the way, Jackie's sense of family and her role as kin keeper will prevent her and her sister from "splitting up." They tried that once, and Sara came back within a matter of hours. "We are the original Odd Couple," said Jackie. "And I guess that's the way it's going to stay. Neither of us is going to change at our age!"

FROZEN MISUNDERSTANDINGS

An overwhelming number of studies have shown that rivalry between siblings diminishes as they age. Possibly because they interact in different ways and place a premium on the renewal or repair of relationships, older siblings engage less in argumentative, bossy, competitive behavior that may have put them at odds growing up. Reconstructing their shared past helps them put their lives in order and provides meaning in the final stage of adult development.

Despite these advantages, a certain percentage of older siblings lose touch completely. These siblings declare that nothing can ever create or reestablish a meaningful, positive relationship. Their negative feelings toward one another have lasted a long time and were often precipitated by one critical event, like a dispute over an inheritance or a serious misunderstanding. Figures vary from three percent to ten percent, but those siblings who never see or talk to one another in later life give us a clearer picture of what can go wrong between brothers and sisters and why.

Take the story of Herbert, now eighty-one and the youngest of three, and his two sisters, Kate and Rita. Theirs was a happy childhood, though the "girls" had different interests and didn't spend "enormous" time with their baby brother.

Kate married first. Her husband, a plastering contractor, became the source of conflict between Herbert and Kate. "I think her husband was a crook," Herbert said.

When my mother was ill, he whittled away the little income my mother had. And after I helped him get a job with the company I worked for, it was discovered down the

111

line that he was greatly overcharging. The whole situation was very embarrassing to me, and it strained my relationship with Kate. As I see it today, I feel she was weak to have been so influenced by her conniving husband. And, years later, when Kate decided that I should take care of our ailing mother, all heck broke loose. It was a Catch-22; I didn't want to care for my mother, who was senile, yet Kate's husband had spent all of mother's money. That was a mess. I did not pay; they did. And all contact with Kate was lost. The last time I saw her was at my mother's funeral. That was more than twenty years ago.

While Herbert hasn't seen his sister Kate for more than twenty years, he hears about her through Rita. "I don't like the rift," he said, "but I'm not big enough to change the situation. It would be very, very difficult to put aside all the hurt and anger. I would not travel a great distance to go to her funeral . . . I guess I wouldn't go."

For older siblings like Herbert, the hurt and missed connections of the past still have the power to rile them. They are not able to change or to make amends. For others, the hostility seems to matter little, and they shrug off the rift. Yet for many estranged siblings, the protestations of not caring a whit cover up a great deal of guilt and remorse. One wonders whether it is possible to ever divorce oneself from a sibling in the way one can forget old friends or even a former spouse.

JUST KNOWING A BROTHER OR SISTER IS THERE

As siblings age and their physical strength wanes, it may not be possible for them to step in and, say, provide day-to-day care for an ill brother or sister. That kind of caretaking responsibility is usually handled by a sibling's children. That does not mean, however, that siblings are not intimately involved in emotional support. They talk frequently and see each other whenever they are able. And if the normal chain of command fails and children are not able to pitch in when needed, siblings usually pull together and care for one another. "We can count on each other," said an eighty-two-year-old sister. "My sister had a heart attack last November and, of course, I was there. I've been hospitalized twice since then, and my sister was right there. Her children are far away; I have a son nearby. I'm really the only one she has right now."

Over and over again, older siblings talk about the importance of staying in touch. Even when they live in different parts of the country and are not well enough or can't afford to see each other often, most older brothers and sisters find the sense of family very compelling. A sixty-five-year-old minister in failing health brimmed with energy when he discussed his three surviving siblings:

> It's something special to have two sisters and a brother at this point in my life because we want to keep the family tree going. We're now coming up on our third family reunion. This brings us together, and we have a glorious time. Our family is a tremendous force. It's hard to get us together, but you talk about a good time! It's as if we'd just seen each other yesterday.
> I say I am blessed to have grown up in a time when people were more conscious of their families, they lived closer, they were more caring. There was a true bond.

I asked Reverend Jones what he feels about siblings who haven't spoken in years: "I say that's wrong as two left shoes. If someone has to bend, someone has to make the first step. And if that's you, then you do it. And don't bring up why you haven't called. Once a brother or sister sees that you're not going to leave them again, they're all right."

The reverend's "down-home" approach may sound naive

to some, yet the importance he places on the sibling bond as he ages echoes the sentiments of the vast majority of siblings in later life. "It's been proven," said Reverend Jones, "that I could go to any of my siblings. My wife and I are on a fixed income, and the money is tight. But if we really and truly need money to tide us over, we can refer to one or two of them. That's saying something!"

THE "LIFE REVIEW"

The "life review" is a crucial process that all of us go through in the later years. As first postulated by Robert Butler in 1963, this process helps us accept that human life is finite by looking back at our own life and connecting all the disparate parts. Life review allows us to resolve old conflicts and come to grips with past mistakes. It can help us achieve what Erik Erikson calls integrity, that final stage of adult development in which one can give a blessing to one's own life.

Ironically, by the time we're ready to review our lives, our parents are usually gone. Who better, then, to help validate experiences than our brothers and sisters who have been there most (or all) of the time and know us in ways no one else can. Through reminiscing about the past with our siblings and reintegrating those events, values, and attitudes with the present, we can more easily face old age and death. Brothers and sisters connect us to our early lives. Talking with them about growing up clarifies events, fills in gaps, and evokes the warmth of early family life.

Despite the rivalry and competition many people associate with brothers and sisters, most of us will find unexpected strengths in this relationship in later life. And this late-life bond may be particularly important to the baby boomers now in middle adulthood. The high divorce rates and low birth rates will push members of that generation to look to their siblings for support in old age. Since people live longer, healthier lives, these siblings will be able to help each other find the solace and peace later life offers. Research on siblings in later life may be sparse, but senior siblings themselves clearly understand the value of the emotional support they give to one another and how that support and link to the past can help each of us see the harmony and order behind the apparent disorder of a lifetime.

7

TWINS AND THE MEANING OF SIBSHIP

Many of us spend our lives searching for
our lost other half, a soul mate who is like
us enough to understand us perfectly.
Twins have that without even trying.
—Letty Cottin Pogrebin

It's easy to get swept up in the specialness of twins, particularly identical twins. To meet two people who look and act alike, finish each other's sentences, share the same interests, boast identical IQs, and often assume the other's successes as their own never ceases to fascinate us. As siblings, close identical twins establish a model for intimacy in which jealousy, competition, and selfishness are foreign concepts. The bond between twins is potentially the strongest and most enduring of human social relationships. In it we find values and behaviors of true sisterhood and/or brotherhood. Investigating the relationship between twins helps us better understand the grand effect siblings can have on one another and how likenesses and differences emerge.

NATURE VERSUS NURTURE: THE ROLE TWINS PLAY

The study of twins not only sheds light on sibling intimacy but affords a better understanding of the interplay between nature and nurture. The debate over which has greater influence on one's personality and behavior—heredity or environment—seems to be taking a decisive turn. Results from studies of twins, specifically identical twins separated at or shortly after birth, as well as findings in behavioral and animal research, have led many scientists to conclude that genes play a role in every phase of human behavior from leadership to fears and phobias.

At the forefront of the research on the role of genes in human behavior is the Minnesota Center for Twin and Adoption Research. Since 1979, hundreds of sets of twins have been tested and scrutinized. "Our studies show," said Nancy Segal, the center's assistant director, "that genetics underlie every aspect of human behavior. The question is, how much is genetic and how resistant is certain behavior to change?"[1] In this view, the human mind, rather than being a clean slate to be filled in by family and society, is wired before birth with a predisposed personality. Such predisposition can be enhanced or suppressed, but not eliminated, by child rearing and other nurturing experiences. Like a diamond that can be smoothed and reshaped but not crushed, we come into this world with built-in traits that encourage us to act in specific ways and to gravitate to certain environments. Extroverts, according to the center's findings, are born, not made. The same can be said for the tendencies toward being conformists, worrywarts, creative personalities, optimists, and paranoids. Other traits such as cautiousness and aggressiveness appear to be determined as much by heredity as by one's culture. Scientists have speculated for generations that people are highly influenced by their genes, but proof was lacking. Now that has changed. Because studies have shown that identical twins raised apart have an uncanny number of precisely the same behaviors and personality traits, there is now solid evidence that the DNA in our genes is often more influential than our environment.[2]

TWIN BIRTHS: A QUICK REVIEW

Identical twins, which account for one-third of all twin births, are formed from the splitting of a single fertilized egg. Each egg half develops into a fetus with the same genetic code. Identical twins are genetic clones. Fraternal twins, on the other hand, are formed by two eggs released at once and fertilized by two separate sperm. The two fetuses can share up to fifty percent of their genetic makeup, the same as ordinary siblings.

At conception, each of us gets a genome—thousands of genes arranged on our forty-six chromosomes, half contributed by the mother, half by the father. Half of the genome is held in common by all people, and this half differentiates us from lions or chimps or dogs. The other half varies from person to person—except in the case of identical twins—and guarantees that each of us will be one of a kind. The personalities of siblings, who are anywhere from 35 percent to 50 percent genetically alike, may be quite different. Variety in personality has many causes (discussed in Chapter Two), but one cause is that certain traits are controlled by the *combined* action of numerous genes.

When looking at fraternal twins, whose genetic makeup is as alike as ordinary siblings, it's important to realize that they share the same intrauterine environment and that they are born at the same time. Fraternal twins come into the family together and go through developmental milestones in synchrony, which places them somewhere between identical twins and the rest of us on the sibling ladder.

While there are many facets of twin relationships yet to be studied, several recurrent themes about the differences between identical twins and fraternal twins have been researched. The most commonly mentioned is the more intimate relationship shared by identical twins. These findings are based on the deep personal loss experienced by most identical twins upon separation, their tendency to live close to one another throughout their lives, and their frequent use of the pronoun "we" in place of "I." When identical twins who were separated at birth or shortly after birth have been reunited, the strength of their bond is obvious. Many of these reunited twins choose to live and/or work together and to remain in very close contact. While some separated fraternal twins also enjoy very close relationships with one another once reunited, the same striking rapport observed among identicals has not been apparent.[3]

"IT'S LIKE TALKING TO YOURSELF ONLY BETTER"

At thirty-six, identical mirror-image twins Paula and Polly are both confident, outgoing women who have not merely accepted their twinship but revel in it. They live in the same city, see each other often, and talk at least once a day. "I can count on her always," said Paula. "If I need somebody, she's there. It's like talking to yourself, only better!"

Though Paula and Polly were interviewed separately many months apart, the similarities in their memories, reflections, and attitudes were uncanny. Both twins described their childhood as "wonderful" and "great." They always had someone to play with, someone who shared the same interests. As tomboys, the girls rode around their backyard wearing cowboy hats and guns, going after snakes and bad guys. "We knew even then," said Polly, "that, even if friends bailed out on us, we always had a built-in friend."

The girls continued to dress alike ("down to our shoelaces") long after they were put into separate classes as first graders. "Being separated was pretty traumatic," said Polly, "and we thought it was dumb. But we survived and, in retrospect, I don't think it hurt us. At some point, it is important to learn individuality." That point came when the girls were around ten or eleven, and they decided to dress differently. "We decided we wanted double the wardrobe, instead of half," said Paula. "We made a conscious effort to dress differently and say, 'You're you' and 'I'm me.' "

But as the twins matured, they both understood that their similarities far outweighed any differences. "As identical twins, we tried very hard to be different, but it was tough," said Polly. "I can remember in college that I really wanted to be different. Paula was in art education, and I tried everything else. But I wasn't good at anything else and ended up in art education with Paula."

As the self-described tomboys grew up, they became avid tennis players and both feel that their twinness encouraged them to excel. "If she can do something," explained Polly, "I say, 'I can do it, too.' " "It's a very strange thing," said Paula, "and if you're not a twin, it's hard to understand. But competition for us doesn't mean doing better than the other; it means doing as well. When I win, it's as if she wins by osmosis. And if something good happens to her, it happens to me. We just wish the best for each other. We would never wish bad because you then wish it for yourself. We live vicariously through one another."

The twins' other sibling is a sister seven years younger. Both Paula and Polly say they are "really, really close" to her. Yet when asked to compare that relationship to the one with their twin, Paula and Polly agreed there is no comparison. "It's just different," said Polly. "My twin and

I look and act like each other. It just isn't the same." Apparently, their younger sister feels the difference. "She used to say, 'Mom has Dad, Polly has Paula, and I have nobody.' "

The relationship between Polly and Paula has been a constant in their lives. They have gone through the same developmental stages together and have always been close. As adolescents, they made a pact about dating the same boy. If one of the twins "dropped" someone, the other would not date him. "If she didn't want to go out with a guy," explained Paula, "I sure didn't want to, either."

One of the boys Paula dated in college didn't like Polly. "He saw Polly as a threat to our relationship," said Paula, "so I did the prudent thing and dropped him. If he couldn't accept Polly, who is such a big part of me, then I couldn't accept him."

The twins' respective husbands accept the special closeness of their relationship. They may roll their eyes at the nightly phone calls, but the connection between all four is a good and supportive one. The year Polly and her husband spent in California marked the first time that the twins were separated for more than a matter of days. "It was tough, really the pits," said Polly. "We talked all the time. I'm sure Ma Bell made a fortune off us." Both Polly and Paula were reminded of a "cute story" when they talked about this separation. Their mother went to visit Polly. Paula took her to the airport, dressed in a new skirt and vest. When Polly met her mother in California, she was dressed in exactly the same outfit.

Is it difficult to form other friendships, given the intimate bond between the twins? "No," said Paula. "It's just a happy threesome. If somebody is my good friend, she is automatically hers." "Anybody that's a friend of hers I automatically like," echoed Polly. "We are attracted to the same kinds of people." Paula described a time when a friend of hers who had never met her sister was on a flight to Las

Vegas, the same flight Polly was on. By the time the two women returned home, they were "terrific" friends. "It can be strange for some people," said Paula, "but if they like one of us, they like the other."

Friends play an important role in the twins' lives. As Paula explained it, she's never been able to be alone. She's always been around other people and likes it that way. Polly doesn't look at it as a problem. "I don't need time for myself," she explained, "probably because I'm an identical twin. Time for myself might be used to play tennis with my sister. Being alone isn't my cup of tea."

Paula started a family first, giving birth to two girls and then a boy. Because her pregnancies were difficult, Polly waited until later to start her family. However, it was Polly who miscarried twins in her fifth month. "It was extremely traumatic," she said, "but I had a terrific support system around me." "It was very difficult for both of us," said Paula. "Even now, I have trouble talking about it." The twins' sense of loss was tempered after the subsequent healthy births of Polly's two girls.

"Our children are more than first cousins," said Polly. "Genetically, it's as if they have the same mother. Our husbands don't look alike, but feature for feature, our kids are quite similar. And they are the best of friends—more like brother and sisters." "They get a real charge out of their mothers being twins," said Paula. "Polly's youngest one still gets confused. I think they all hope they will have twins when they grow up."

And as Paula and Polly face middle age, their hopes and dreams include maintaining the same close bond, living near one another, and sharing the joys of family. "Some twins really fight for their own identity," said Paula, "taking up separate interests and trying to fight the mold. We've accepted our twinness and marched on. It's fun. My twin is my best friend!"

* * *

If the basis of a healthy relationship is established in childhood, Paula and Polly got off to a fine start. They played together, enjoyed the same activities, and considered each other their best friend. Their relationship was good practice for future relationships because they learned how to love and share and seemed to avoid competition and conflict. The task of solving conflicts, of course, was made a lot easier by the twins' attitudes about competition and their stance, apparently unique to twins, that one's successes were the others and that, if one could attain a certain level of achievement, the other twin could, too. The absence of jealousy that marks their relationship (again consistent with many identical twins) encouraged a cooperative, altruistic spirit that carried over into all of their personal connections.

As "genetic clones" whose physical appearance, behavior, and personality were virtually identical, Paula and Polly did not experience parental favoritism, which often drives a wedge between siblings. According to both twins, their parents treated them equally and never compared one to the other. And the twins' own attempts to be different from one another ultimately led to the realization that neither could fight the nature of their relationship. They had been dealt an even hand and decided to work with it, not against it.

Important marker events, such as moving and marriage, did not disrupt the tight bond between them. Separated for only one year, Paula and Polly now live in the same city and plan to keep it that way. Unlike many siblings who leave their parents' home for parts far and wide, these twins have made a conscious choice to remain in close proximity. And unlike many siblings whose relationships are diminished when one or the other marries, Paula and Polly made sure that their respective husbands liked the twin as well as each other. Theirs appears to be one big, happy family.

WAR AND PEACE

Twins, like other siblings, have their share of arguments. As one identical male twin put it, "If there is competition, a hankering to stand apart, among all siblings, between twins the heat is turned up, the stakes higher and the connection between competition and intimacy more pronounced. After all, the closer two people are, the more likely they are to be standing in each other's shadows."[4]

As twenty-eight-year-olds looking back on their childhood, Tim and Tom agree that they came to physical blows every day of their lives until the age of twelve or thirteen. "We fought a lot over noises," Tom said, "like the noise I made when I chewed my food or when I snored. And when we fought, we were out to hurt each other. We wouldn't stop until one of us started to cry, usually me, or until a parent threatened us with some kind of punishment. When our rage was triggered, nothing could stop us."

"We were known for our dramatic outbursts," said Tim.

> We were terribly bothered by each other's noises. We shared a bedroom and Tom was snoring so loudly one night that he woke me up. I went over to him and saw that his nose was plugged up but that his mouth was open. So I stuffed his mouth with a towel, and he blew up like a balloon. The next night, he was snoring again. I crept over to his bed to suffocate him again. But he had set me up and yelled at the top of his lungs, knowing that he'd wake my father, a serious taboo in our house. It was two o'clock, and there I was hunched over Tom. My father threw open the door and sentenced me to thirty days of no television, much to Tom's delight.

Something changed between the twins when they started junior high school. "We'd come home after school," recalled Tom, "and lie on the floor together and talk for hours. It was the first time we related as people who could communicate on an intellectual basis. It was also the first time we had gone to the same school."

Attending the same school and being involved in many of the same activities, plus the natural maturation that takes place during adolescence, helped Tim and Tom to draw closer together. "We respected each other more," said Tim. "It was a strange thing . . . I wanted to protect him, to look out for him. I've always been more dominant, and I took on the role of protector."

According to twin research, it is not unusual for one twin to be dominant and extroverted, while the other is submissive and introverted. These appear to be traits that some twins use to assert their individuality. "Tim was always much more social and verbal," commented Tom. "I was always the shy one and less aggressive. I stuttered, and he never did. Tim is more of a responder, whereas I'm more inclined to sit back and analyze a situation before responding. I may be more content, but he has an easier time meeting people."

Both Tom and Tim are very sensitive about comparisons. "We don't like people comparing us," said Tim. "And I've noticed that even today, when we're together with other friends, one of us will take the role of the clown and the other will be quiet. It's uncanny."

Unlike many twins who choose to live close to one another throughout their lives, Tom and Tim have lived in different places since high school, except for a six-month period between undergraduate and graduate school when they lived with their parents. That was a difficult time for the twins. "I thought Tim was inconsiderate and selfish," said Tom. "I regressed and didn't handle it well at first. I did a lot of yelling. I would have behaved differently if he had been a roommate and not my brother. I felt the liberty to go right in and be a 'dick.' With intimacy, there's a liberty to let it all hang out."

"Tom was out of control over many aspects of his life at

the time," said Tim, "and I think he tried to compensate by controlling me. I didn't feel like coming to blows but was really insulted. He brought me to tears many times, just like when we were kids. I was shocked. I was glad to see him go at the end of the six months."

Despite such a difficult period, both twins see themselves as more alike than different; they have the highest regard for the other. As adults, they have similar political opinions, interests, and kinds of friends. "We both share a sensitivity to other humans," said Tom. "We look at the world with similar glasses," Tim agreed.

The possibility of women looking at *them* with "similar glasses," however, is disquieting to both twins. There is always the question in the back of their minds: "If she finds me physically attractive, what does she think of *him?*" "There is still an insecurity with us over women," said Tom. "I'm getting better about it, but it's still an issue." "I might even prefer," said Tim, "that the woman I marry not be particularly close to Tom. It would fill me with jealousy, if I felt she were attracted to him."

While neither of the twins has experienced anything that could be remotely considered ESP, they describe their special connection as "empathic." "If something were to happen to him," said Tom, "I'd know how he was feeling."

Tim described a unique physical bond he and Tom share.

When I'm around him, I feel a huge sense of comfort . . . more a tease. And when we get physically close—put our heads together—there's a certain wave of joy, a complete calm, that makes me overjoyed to be a twin. It's a feeling that I've never felt with anyone else, only with him. There's only one person in the world I feel as comfortable with, and that's my twin. No matter where we are, I know I can trust the relationship. No matter what, I know he'll love me.

126

It is difficult to make strong generalizations after looking at the fights and arguments between Tim and Tom, and the absolute harmony between Paula and Polly. There has been little research on the difference gender makes, for example. Therefore, it would be wrong to draw the conclusion that female twins are closer than male twins.

Although neither of these sets of twins reported extra-sensory communication, many other twins have. But because their ESP experiences are usually recounted after the fact, they are difficult to substantiate. What researchers do know is that identical twins are remarkably similar in the kinds of brain waves they produce, indicating that genetic factors influence brain activity. The results of brain-wave and ESP studies leave researchers with the task of offering other explanations for the amazing resemblances and co-incidences that many identical twins report. Nancy Segal, of the Minnesota Center, wonders whether similarities in behavior, close social contacts, or constant awareness of one another result in "ESP-like" events in the lives of many identical twins. LaVelda and LaVona, the next set of twins to be discussed, related several experiences that they feel were much more than coincidences.

TREASURED COMPANION

LaVelda and LaVona Rowe-Richmond were born in Iowa fifty-six years ago, eight months after their next oldest sibling, a sister, had died in infancy. When people ask which of the two mirror-image twins is the oldest, both LaVelda and LaVona will say the six-minute difference is "not enough to count." "We are the same," said LaVelda. "We feel we are an extension of each other," said LaVona.

Despite the family upset when World War II took their father overseas for four years, LaVelda and LaVona described an idyllic childhood and a family that was extremely close. "We were and still are very, very close to our older brother and younger sister," explained LaVelda. "But we're even closer to each other. We share things that we won't share with them, like our deepest feelings. There is a psychic bond between us." "The connection with Sis," said LaVona, "is closer than anyone would hope to be. What affects her affects me, and what affects me affects her. We love being together."

The only time LaVelda and LaVona were separated was during their sophomore and junior years in high school. The school administration got the "bright idea" to separate the twins in order to prepare them for "life." "We were completely lost," said LaVelda. "Mirror-image twins do better if they can see their twin and know she is okay," said LaVona. "We made it as miserable for the teachers as we could. They finally let us go back together our senior year."

During their senior year, LaVelda and LaVona worked at different variety stores to earn money for college. Neither of their employers would hire them together. As LaVelda tells it, she had an appointment and needed the day off. Not wanting to miss a day's pay, she asked LaVona to take her place. All went smoothly until the next morning when LaVelda's store manager asked why she hadn't done something. "I forgot to tell Sis, so I fibbed and told him that *he'd* forgotten. He looked at me rather strangely but said that maybe he had forgotten." A couple of weeks later, the twins switched places again. This time the store manager, who had suspected some monkey business all along, stopped LaVelda in her tracks. When he asked why she hadn't done something and she again told him that he'd forgotten to ask, he pointed to a calendar on the wall, where he'd jotted down his request. "Tell your sister," he said, "that I want to see both of you in my office." Afraid of being fired, LaVelda "fessed up" to the switch. But instead of losing her job, the store manager put both twins to work. "That way, I'll know where you both are!"

In the past fifty-six years, LaVelda and LaVona have never dressed differently, except for two weeks when a minister told them he would be interested in one of them if they did not dress alike. "We did it for two weeks," said LaVelda, "and then told him he wasn't worth it." "We dress alike," said LaVona, "which shows our individuality. Society says it's 'cute' until about the age of five. Then they try to force us apart to fit its mold. We dress alike out of a kind of defiance. We're expressing our own desires, our individuality."

During college, LaVelda and LaVona fell for the same man. "I was working different hours from Sis," said LaVona, "because they split the classes alphabetically right between Sis and me."

The boy I was dating never believed I was a twin. So I sent him off to where she was working. There she was, looking just like me, and they got to talking and she served him an extra piece of pie. One day, she came home and said, "I think I'm going to get engaged. Will you be my maid of honor?" I said, "Oh, I'd be thrilled to! I'm so proud, so happy. Who is it?" When I found out, I told her that was the boy I was going to marry!

That was the only time we really fought. She wasn't convinced that I had also dated the young man. Then one night she went uptown and ran into him with another girl. She dropped him, and I dropped him. Convinced it was the only thing that could break up our twinship, we made a pact that from then on we'd let the other know who we were dating and, no matter how we felt about that man, it was hands off for the other one."

LaVelda and LaVona married the thirteenth set of twins they dated, mirror-image twins Alwin and Arthur. "We saw them walking down the street and had a girlfriend find out who they were," said LaVelda. "We gave them a call and invited them to a twin convention." "They acted so settled in their ways," continued Darlene, "that we thought they were married men. It took us three years to find out that they weren't, and then we went after them. Sis had talked to Arthur on the phone, so they paired off. That left Alwin and me. We felt from the very first that we belonged to that person, and nothing could have made us switch."

They were married six months later in a double ceremony attended by thirty sets of twins. LaVelda, Arthur, LaVona, and Alwin shared the same home, the same bank account, and the same car. "The boys were in their fifties," said LaVona, "and had always lived together. So had Sis and me. You couldn't ask for a nicer relationship. You have to be a twin to understand it." "The only difference between the two boys is the special feeling I have for mine and she has for hers," said LaVelda. "Things worked out beautifully."

Both couples tried very hard to have a family. "We wanted very much to give our husbands children like them to carry on their family name," said LaVelda. "They are the last males in their line, and it was our turn to have twins." "Both of us miscarried five times," said LaVona. "We both lost a baby within a day of each other. We were told before one of the miscarriages that we might be carrying twins. We even tried to adopt. But our ages put us out of the running, even for Siamese twins that had been abused by their mother."

"We thought we were going to live to be the oldest twins in America," said LaVelda. "We had a beautiful life together and believed nothing could destroy it." But three years ago, LaVelda's husband Arthur died of brain cancer. "It made it easier to have LaVona and Alwin with me. They were going through the same grieving process—Alwin probably to the same extent I was, if not more, because he lost his twin. Alwin is much more quiet now, much more serious. He was never serious before. I'm still living with them. The only difference is that we don't have Arthur here."

LaVelda and LaVona are no strangers to paranormal experiences. When they were nineteen, LaVona "saw" her sister in distress, though they were separated by many miles. LaVelda was in a car with a young man, who supposedly wanted to take her to a coffee shop uptown. Instead, he drove into the country. "When I realized what he was up to," said LaVelda, "I tried to get out of the car. He drove faster, and we ended up in a ditch."

"I was 'seeing' the accident and feeling her pain," explained LaVona. "I asked Dad to call the police, but he thought I was making things up. When Sis came home all muddy and shook up, Dad made sure she was okay and then told her not to say anything and to get in the car. He made me direct him to where the accident was, without LaVelda saying a word. I directed him right to the tracks where the car had gone into a ditch."

To this day, LaVelda and LaVona feel each other's pain. When LaVelda was operated on recently, LaVona was able to tell the doctor the exact time he started cutting and the exact time he started sewing her sister up. "There were two different kinds of pain," said LaVona "and I could feel them both."

"We have a close psychic bond," said LaVelda, "and know what the other is thinking. I'll start a sentence, and she will finish it. She always starts or ends exactly the way I would have. We complement each other; we never compete. And we never experience jealousy—we don't understand it." "Not everybody can be an identical mirror-image twin," said LaVona. "Only one thing could beat it—being a triplet!"

* * *

For some, the joy expressed by LaVelda and LaVona in their twinship may sound surreal. How can two women in their mid-fifties dress alike, live together under the same roof with their respective twin husbands, and describe a complete lack of competition and jealousy in their relationship? For many identical twins and the researchers who study them, the possibility of such a harmonious, selfless relationship is quite real. And while there are some potential drawbacks to such intimacy (the possible difficulty, for example, in forming relationships outside the twinship), the existence of such idealistic cooperation and altruism professed by LaVelda and LaVona has been supported by twin studies. The pleasure many identicals find in cooperative effort and willingness for self-sacrifice for the benefit of the other is commented on again and again.

As noted, competition can be an entirely different thing for identical twins. Instead of wanting to outdo one another, many identicals want to maintain the same level. So if one twin does something a little better, the other figures, "I can, too." If one should win something, the other regards it as her/his victory. LaVelda and LaVona, for instance, competed together and won the title "Miss Iowa City." But when the heads of the Miss America contest wanted them to compete separately, they dropped out. "We choose to complement one another," said LaVelda, "and not compete."

LaVelda and LaVona describe themselves as each other's best friend with whom they share their innermost feelings. "If we ever argue," said LaVona, "we end up crying in each other's arms. We never go to bed on a sour note." And when asked about the extent of their outside friendships, LaVona said that neither of them "knew a stranger," that they trust everybody to a fault. "We have friends all over the world," LaVelda said proudly. "Why, we know over eight thousand sets of twins."

THE PROS AND CONS OF BEING
A TWIN

Identical twins David and Bill are the same age as LaVelda and LaVona, yet their attitudes toward their twinship are much less idealistic. The two men, commercial artists who run their own design firm, talked openly about the pros and cons of being a twin.

Question: Who is the oldest?

David: I am. I'm twenty minutes older.

Bill: You can tell because he's always mistaken for my father.

Q: How has that made a difference?

Bill (laughing): He's a bully . . .

David: Yeah, we went through all that stuff.

Bill: The prototype of anything never works too well. It's the refined model—the one that comes later—that's better. Seriously, though, when you're born a twin, you do a lot of sharing. People accept you as two, not as one. Sometimes you're taken into places as a decoration, not as real people. As twins, we didn't really learn how to communicate. We talk in abbreviated terms and understand each other very well, but other people can feel left out.

David: And you can sense when the other guy is in trouble.

Q: ESP?

David: Yeah, it definitely exists. For example, during the years, we've had some trouble with alcohol. We could tell when the other was in trouble.

Bill: You can tell something's wrong . . . like a sixth sense that a mother might have.

Q: Do you have other siblings?

Bill: No other siblings. Mother had a miscarriage, then us.

David: There isn't much jealousy when one of us gets something and the other doesn't. We've always shared, and we don't believe that anything is anybody's. You don't own anything in this world, and this goddamn attitude of having all for myself just galls me.

Q: In what ways are you alike?

Bill: Ornery, bull-headed, impatient . . .

David: Yeah, impatient as hell. And we're loud . . . and we share the same career.

Q: How did that happen?

Bill: Safety. Let's go back and explain. When we were growing up, the thing to do was to keep twins together. For example, we dressed alike until we went to college. Our parents didn't know what the hell they were doing.

David: They did the best job they knew how.

Bill: Anyway, we went to the same college, joined the same fraternity, and went into the service together during the Korean War. After the war, we took advantage of the GI Bill and both got our M.A.s in commercial art. We've always been self-employed. Never made a lot of money . . .

David: Nah, you can't in this business.
        What about friends?

David: We had the same friends—the same friends all the way through.

Q: Who got married first?

David: I did—a month earlier.

Bill: Marriage ended a lot of fighting.

David: But then it created a lot of other problems.

Bill: We used to argue a lot. We were living together and working together. Used to have a lot of battles . . . knock the other guy down the stairs . . . all kinds of stuff.

David: We didn't have a lot of personal space. After we were married, we went our own way on a lot of things.

Q: Are you both still married?

David: No, my wife died three years ago of cancer.

Q: What was the relationship like between your wife and your brother?

David: Wasn't good . . . probably a lot of jealousy.

Bill: Also a tendency to criticize the spouses instead of each other . . . takes the pressure off. And the two women were very different. I married someone just like my mother.

David: That's what he thinks.

Bill: My wife is more conservative; his was more liberal.

Q: So you chose different kinds of women. In what other ways are you different?

Bill: Oh, we're different in a lot of ways.

David: That's been good over the years because it's helped separate us a lot. But we still work together.

Bill: Too late now to change.

Q: Was it an advantage or disadvantage to have a twin when your wife died?

David: The relationship was strained . . .

Bill: It made it difficult for me to give him support.

Q: Do you spend any more time together since your wife died?

David: No. Never. We don't spend any free time together at all. We go our separate ways. We had some Christmas shoot-outs, but we don't even do that anymore.

135

Q:	Does that mean your children are not close?
David:	Unfortunately, they're not.
Bill:	A lot of that was caused by us. The wives made certain distinctions along the line, and we allowed it. That separated them. It's sad.
David:	Yeah, I always felt that was a bad deal.
Q:	Do you think it's too late to change that?
Bill:	The last few years, we went through a lot of financial strains. It's all added up . . . a lot of problems.
Q:	What do you do to relax?
Bill:	Not a hell of a lot. I go to bed at nine o'clock.
Q:	And you, David?
Bill:	He's got this new girlfriend. (Both laugh.) He's in better shape than he's ever been in in that department.
Q:	In what ways can you count on your brother?
Bill:	In work, I think I can count on him.
David:	Implicitly.
Bill:	That's why we work together.
David:	Every now and then, I accuse him of having one foot in the boat. It's because when he goes home, he gets his mind changed. He's okay as long as he's here.
Q:	Has it been hard to become two separate people?
David:	I think it's been a struggle, but not so at this age.

As twins approaching their sixties, David and Bill concur that the struggle to become two separate individuals is no longer an issue and that the difficulties of the past have been tempered with the passing of time.

Interviewing David and Bill was a little chaotic. The two talk at the same time, and the one who raises his voice higher usually takes the floor. Their barbs back and forth seem to be offered with a sense of genuine humor, though I got the sense that their teasing must have been hurtful as they were growing up. It was clear that the fight for personal space plagued their relationship when they were younger, working and living together. And while their respective marriages ended a lot of the fighting, their wives seemed to have driven a wedge between the two men and between the two families. Both Bill and David expressed regret at that turn of events, particularly about the distance between their children. However, both appeared resigned to the situation and unwilling to do anything to change it.

On the positive side, neither Bill nor David understands jealousy and both rail against what they see as the "Me Generation" and its unwillingness to share. Even though the twins no longer share their lives outside of work, the design firm they own keeps them together five or six days a week. There are volatile moments, to be sure, but they enjoy working for themselves, convinced that their "ornery," "bull-headed," "impatient" personalities would not be easily tolerated by anyone other than their twin. "Besides," said Bill, "we're a novelty and, in the beginning, people hire us because we're twins. Afterwards, the proof is in the pudding."

"PEOPLE DON'T KNOW WHAT THEY'RE MISSING"

Identical twins Beth and Bess have been each other's best friend for seventy-three years now. "We don't like people to know our age," said Beth, "because we're so active in the community and in support of our university's basketball team." "Our hair is red," said Bess, "if we can find the right bottle. We don't look our age."

Beth and Bess grew up in a little mining town in an age when the emphasis on family and strong moral fiber guided many people's lives. Theirs was an extremely happy childhood, shared with two older brothers and loving parents who always treated the twins exactly alike. "I remember the twenty-two-mile bus ride to and from school each day," said Beth. "The four of us attended a two-room school until we went to high school. Sis and I had nearly identical academic records, though I was the state typing champion my junior year. According to a teachers' journal, Sis would have won second place, but she got confused and retyped a paragraph." "I was just as pleased as if I'd won the title," said Bess. "We don't seem to have any jealousy toward one another at all. It's been that way all through our lives. Her successes are mine, and mine are hers."

Some years after she married, Beth moved with her husband to Minnesota. It was the first time the twins had been separated, and they missed each other terribly. When Bess's first marriage failed, she and her son ultimately moved to Minnesota to be near Beth and her husband. Bess met her second husband there. The relationship between the foursome was so good that they owned and ran a neighborhood bar together for seventeen years. "It might be too close for comfort for regular brothers and sisters," said Bess, "but not for us."

Their husbands' deaths within four years of one another have pushed Bess and Beth even closer. They've started dressing alike again and buying exactly the same things. They are moving soon to the same new apartment complex, where they have chosen the same model and the same carpet. "We like so many of the same things," said Beth. "And we share the same friends. We're both outgoing but don't seem to need other friends so much. And I've had so many people say, 'You girls don't know how lucky you are, especially as you get older.' "

There is one difference the twins admit: Though younger by twelve minutes, Bess is more precise and a little more sure of herself. "She's been in business more than I have," explained Beth. "That made her a little more forceful or aggressive." Bess agreed: "If things don't turn out exactly as she wants it, she'll accept that, whereas I'll fight it to the end. I have high blood pressure, and she doesn't, probably due to more stress in my life from business. I take medication, but it doesn't slow me down. We're on the go all the time."

While neither twin has had an ESP experience, they both describe themselves as "on the same wavelength." "We'll start to say something at the same time," said Bess, "and it's exactly the same thing. We often laugh about it." "I think we're more alike than most twins," Beth said.

"People don't know what they're missing having someone so close, someone you can tell your innermost feelings, somebody who always knows how you feel. Others survive, but they miss so much. As time goes on, I don't know how it would be if something happened. Of course, she still has her son, but he's busy with his own life."

As "seniors," Bess and Beth have begun to confront their own mortality and the possibility of losing the other. New findings from the Minnesota Center for Twin and Adoption Research have confirmed that the death of an identical twin is a greater loss than any other relative, including a spouse or a parent. Both Bess and Beth were devastated by their respective husbands' deaths and can only imagine the frightful pain of losing their twin. "It's been so helpful to have Bess throughout my life," said Beth. "You can't understand unless you're a twin."

Like most older siblings, Bess and Beth love to reminisce. Not surprisingly, their memories of the past are identical. They both described the same happy events in their childhoods, and their feelings toward their two older brothers (one of whom died in WWII) are identical. Being "on the same wavelength" includes their memories: They like to tell the same stories and narrate the details in the same

139

way. Unlike other siblings who rarely see their past through the same eyes, Bess and Beth seem to have carbon-copy memories.

Looking at twins across the life span crystalizes the issues of closeness and distance faced by all siblings. Twins, particularly identical twins, highlight the meaning of sibship and all of the relationship's pushes and pulls. Observing how twins strive for individuality while remaining part of a whole teaches us all about the meaning of intimacy and how we might better achieve such strong relationships in our own lives.

One thirty-five-year-old identical male twin wrote that his father, now deceased, once told him that family is where he would return in life when he was most secure. "And as I get older and see the effects of the years mirrored in my brother's face," he wrote, "I want to strengthen our remaining bond, conscious of how few lifelong ones there are."[5]

8

ADULT ONLY CHILDREN

*When a person finds out that someone is
an only child, they make certain
assumptions about them, perhaps that
they're antisocial, shy, or egotistical. Yet
when looking at hundreds of studies, I was
able to conclude that, on average, only
children are like other people. If there are
any differences, they are that onlies are
more human-motivated and have more self-
esteem.*

—Toni Falbo, *The Single-Child Family*

As the mother of an only child, I find great solace in
the knowledge that only children grow up to be just
like the rest of us. As the author of a book on siblings, however, I needed to understand what this portends
for those who say that siblings are tremendous influences
in our lives. Toni Falbo helped me set the record straight.
"A lot of people," she said in a phone interview, "see life
as a zero-sum game, in which there is only one answer, one
winner, and many losers. So if I say that only children grow
up to be like the rest of us, they see it as if only children
have won and everybody else has lost. Or, conversely, if
somebody says that having siblings is great, then not having
sibs is terrible. In fact, life isn't like that at all; there are

many ways of living and growing, of having social networks."[1]

I wanted to kick myself. There I was, making the same mistake I warn people against in the Introduction. We are a culture that likes to see issues in black and white, good and bad, right and wrong. We tend to seek easy answers to complicated questions, closing our eyes to the complexities and interconnectedness of many factors that shaped who we were and who we've become. As siblings we cannot ignore the variety of influences that shed light on our personalities and the way we approach the world.

For example, the attitude of an only child's parents about having one child can make a tremendous difference in how the child sees the situation and whether he or she grows up feeling that perhaps something has been missed by not having siblings. If the parents regret the fact that they have only one child, they will more than likely communicate that regret to the child. And the child will feel he or she really missed out. But if the parents are happy and content with their only child and allow plenty of opportunities for their child to be with other children, there is no reason the child should feel unlucky or lost.

The popular myth that only children are emotionally or psychologically handicapped is not supported by scientific research. Yet such notions persist. "Only children are spoiled." "Only children have trouble making friends." "Only children are self-centered." Why have Americans clung to these assumptions when an impressive number of studies have refuted every one of these stereotypes?

An article in *The Single-Child Family*[2] cites pronatalism and the mass media as major culprits in the largely negative folklore surrounding only children. For generations of Americans, society has constrained us to marry rather than to not marry, to have children rather than to remain childless, and to have at least two children instead of only one. One-child families have been viewed as "incomplete" or

142

"hardly real families."[3] Yet as many observers point out, single-child families also seem to have some distinct advantages: namely, lower expenses, fewer restrictions on the parents, and less years spent on childrearing. Why, one might ask, aren't more couples choosing to have just one child? The answer, contend the researchers, is that the media continue to perpetuate the negative stereotypes surrounding only children. Newspaper columns, cartoons, and even movies warn us to watch out for only children. We're advised that they make difficult spouses because they crave attention and need to dominate. We're warned that only children often turn into miniature adults who really never grow up.

Such negative "scientific" opinion convinces us that only children should be and, in fact, are different. Only children, who reap the benefits of their parents' time, money, and attention, are expected to be overindulged or spoiled. As the receivers of such concentrated attention, only children are expected to be more susceptible to family stress and, therefore, "insecure." They are expected to have problems socializing outside the family and to achieve less intellectually and academically because they don't have the chance to tutor younger siblings. And, finally, only children are expected to become more demanding and inflexible than others, because they were involved in family decisions at an earlier age than children with siblings.[4] Yet after exhaustive study of only children as adults and after hearing their own views, it is clear that they are as diversified a group as the rest of us, with very different views about the meaning of having been raised as an only child. Actress Eve Arden, the only child of a divorced mother, wrote, "My desire for siblings had been demonstrated at the age of four, when I kidnapped a baby parked by its trusting mother outside the Mill Valley Post Office." However, seeing her own childhood in a completely different light, philanthropist Brooke Astor wrote, "I had the priceless

143

advantage of being an only child. All the love that I might have had to share with rival siblings was mine alone."[5]

The adult only children I interviewed ranged in age from thirty-five to seventy-eight. Their stories were unique and painted with the many different colors of life. Some had wished for a brother or a sister; others never felt the need for a sibling. Some reveled in the attention they received and the boost to their self-esteem; others felt a "burden" in balancing the family. Yet, in the end, only one of those interviewed expressed serious regrets for having been raised as an only child. For the others, every negative seemed to have a positive; for each regret, there was a fond memory or beneficial outcome. "The only way we're different," said one woman in her thirties, "is that we're better!"

"IT'S A WONDER I'M HERE!"

Growing up, Sarah S. never knew why her parents didn't have another child; as an adult, she now understands that her parents had a very difficult time conceiving. "My mom says it's a wonder I'm here," Sarah said. "That partially explains why I had a real sense that I was valued as a child."

Basking in her parents' attention, Sarah got all the glory and has continued to search for the glory in her adult life. "I was propelled to excel in the real world, continuing to shine and getting the positive feedback I received as a child. I am not an overachiever, but being an only provided me with a standard of excellence that I continue to pursue."

The downside of her parents' focused attention, Sarah explained, was that they made it harder for her to exercise the independence she learned as a result of being an only. "I've always been much more comfortable making my own decisions and living with them, no matter how they turn out. There was a conflict between my independent nature and parental authority. As I got older, I rebelled against it more and more."

As an only child, Sarah learned how to rely on herself without a lot of outside structure. Never forced to be in a certain position in the family except "the child," she played all the roles. "I could be the clown, the victim . . . whatever. There was tremendous freedom in not being typecast." She wondered whether having had siblings would have changed all of that.

What did not change was the unique relationship she had with each parent. She was "Daddy's little girl" and enjoyed a very close bond with him until his death from cancer when she was twenty-four. "He was ill during most of my childhood," Sarah said. "He had his first operation when I was two. That probably made things a lot different between us."

On the other hand, her mother and she had very different personalities, something Sarah didn't understand as a child. "It was hard on both of us," she explained. "We were both struggling to mold the other into what we thought she should be. I'm very laid back, and she's go, go, go. We still have the same conflicts, but we usually cope much better now."

Coping with her father's early death was difficult. Though it was not unexpected, losing the family member she was closest to took its toll. "I don't know if anything really could have helped, but it would have been nice to have had a brother or a sister to lean on. Of course, that's hard to know. I may have hated my brother or sister."

Most of Sarah's adult friends are men. "Maybe I'm looking for the older brother in them," she offered. "I consider my husband to be my best friend; we're pals. And I like his two brothers a lot. We would spend more time together if they lived in the same city. I must say, however, that I never developed a tolerance for chaos. When I'm at my in-law's home and all the relatives are there, I could scream

145

after ten minutes. I like quiet and peace in personal relationships."

Sarah's desire for quiet and peace may have something to do with her lack of interest in having children of her own. "I've never been around children to speak of," she said, "and I can't get excited by it. If I were to have a family, I think one would probably be all I could handle. I would try to encourage the positive things I got from being an only and hold back on what I felt was my parents' overprotectiveness."

To Sarah, a woman in the prime of her life, growing old is not a pressing issue. However, she has thought about aging and the fact that she won't have siblings or children of her own to rely on. "I'll have to figure out alternative means of getting myself taken care of or, preferably, go until I drop. There are financial things you can do to protect yourself, and I'll definitely plan ahead."

It might help Sarah and other adult only children to know that many childless, elderly only children whose spouses have died do just fine. They make friends easily and have established a supportive social network that helps them stave off loneliness in the later years.

Recently, psychologists who study adult only children seem to be saying that the similarities between only children and those with siblings far outweigh the differences. In areas of health, intelligence, self-confidence, and emotional stability, only children do just as well as those with siblings. In fact, only children tend to be better educated. But reducing people to statistics diminishes the human component. Like the rest of us, adult only children have their share of good traits and bad, some of which can be attributed to genetics, some to parents, some to social environment, and some to chance. There are adult only children who can spend a month by themselves and enjoy every minute; others are eager to create an extended family. There are adult only children who are socially facile, no matter the circumstance; others are terribly shy. To generalize about the character of the adult only child is as foolish as counting on balmy weather in Alaska in the middle of February.

"I WOULDN'T CHANGE
THE THINGS I GAINED"

Peter is forty-one, and the director of a nationally recognized independent film theater. As a child growing up in Czechoslovakia, Peter was one of very few only children and was made acutely aware that he was different. "I had a dual response to being an only," he said. "Because of the stigma, I felt guilty. On the other hand, there was a feeling of disbelief because I didn't really think there was anything wrong with me. I wondered what it would be like to have a sibling. Where would he sleep? What would the rituals be between us? Would he get my hand-me-down clothes? I was isolated from the experience, but I wasn't unhappy."

Peter's father left Czechoslovakia, having promised his then pregnant girlfriend that he would return soon. But the political climate changed, and he was not allowed back in the country. With his mother working to support her young son, Peter was basically raised by his grandparents—a very warm and supportive grandmother and a harsher but intelligent grandfather whom Peter looked up to and respected.

I was very popular as a child and had lots of friends, including a cousin five years younger for whom, in an informal way, I was made responsible. I was certainly not lacking in social skills, but I spent a lot of time by myself. I had the opportunity to learn how to structure my time and

147

to be extremely happy by myself. The skills I gained as an only child have been extremely valuable to me as an adult. I have an ability to think intuitively, to go from nowhere to somewhere out there in outer space—to make that leap. I trust my own daydreams, my own imagination. There's a real thrill in that.

The negative side to that is that I can be incredibly depressed. I don't know how to talk about day-to-day personal problems, things that I think are resolvable on my own. So I reach out later than others, yet I've rarely doubted my ability to go through something and ultimately reach a solution.

Like most adult only children, Peter is acutely aware of the negative stereotypes. Understandably, he refutes most of them, including the idea that adult only children are spoiled and not used to sharing. "I think it's quite the opposite," he said. "I tend to be much more generous because when I give, I give much more naively, as an expression of affection. I haven't been through the problem of someone else coveting what I have. And I have no experience with the parceling out that goes on among parents and their children. I've never been obligated to share and have never experienced the down side."

What about Peter's ability to solve conflicts? After a pause, he made a distinction between solving conflicts for others and resolving his own problems. "I think onlies can quite often be better at resolving conflicts for others," he said, "because we don't bring any kind of agenda with us. The ability to listen is key, and I think many onlies do that better than siblings. However, with personal conflicts, I think I'm probably more limited in skills because I didn't have as many opportunities to practice."

When Peter was twelve, his father entered his life for the first time. By then, Peter was "totally unequipped" to relate to the father he had never known. "I had been set up by my mother," he said. "The father-son relationship had been idealized for me. Yet the reality was painful and not anything like I'd been led to believe. I did the most radical thing in my life, as a result, and ran away from home when I was sixteen. I think if I had had a sibling, that would have taken some of the burden off. There would have been a sense of solidarity, someone to talk to, to share my feelings with, to analyze the situation. As it was, I was completely isolated." And when his father died earlier this year, Peter experienced the same kind of isolation. "A sibling could have been an equalizing factor," he said. "We could have shared the responsibilities, instead of all of them falling on me."

Peter, who is separated from his second wife, married for the first time when he was just eighteen. In many ways, his marriage was a continuation of his running away. Still, even as a teenager, his experience as an only child affected his choice of a mate.

I was aware of, and had great respect for, introspection. I was looking for an intelligent woman with some creative ability. In both my first and second marriages, the women came with social expectations of what couples should do together. As an only child, I understood the need to be alone and didn't take that need in others as a personal insult. I understood that time spent separately did not translate into loving someone less.

Peter's ability to be alone and his joy of "fashioning something from scratch" shaped his professional career. He sees his work as a fulfillment of the skills he learned as an only child. "I work best independently of outside structures," he said. "My job allows me to utilize my love of starting things; it's the happiest time for me. The playing and imagining I did as an only child allow me to trust my imagination and give me the impetus and support to try new things. I learned self-trial and -error, which I think is a very unique way of learning."

149

Like many adult only children, Peter sees both sides of the coin when he contemplates growing old without brothers and sisters. "On the one hand," he said, "I will have no immediate family to be there. On the other and, I don't know if I'd want a blood relative there in that capacity. Friends are one thing; they represent chosen relationships, not obligatory ones. Yet it is a bit frightening to realize that there are no built-in caretakers. But who says anyone can cure the loneliness or fear of aging or illness?"

If it had not been for the social stigma of being an only child growing up in a predominately Catholic country, Peter would have been quite content not having brothers or sisters. He was curious about what it would be like to have a sibling but did not covet one. Even as a child, he enjoyed spending time alone, though certainly not at the expense of his social development. He was well liked and never lacked for playmates.

Peter appreciates his ability to think intuitively and the trust he has in his own daydreams and imagination—skills he firmly believes he developed because he was an only child. "When I worked for other people," Peter said, "I was very successful. But I had many, many conflicts. I'm much more comfortable working for myself." The most difficult part of his current job is having to depend on so many other people. If he could juggle all the responsibilities himself, he would gladly do so.

Although he is used to working for himself and spending time alone, Peter was quick to point out that his "naively heroic" tendency to solve his personal problems by himself can sink him into depressions that may last longer than they need to. His discomfort in reaching out for help sometimes slows him down. Perhaps if he had had a sibling, he would have learned to trust others almost as much as he trusts himself.

Peter's concept of sharing—one echoed by many of the adult only children I interviewed—is reminiscent of the way many twins view sharing. There appears to be a more altruistic attitude when it comes to giving. Unlike siblings who are obligated to share, only children are, for the most part, unused to the concept of sharing in order to get something back and can be more genuine in their desire to give, not receive.

Unused as they are to the challenge of solving conflicts with their siblings on a regular, if not daily, basis, adult only children might be expected to lack the skills for conflict resolution. They aren't called upon as often as siblings might be to fight, negotiate, compromise, and ultimately resolve problems. Conversely, it could be argued that precisely because adult only children are not jaded by a process that can go bad among siblings and lead to poor and ineffective problem-solving skills, adult only children are in a better position to approach their peers with a clean slate or, as Peter put it, without "any kind of agenda." The reality, it seems, is that one's ability to solve conflicts is dependent on a number of factors, not simply whether or not one is an only child.

Psychologists are just beginning to investigate various crises in which not having a sibling might pose a problem. Initial evidence suggests that the main disadvantage for adult only children comes later in life when they alone have the burden of caring for their aging parents. However, the evidence of a pattern is not yet clear. What *is* clear is that many only daughters are the equivalent of an only child when it comes to caring for parents. Brothers, it would appear, tend to shirk their responsibilities, leaving the sister on her own to handle the many challenges and decisions. And as Toni Falbo pointed out, having a sibling or not may not be the major factor here; rather, the nature of the relationship between siblings and/or between the parents and children (child), the financial situation, and the nature of the parent's illness will determine the ease of the situation.

"I'VE LOST SOMETHING OF MY PAST"

When I asked Amy, forty-three and a sales representative, about her first thoughts on being an only child, she didn't skip a beat.

> Being an only limits my recall of the past. I see my two daughters . . . how one will recall something and the other will embellish the event, and how that often brings another memory to mind. It's really different for me without any siblings. The only person I really have is my mother, and of course, hers is an adult point of view, not a peer's. I've lost something of those memories from my past, the ability to take a step back and look at where I came from and laugh at the things that happened.

The choice to have one child was a conscious one made by Amy's parents. Living, as they did for many years, with an extended family that included Amy's grandmother and an uncle, her parents felt it was an "imposition" to have more than one child around the house. "My mother said that when I was an infant and I cried during the night, she felt uncomfortable. And then I think my parents started drifting apart and didn't want any more kids."

Amy wanted a brother or a sister but managed to compensate by spending time with a good friend who had two sisters. "I had the real sense of kids about the same age sleeping together in a house, eating around a big table . . . Those were some of the happiest memories for me."

Not that Amy spent a lot of time alone in her own house.

152

"There was always someone around," she said. "Yet it wasn't the same as having sibs. I think being an only child made me a little more self-conscious with my peers. I don't think I was as good at being silly. And in terms of socialization, I was always active but felt that I was somewhat on the outside, that I couldn't get as close to friends as others could."

As an adult only child, Amy thinks her tendency to avoid conflicts "at any cost" may, in part, be due to being raised without siblings. "I'm not a good fighter. My parents never fought in front of me, though there was a lot of friction in the house. And I never had brothers or sisters to fight with. Today, I don't ignore conflict, but if it's something I can let pass, I'll do that."

There are certain tendencies that Amy sees as advantages of having been raised as an only child. The fact that she spent a lot of time with adults, including many of her parents' friends, taught her about the variousness of people and how their differences can be interesting and beneficial.

I listened to their conversations because I wanted to know what people are all about. As a result, I'm a good listener and appreciate diversity. I think that's a real plus.

And, as an only, I always felt that I was supported in terms of everything I did. There was always a lot of praise. Whatever I accomplished was an important event, and I knew it was important. I've never been afraid of failing, just afraid of not trying something. Not having a sibling to compete with meant I didn't have to worry about being as good as someone else.

The main thing that drew Amy to her first husband was that he came from a large family; he was one of five children. "I liked the idea of marrying into a big family. That was something that I definitely had on my mind. And the last thing I wanted to do was have just one child. I didn't want the child to be an only like I was. Not that it was

153

terrible. Part of my motive was a selfish one; I wanted to have lots of people around me. I like the feeling of people sitting around the table at mealtimes, at the holidays."

Amy was thirty-one and divorced from her first husband when her father died. Because he left almost no insurance and no money, the financial burden on her mother was tremendous. "My mother," said Amy, "started to turn to me to solve all her problems."

I wasn't financially capable, but what really bothered me was that she assumed I was *supposed* to bail her out. The more she pushed me, the more I didn't want to help. It felt very unfair to me, coming at a time when I had two small children to raise and had to go back into the work force to make ends meet. There was a lot of guilt on my shoulders and no siblings to turn to for support. Yet a lot of people say they have a brother or a sister and that the siblings do nothing during a crisis like mine. The responsibility seems to fall on one person anyway.

Not having siblings with whom to share memories about her father has also taken its toll. "There's a blank," said Amy. "I don't think I've felt the full sorrow of my father's death; his memory is hard to keep alive. My mom doesn't talk about him much, and, while I know I miss a lot of things about him, I almost forget what they are. If I had siblings, there might not be that blank."

Watching her two daughters interact over the years has reaffirmed what Amy thought having siblings would be all about. "There's something there that they can see or feel or touch that binds them together. Sure, they fight, but they've taught me that it's okay. If you really love each other, love is stronger than any problems. My two girls reinforce each other's thoughts, validate the past, and compare notes. I realize more and more how much I would have enjoyed having had siblings. I live the sibling experience vicariously through them."

*   *   *

For many the sibling connection is the only intimate one that seems to last. As constants in their lives, siblings provide a reference against which to judge and measure themselves, and they share a history that can bring understanding and a sense of perspective in adulthood. For some adult only children, like Amy, there exists a keen realization that a part of their past has been lost forever. Parents and other relatives can help fill in the blanks, but as Amy said, their adult perspective is different from that of a peer within the family.

Environment and genetic makeup combine to shape behavior and personality. Being an only child cannot be isolated from the many other influences that mold one's character and general worldview. Amy speculated that not having siblings made her a little less sure of herself when socializing with her peers. Making and keeping friends was (and still is) very important to her. Yet, as a child, she always felt "on the outside." Even today, she tries her best not to "rock the boat" in her personal relationships, a carryover from childhood, when being "nice" dictated the way she interacted with her peers. The question remains how much of this tendency is genetic, how much environmental, and how much a result of being an only child.

The same question ought to be asked when evaluating Amy's self-described tendency to avoid conflict at all cost. Indeed, Amy saw the error in attributing her fear of fighting to her status as an only child. "My husband," she said, "is the same way. And he was raised with two brothers."

The fact that she had no siblings with whom to compete gave Amy the freedom to try anything, without the fear of being compared to a brother or sister. She was the center of her parents' attention and thrived on their undivided support and encouragement. On the other hand, not having siblings to help defray the pain and responsibilities after her father died felt like a huge burden. All of the financial

155

and emotional decisions were hers, at a time when she was trying to pick herself up after a divorce. "There was no one I could turn to," Amy said. "It felt very unfair." But here, too, she realizes that caring for parents usually falls to one sibling in any case, and most often it's the oldest daughter.

AN ONLY CHILD IN A DISRUPTED FAMILY

Research has shown that an only child's ability to adapt to a divorce and to the subsequent years living in a single-parent household often reflects the mother's response to the situation (assuming that the child's mother has custody).[6] If the mother is autonomous, financially stable, and generally happy with her life, chances are good that her only child will accept the situation and continue to thrive. If, on the other hand, the mother is tired, strapped financially, and generally lonely, chances are that her only child will reflect her unhappiness.

Art F., a forty-six-year-old arts administrator, described his mother as a frustrated artist who, after her divorce, had to work at a low-paying job that did not challenge her full creative potential. He also said that, because of her own childhood, his mother had a lot of problems asserting herself. As a young child, he witnessed her chronic bouts with migraines and with functional breakdowns. And although there was never any doubt of her love for him, Art, at a very young age, had to absorb his mother's stresses as she struggled to survive as a single parent. "I was her son, her companion, her little brother, her confidant, and in some ways her caretaker. Ninety percent of the time, my mother was my mother—the parent, the disciplinarian, the one to watch over me, feed me, clothe me, and protect me. But because of her own emotional fragility and needs that were not always met, I heard perhaps more than other kids about her longings and shortcomings." Whether having siblings would have, in reality, lessened the pressures he felt as the sole bearer of his mother's "longings and shortcomings" is anybody's guess. What matters is Art's fervent belief that it would have.

As has been mentioned, those only children whose mothers are disappointed about not having more children tend to be more concerned about having brothers and sisters.[7] Art clearly remembers times when his mother expressed a desire for more children. "She didn't do it with tears," Art said, "nor with a great deal of emotion. Rather, she talked about it with a pang of reality. But I can remember her saying that, if things had been different, she would have liked more children. And I can remember saying that I'd sure like to have brothers and sisters like other kids." For a sensitive child like Art who already longed for siblings, his mother's sadness about their circumstance obviously made an impression.

Lest too much is made of Art's mother and her attitude toward being a single parent and the subsequent effect that may have had on Art, other factors like Art's basic nature should be considered. If, indeed, a person "makes" his or her own environment based on genes, interests, and personality, it is not so much what happens in one's life but the meaning one attributes to the events that makes the difference. Differences in emotional responses and in the ability to cope with changes and stress mean that some only children will be more affected by divorce, separation, and loss than others. When, for example, Art's mother and stepfather were killed in an automobile accident, Art, who was in his early twenties, felt an intense need for a sibling "to lean on and with whom to share the burden of that pain and loss." "I had good friends," Art said, "I had relatives, and I really had nobody. The only person who could have shared the measure of my grief and the feeling of being lost completely would have been a brother or a sister."

Art can think of very few positive things about having been raised an only child. He feels he got "shortchanged." As he said, "Everything else is transient except brothers and sisters." When he thinks about the importance of siblings and the role they play as we age, he worries about dying alone. "I have this ideal notion that, no matter what the hell happens in your life, you have a brother or sister who will take care of things and be at your bedside."

AN ONLY CHILD IN AN
EXTENDED FAMILY

We know from accounts of growing up in a kibbutz that the extended family made up of relatives and nonrelatives, young people and adults, can provide the warmth, affection, and discipline children need to feel loved and well taken care of. While the system of housing children in a children's house away from their parents and entrusting their care to "nurses" and teachers may make many of us uneasy, studies show that adult *sabras* view their childhoods as happy and view each other as siblings.[8] The strong relationships these children share with other children and their parents and siblings (as well as with their own) provide a network of support and community essential to their well-being and growth.

If we apply these same principles of extended family to only children raised in this country (or anywhere else, for that matter), it would seem good advice that parents of only children surround their one and only with a loving array of relatives and nonrelatives who can supply a greater sense of family. Whether these members of the extended family can take the place of brothers and sisters is not the point; rather, it is that they can provide warmth, support, discipline, and a more secure feeling of belonging.

Born in 1912, Sadie G. enjoyed the benefits of an extended family that many of today's only children sorely miss. "First of all," Sadie said, "my father's two sisters, seven and nine at the time, moved into our house shortly after I was born. I had built-in sibs. And you have to remember, those were the years when a lot of people immigrated from Europe to the United States. Our house was a halfway home for a lot of people. So in addition to aunts, a great aunt, and cousins who lived with us, there were so many other children who passed through my life. When I was six, my mother's niece who lived with us had a son. I was the proud 'sister' and for years never felt that I was an only child." Not only did relatives live in the same apartment, but Sadie's mother came from a large extended family that was very close, and her father was a very social man who loved to take Sadie along to all kinds of events. "I didn't fit the mold of the shy, quiet only child," Sadie said. "People were always surprised to find out that I was an only."

There were times, however, when having a loving extended family did not meet the special challenges of being an only child. Sadie felt that trying to please her parents was sometimes a burden. "I somehow felt it was up to me to maintain a good balance between my parents. I don't know how it would have been with a sibling or two. But I don't remember it as a joy to always be the center of attention. There was a responsibility there that may have been less burdensome if I'd had a brother or sister."

The time Sadie was most conscious of being an only child was when her mother was ill. At that point, caring for her aging mother was a full-time job. "I didn't think I should put that on my own children," she said, "as long as I could think it through myself. And there were definitely times when I wished there was somebody else. But then again, I would think of friends who had siblings and were in similar situations. Many of their sibs were not supportive. They had bigger heartaches than I did!"

Today as a seventy-eight-year-old living alone, Sadie is

a prime example of an adult only child who has fostered an active and happy life based on many friendships and a loving family. She swims, plays the piano, and her social calendar includes lectures, plays, and concerts. Her ability to listen and to gently offer sound advice are qualities her numerous friends admire. Growing up in the midst of a supportive extended family that placed a high priority on closeness, as well as on intellectual and artistic pursuits, appears to have helped mold a happy, self-fulfilled adult only child.

According to the most recent statistics available from the United States Bureau of the Census (1988), ten percent of women between the ages of eighteen and thirty-four said they did not want any children; 13.5 percent said they wanted only one. And of women between the ages of eighteen and forty-four (the age at which most women have completed their child bearing), twenty-two percent who had ever married had only one child. Baby-boom women in their thirties or early forties who delayed having children are now raising their first child. Until these women approach the end of their child-bearing years, we won't know what percentage will decide to have a second child and what percentage will decide that one child is enough.

For those who choose to have one child or who, by circumstances beyond their control (divorce, death of spouse, financial concerns) have only one child, they should take heart in the knowledge that, as adults, only children are as adjusted, happy, and self-fulfilled as those who grew up with siblings. And potential parents who are contemplating how many children they would like to have and who are concerned about the quality of social and economic life should look at the "only-child syndrome" cliché in light of these findings. Perhaps, as the authors of a book on the only child claim, "the time for the one-child family has come."[9]

9

THE DEATH OF A SIBLING

Death ends a life but not a relationship.
—Robert W. Anderson, "I Never Sang
    for My Father"

In a culture that has been slow to recognize the strength of the sibling bond, the death of a brother or sister is often viewed as a singular event to get through quickly with a minimum of grief coupled with an almost saintlike concern for the pain of other survivors. This is particularly true for children and adolescents, whose capacity for grief and long-term reactions to death have typically been overlooked or denied. There is a body of literature suggesting that grieving is a necessary and healthy response to loss, and this process has been fairly well researched in adults. Yet much less is known about the process in children. It is evident to even a casual observer that children do experience grief, but family, friends, and our society make it extremely difficult for children to mourn.

The grief of young siblings is most often ignored—albeit unintentionally—by parents so consumed by their own loss that they are emotionally unable to reach out and provide solace for their surviving children. Friends, relatives, teachers, even clergy who might step in for the "absent" parents place a double whammy on these "forgotten grievers" by urging them to be "strong for their parents" and on their "best behavior." These extended family members unwittingly saddle the young siblings with additional caretaking responsibilities at a time when they desperately need attention. Predicated on the assumption that the loss of a brother or sister is not that serious and that the surviving siblings will get over it in no time, the well-intentioned but misguided advice prevents younger children from sharing their feelings with anyone at the time of the loss and for a long time after.[1] It is not uncommon for siblings who loss a brother or sister in childhood to move into adulthood with an unresolved loss that can block productive behavior and make achieving intimate relationships more difficult.

The lack of cultural supports for the expression of grief or the recognition of loss extends to older siblings as well. The death of other family members, particularly parents and spouses, is considered more difficult, and grieving for those losses is more culturally acceptable. It is not surprising that many adult brothers and sisters minimize their show of grief over a sibling's death because they assume that the spouse and children have more cause to mourn.[2] Such an altruistic response that ignores or represses the depth of the sibling connection is once again reinforced by relatives, friends, even therapists, all of whom tend to overlook the importance of a sibling's death and the need to mourn the loss in order to come to grips with it and get on with the business of life.

TWELVE YEARS LATER

My family still doesn't talk much about my brother Robin. His death remains a delicate subject around which we tiptoe like a lion circling its prey. After twelve years, sharing our grief still does not come easily.

And sharing the process of grieving with those outside my immediate family hasn't been much easier. Talking about death, particularly a suicide at age thirty, requires people to confront their own mortality, the logic of "natural order," their attitudes about suicide, and their ambivalence about the sibling bond. It's safer to remain silent. Almost never have aunts, uncles, cousins, or longtime friends who knew my brother attempted to share a fond memory or acknowledge the void his death has left—not at my second wedding, at my son's Bar Mitzvah, nor upon the publication of my book on suicide. Talking about the dead is uncomfortable and risky business, a subject better left alone.

Our culture is impatient with the bereaved; there is undue pressure to "return to normal" as quickly as possible, often within twelve months or less. To not complete our grieving after a year's time is interpreted to mean that we survivors are unstable wallowers in our own unhappiness. (One study showed one-third to one-half of adolescent siblings still experiencing guilt, confusion, loneliness, anger, and depression almost two years after a brother's or a sister's death.)[3] I resent the implication that I'm maladjusted because I still miss my brother and because I want to explore how his death may have altered my capacity for intimacy, my understanding of the fragility of life, and the importance I now place on family, specifically on my two surviving siblings.

As older relatives die and my extended family shrinks, I turn more and more to my sister and brother for their side of the story. That their recollections mirror mine validates the past; that their memories differ reminds me that each of our experiences is unique but no less valid or important. If only Robin were around to add his two cents' worth. That he is not means a major piece of the life review puzzle will never be recovered. So I march into the second half of my life with a part of my reality check lost forever, and, for someone who spends a lot of time checking reality, that is one hell of a loss.

LOSING A SIBLING IN CHILDHOOD

There is never a good time for a sibling to die, but it appears that losing a brother or sister in childhood can be a devastating experience. Many younger siblings, in fact, suffer a double loss—the loss of a sibling *and* the loss of their parents. It's easy to understand how these young survivors can feel neglected, put upon, and misunderstood, surrounded as they are by a culture that ignores their pain. In many ways, the death of a sibling can mean the premature ending of childhood for the surviving siblings. Called upon to be strong, responsible, and perfect, many surviving brothers and sisters learn to suppress their feelings while harboring a deep sense of insecurity that can affect their level of trust and self-esteem.

"THERE'S SO MUCH STUFF IN THERE"

Sandra's parents never told her that her five-year-old brother was going to die. They just said he was sick and had to go to the hospital to get better. That he had leukemia and was given a short time to live was not information shared with six-year-old Sandra. Only when the weeks turned into years—three and a half years—did Sandra begin to comprehend that her brother was going to die.

"The night he died, I had a dream. When I woke up, I knew my brother was dead. I was never told he was near death, but I knew. And I remember the morning as clear as a bell, what my dad had on, what I ate for breakfast, the weather, my babysitter, everything. And I remember my father telling me, and that I never cried. Never. I just got back in my old routine like nothing had happened."

Three years ago when she was thirty and on a visit to her father's, Sandra stumbled upon a box full of old photos.

> I came across a group stapled together and I freaked. There were pictures of my brother . . . there was one in particular that was a close-up of his face. And I'd forgotten that look that he had when he was full of cortisone. He was all swollen, and his eyes had this certain look. When I saw that picture, I started shaking from head to toe. I've never had a physical reaction like that before. And that's kind of what began my search that eventually led to therapy. I realized . . . God, there's so much stuff in there . . . so many feelings I need to let out.

Sandra's story is a familiar one to many siblings who have lost a brother or sister in childhood. With her parents immobilized by their own grief, she was left to deal with Ken's death on her own. As a means of survival, she repressed her emotions and tried to win her parents' love and attention by being the "perfect" child who excelled in school and looked after her younger sisters. Sandra became a substitute parent, particularly after her parents' divorce. While her mother slipped into alcohol-induced stupors, Sandra took charge. From the outside, it appeared as if she had everything going for her. She was bright, responsible, and well liked. Yet if anyone had bothered to look more closely, they would have recognized a young girl out of touch with her own feelings.

A MAJOR LIFE HAPPENING

It took Sammy twenty-five years to mourn the loss of his brother, Zack, who died in an accidental shooting incident when he was seventeen and Sammy was eleven.

165

"I felt abandoned and very angry about losing my brother. Both my parents were devastated and sank into deep depression. They were 'old school' and didn't talk about feelings a whole lot. So my memories are of eating breakfast in silence. I can still see the gray, drab mornings. And I think I felt fairly responsible to try to help my mother especially. She was completely immobilized."

A model student before his brother's death, Sammy became a "terror" in school. All of his teachers knew that his brother had died, yet not one of them connected his marked change in behavior to Zack's death. And none of his many friends ever encouraged him to talk about what had happened. "As I got older, I made a lot of acquaintances but few real friends. I think part of that must have been the recognition of being able to lose somebody who is very close and how devastating that is. I was wary of being hurt again."

To compensate for the abandonment he felt by friends, teachers, and his family, Sammy threw himself into a whirl of activities. "I was compensating for what I had lost by putting my energy into a lot of things and staying busy. That way, I didn't have to think as much." Sammy's inability to concentrate and his desire not to think too much led to a disappointing high-school academic record, a false start in college, a stab at becoming a writer, an eventual degree in English, marriage, divorce, travel, and a variety of jobs.

I was frantically hopping from one place to another, taking the job that nobody else wanted or getting a degree that was some kind of achievement. I was proving myself while desperately wanting to figure out how to deal with my own pain.

I learned through therapy that the depression plaguing me and my inability to settle down and form intimate ties were directly attributable to the loss of my brother and my never having worked through his death. Therapy was very painful for me. I spent a lot of time crying, something I didn't do after Zack died. My therapist was sensitive to the issue and encouraged me to express my feelings for the first time. I was very fortunate. I hear all the time from people who go into counseling and are told that they have had ample time to grieve for a dead sibling, that their problems have nothing to do with that loss. Losing a sibling is a serious, tragic experience that has a huge impact. Such a loss is a major life happening. It certainly was for me.

Grief is a normal, emotional, and often irrational process. So that the outcome can be as healthy as possible with few complications, children should be encouraged to let out their feelings and to express them in as deep a way as possible, as soon as possible. Unfortunately, grieving children are at a disadvantage. There is the tendency to deny death and the painful emotions, common to all children, that it evokes. Their grieving, then, is done piecemeal, if they react at all. One minute they may feel deeply sad or guilty or angry; the next minute, they may go out and play. This kind of on/off grieving can make parents and other adults furious. Surviving siblings are often seen as hypocritical and disrespectful, as if they don't really care that a brother or sister has died. Nothing could be further from the truth: Younger siblings are deeply affected by the loss and suffer intensely but express their grief differently. They are poorly equipped to handle loss and often act out their feelings instead of analyzing them. And as we've heard, parents and other adults are not very helpful in encouraging surviving siblings to express themselves.

At that point, a separation often occurs between the child and his or her peers. One woman said she felt like a "freak" because none of her friends had experienced the death of a sibling. When people lose their parents, others can share that. Either they've lost a parent themselves or know someone who has or know that it will happen to them sooner or later. But the death of a young sibling is unanticipated; it's not part of our normal expectations, and most of us don't know how to react.

To retreat from children who have experienced the loss of a brother or sister makes them forgotten grievers, leaves them alone to muddle through the maze of feelings that even most adults find difficult to handle. By recognizing the ways in which we make it difficult, if not impossible, for children to mourn—lack of communication within the family, and direct exhortations from non-family members to "be strong"—we can begin to encourage young siblings to talk about their feelings, acknowledge their grief, and provide healthy ways of coping with what is a significant and painful loss. As one surviving sibling said when asked how grieving children should mourn, "Don't be afraid to let out everything you feel, even those crazy feelings. If you feel like crying, laughing, or being angry, do it. Just don't hurt anyone. Go ahead and scream and stomp and kick doors if you have to. I swallowed my feelings and it damaged me and my relationships with a lot of people. It's important and comforting to know that you're not alone in this. There are lots of us who know just what you're going through."

LOSING A SIBLING IN ADOLESCENCE

Adolescence as a developmental stage is a fairly recent idea. The classification did not exist throughout much of American history and still does not exist in many cultures. It appears that adolescence came into being in western cultures with the realization that the end of childhood did not automatically lead to the beginning of adulthood.

Not only have our notions of adolescence been changing, but so have our experiences with dying, death, and mourning. The average life expectancy has increased, mortality rates have declined, the principal causes of death have changed from communicable to degenerative diseases, many bereavement rituals have been abandoned, and dying has in many ways become institutionalized. When it comes to death and dying, adolescents, generally sheltered from "real-life" involvement in death-related matters, are often treated in conflicting ways.[4]

If we accept the view that adolescents are no longer children and not yet adults, we treat adolescents as individuals with characteristic needs, problems, and tasks. Their thoughts and feelings about death, the way they behave, and their coping skills are, in many ways, unique.

SO ANGRY AND NOT KNOWING HOW TO COPE

"I got so much support for being 'mother's little helper' that I became completely hostile," recalled Rita, whose next youngest sister died of leukemia when Rita was a high-school senior.

I was so insulted that people thought I was special because I could put a meal on the table. These same people acted stupidly, telling me that they were praying for Beth and that they knew she wouldn't die. And I'd say, "Are you kidding? Haven't you read about leukemia? It's a hundred percent fatal." Or some misguided friend of the family would say, "She's very young. I know she'll grow out of it." And I'd respond with, "I know she will. She'll go directly into a coffin." I said these things because I was so angry and didn't know how to cope.

Beth died in March. Rita was "*so* relieved!" Three months before she died, Beth's condition had worsened to the point of a "living hell." She'd lost all her hair from

169

chemotherapy, was emaciated except for a bloated stomach, had what looked like "zits" all over her face, and couldn't walk up a flight of stairs.

"I just didn't understand why arbitrarily this fourteen-year-old died and that one didn't," said Rita. "Rather than try to deal with unanswerable questions, I directed my anger toward people I thought were acting like fools. I knew they were trying to be helpful, but their good-intentioned comments set me off. I'm sure the town was probably thrilled to see me leave for college."

By the luck of the computer draw, Rita's college roommate was a "wise saint" who "figured out she was living with a maniac" and did her best to get Rita back into the human race. "I'd go into two-month depressions where all I'd do was eat popcorn and chocolate and complain about my life. Instead of saying 'You're too weird to deal with,' my roommate became a very close friend who listened nonjudgmentally. She stayed with me for two years, and I credit her with restoring my mental health. I never sought professional help; I thought my reactions to Beth's death were appropriate."

Rita lived at home during the summer between her freshman and sophomore year. She worked and earned enough money to buy a car.

> The day I drove away at the end of the summer was the day I got on with my life. I knew I'd never live at home again. One of the problems we had as a family was that we never talked about Beth either during her illness or after her death. It was a closed topic. While I'm sure it was a defense mechanism against the pain of having lost a sister and not being able to turn to my family for support, I felt I had to close that chapter of my life and get on with it."

Like many adolescents trying to cope with death, Rita had difficulty sustaining certain emotions. She converted her sadness and guilt into anger, anger directed toward outsiders who either patronized her efforts to help out at home or who tried to minimize the seriousness of her sister's illness. There's no doubt that she had a right to be angry with those who mishandled the situation, yet Rita herself acknowledged that her anger was out of control and that, looking back, she is still embarrassed about the hostile way she responded.

Rita, like many grieving adolescents, was hampered by a society that turns away from the face of death. Because of anxiety and ignorance of what to do at a time of grief, her immediate family withdrew, never talking about their loss. The rituals for handling dying, death, and grief were not taught, and Rita was left to find out what they were on her own. By sheer luck, her college roommate was a sensitive young woman who actively listened to Rita's feelings without judging them. She encouraged Rita to express the full range of her emotions, even the "weird" and "crazy" ones, while exploring viable alternatives for handling her grief. Rita's roommate stuck by her at a time when it felt as if her family and their friends had abandoned her. The roommate intuitively understood that much about the normal grief experience is frightening, even terrifying, and that the life-and-death questions Rita was dealing with as an adolescent created a sense of vulnerability that most of us spend our adult lives trying to conceal and forget.

Grieving adolescents, like grieving children, need to develop their skills in verbalizing thoughts and feelings about death. In most cases, adults must take the lead. They should be alert to the adolescent's nonverbal behavior, particularly at a time when a teenager's heightened awareness of death may make talking more difficult. And they should try to accept the adolescent's feelings as real, important, and "normal." This is not always easy. Adults tend to respond to young people with instruction about the "right" or "appropriate" behaviors and attitudes, or with overprotectiveness and avoidance. The key is to communicate openly and

171

empathetically, projecting a belief in the adolescent's worth and her or his ability to find solutions to the ongoing pains of losing a sibling.

UNATTENDED GRIEF

That unattended grief from childhood or adolescence can sit just below the surface, making an impact on survivors' behavior and feelings throughout their lives, was attested to over and over again by surviving siblings from thirty to eighty. Forty-eight-year-old Judy's story is one poignant example.

Judy was the second born of four sisters, two and a half years younger than Karen, the oldest. In Judy's eyes and apparently in the eyes of the rest of the family, Karen was very special. She was the first child and the first grandchild. "I always felt she had the upper hand. Karen was the special one. She could beat me verbally in any argument we had, and I always felt competitive in trying to be as good, smart, and talented as she was."

Karen attended Brandeis University for two years and dropped out to get married and start a family. She died of complications from a viral infection when she was twenty-four. "Initially, I felt tremendous grief. I didn't allow myself to feel any ambivalent feelings, feelings that might seem inappropriate. To the outside world, my family and I looked like strong individuals coping well with her death. In reality, my youngest sister had a nervous breakdown, my parents became engrossed in their store, and I stuffed the fact that my sister's death made me the oldest and changed the way everyone responded to me in some very positive ways." The change in Judy's sibling position from second child to oldest often worked to her advantage. Almost everything she did was looked upon favorably, yet there was (and is) tremendous guilt attached to her accomplishments. Karen had to die before Judy felt more comfortable and confident within her own family and within herself.

But the comfort was fragile and was easily disrupted by an illness in the family, a family occasion, and her son's twenty-first birthday. "I was consumed by a sadness that I didn't understand. Here was my son celebrating his adulthood, and I couldn't stop crying for a week." Only later when she attended a grief recovery weekend did Judy discover that her "time clock" was very accurate, and that, like many surviving siblings with children, she was reexperiencing her sister's death as her own son approached the age at which her sister had died.

"The greatest sadness of having lost a sister so early in life," said Judy, "is not having the completeness of our lives together, to fight and love each other and resolve the things that went on in childhood and early adulthood. I still feel that competition with Karen, and I think that if she had lived, we would have come to an understanding."

For anyone who doubts the influence and power of the sibling connection, stories like Judy's underscore the importance of the relationship both in life and after a sibling dies. The competition between Judy and Karen growing up still has power over Judy decades later. That the two sisters were unable to resolve their differences before Karen's death leaves Judy adrift and enmeshed in feelings of inadequacy and abandonment. Even though her change in position from second oldest to oldest has afforded her many "firsts" and the accompanying approval from family, the guilt she often feels diminishes her successes and undermines her ideals of love and caring. Karen has been dead for twenty-six years, yet the relationship between the two sisters continues.

LOSING A SIBLING IN ADULTHOOD

Unlike young children, who may not comprehend the finality of death, and adolescents caught between understanding and acceptance, the vast majority of adults who lose a sibling have already experienced the death of a loved one. The personal pool of grief is reactivated and, depending upon how the survivor mourned in the past, old wounds fester, making a resolution more difficult, or healthy patterns of mourning are repeated to encourage resolution of the current loss.

You'll recall the story of Rita, whose younger sister died of leukemia when Rita was seventeen. The process of grieving was replayed with new twists when her brother Ken took his life six years later.

They were only eighteen months apart, and Ken was *Rita's* brother.

> I knew him better than anyone else in the family. Yet I had no idea he was suffering; in fact, he appeared to be just fine. But he planned his suicide very carefully, buying a gun four days before he shot himself, packing all of his belongings, writing all the appropriate letters. I never had a feeling of disbelief when Beth died. I didn't like it, but I knew it was real. With Ken, it was different. It took me months to even accept that it happened, let alone deal with anything beyond that.

At the wake, Rita refused to look at her brother's body. "If I didn't look, he wouldn't really be dead." And if she drank enough, *she* wouldn't have to begin the process of healing. "I drank like I never had in my life. Four or five months later, I woke up enough to rejoin the human race on a fairly superficial level. I spent the first year denying; I was numb."

Anger was the first emotion Rita felt, and she was astonished at the intensity. She cried and carried on and was so angry at her brother that she could barely speak. Rita saw Ken's suicide as the height of selfishness, the ultimate egotistical act. "I saw his taking his own life as saying to me and to the rest of the family that his problems were more important than anything else in the whole world. I felt there was no excuse, coming as he did from a family where he was loved. If he had arisen from the dead, I would have punched him out!"

The family that loved Ken (and Beth) were incapable of discussing his death. "We still didn't know what to say. We each felt helpless, with no tools for dealing with our grief." And as before, Rita did not seek professional help; she was convinced she could get through the pain on her own. She never connected the migraine headaches that lasted from the end of one year to the end of the next March to either of her sibling's deaths, nor did she understand how many of her other problems might be part of unresolved grief.

Ten years after Ken's suicide, Rita heard about the Rothmann-Cole Center for Sibling Loss. She approached the sibling recovery group, she says, as if she'd gotten through both deaths and would be a shining example to everyone else. But when talking with Jerry Rothmann, the director of the center, she started to cry. " 'Don't worry,' I told him. 'I always cry when I talk about my brother.' I was stunned to discover that after all this time I wasn't over this."

After working with the group for three months, Rita was astonished to realize that she was no longer mad at Ken. "I miss him and I'm sad, but I'm not angry." Possibly more surprising was the discovery that her migraines are holiday/anniversary reactions to both deaths, beginning around the time Ken took his own life and lasting until the anniversary of her sister's death. "Recognizing the connection between my health problems and their deaths has provided me a certain amount of control. I have a physical problem with my mouth that is aggravated by my clenching my jaw and

175

grinding my teeth. Now I can keep my mouth open when I'm feeling stressed and wear a retainer at night. And when I get a migraine, I can recognize that I'm thinking about Ken and can call my sister or someone else close to me. I still get the migraines, but knowing why helps."

After ten years, Rita, her parents, and her surviving siblings have begun to talk about what has happened. Rita made a point of letting her family know about the grief recovery group, and they all asked her about it. The subject is now on the table. "This all would have been so much easier if we'd been able to talk and had help from the outside. I would have understood that I wasn't the only one feeling the way I did—that I wasn't alone."

MORE CONSEQUENCES

Small children and adolescents are not the only ones who experience the loss of their parents after a sibling dies. Adult sibling survivors who are married and have children of their own may still be forced to deal with "absent" parents so involved in their own grief that they cannot reach out to their other children.

One thirty-three-year-old whose sister was murdered comes to mind. Joe talked about how, under the stress of his sister's disappearance and the eventual discovery of her body three long months later, all of the family conflicts reemerged—how to deal with one's own feelings, the feelings of others, and each family member's character. "My father," said Joe, "was very self-absorbed in his grief. And my mother was concerned that no one cared about her loss—only my father's. There was conflict between them, and their conflicts made it too difficult for me. My mother felt 'Woe, is me.' I couldn't give to her after my sister's murder and I still can't. It's too had to be empathic with her. My parents' self-absorbed positions colored our helping each other. I had to go off on my own to grieve."

The expanded-life-experience vision of adult sibling survivors, unlike the tunnel vision of children and adolescents, brings with it a much broader understanding of the meaning of death. For Joe, there's a "real sadness that my sister and I couldn't age together." Joe has a one-year-old daughter, and his sister will never know him as a parent or know his child. "And we lost the opportunity for me to appreciate her being a parent."

For other adult surviving siblings, the sadness centers on the loss of family history. One fifty-one-year-old brother talked about his older brother who died of heart problems: "Our parents were both born in Europe. As a younger person, I was never concerned with the details of our roots. In the last few years, I've been very concerned because my kids have been asking me. I always depended on my brother, but he's not here. My historical roots . . . my local historian is gone." The same fifty-one-year-old, in talking about how the death of his brother, a well-known social psychologist, led to a study he coauthored on siblings of famous people, discussed other studies he conducted on the effects of the death of a sibling in late adulthood:

As their siblings died, they represented the only existing reality, the only verification of their previous life. It's almost as though we have to hold on to the people who experienced our pasts with us as proof of its reality. As we get older and our memory is not as sharp and some of our stories are believed and others are not, who is our checkpoint? Not parents who are old or dead, nor spouses who entered into our adult lives. Our siblings are the only verification of our previous life.

Verifying the past, resolving long-standing conflicts from childhood, and pulling up family roots are tasks cut short when an adult sibling dies. Survivors are faced with the additional challenges of shifting family alignments and confronting their own mortality. For many adult survivors, the death of one sibling can prompt attempts to strengthen the connections between their other brothers and sisters. As one adult survivor said, "I've gotten closer to my sister. So instead of talking two times a year, it is four times. My mother is very old and will probably pass away in two or three years. Then it will be just my sister and me. And I bet after my mother passes on, we'll talk eight times a year."

THE DEATH OF AN ELDERLY SIBLING

The loss of a sibling is probably the death most frequently experienced by people over sixty-five. Yet gerontologists and other professionals have shown minimal interest in siblings because few adult siblings live together, few provide more than a fraction of health care, and the elderly rarely seek counseling around issues of sibling ties.[5] Conversations with elderly siblings, however, make clear that mourning the death of a brother or sister is a continuous process that has an effect on the survivor over time.

For some elderly siblings, the loss may lead to an acceptance, resignation, and anticipation of his or her own death. "I feel I'll go the same way," said an eighty-three-year-old man in a 1987 study. "I've left instructions to my children. My daughter will take care of everything."[6] Another woman in the same study suggested that the time of her death was in the hands of fate. "I lost my husband in 1973, a brother in 1974, and a sister in 1975. When the time's up, I guess we go. There's no choice."

For other siblings, the death of a brother or sister may be viewed with some sense of relief at having been spared, of having survived. One woman in the Moss and Moss

(1989) study said, only partly in jest, that she would "live forver." "Perhaps the strength evoked by survival in and of itself," wrote Moss and Moss, "adds to a heightened sense of invulnerability and possibly a fleeting fantasy of immortality."[7]

As was pointed out in the beginning of this chapter, there are few cultural supports for the expression of grief or the recognition of loss of a sibling, and that lack of support extends to elderly siblings as well. For that reason, some siblings tend to minimize their grief, convinced that other relatives have better reason to mourn. One seventy-nine-year-old man whose older brother died four years ago said, "I still think of him, but he was not living with us, so his death didn't change my life." But as we continued to talk, his rather stoic attitude softened. "It is sad, though. There's no one left in my original family. I'm still in touch with my brother's wife, and I take a look at the belongings of his that I kept every now and then. I realize now that, as the youngest, I profited by his mistakes in that I didn't make them. I certainly owe him that."

A sixty-five-year-old whose older brother died last year talked about how he was affected by his brother's passing. For him, the grief was almost unbearable.

> It was heart-breaking. I was sick at the time and unable to go to his funeral. They thought maybe it was going to be me who was going to pass on. It was just a shock because he had a heart attack and died so suddenly. It means all the world to me to lose a brother. It was more touching than when I lost my mother because I was younger then and not conscious of passing. But as you grow older, you grow closer to family. I'll tell you that my brother's death was so shocking that I had the thought that maybe the Lord should have taken me instead. But then I said, "Oh, no, I've got to go on." And I did everything in my power to stay alive.

179

The same elderly man spoke about another significant family death: his mother's. He compared the impact of the two deaths (his brother's death was "more touching") and explained why the loss of his brother affected him more profoundly. As we age and experience more deaths, our grief tends to grow with each successive loss. Each new loss intensifies our painful memories of the earlier losses.[8] Older siblings tend to reflect upon earlier losses more readily and to repeatedly compare the effect of the successive deaths over a lifetime.

The death of a sibling may ironically help to maintain family ties. Most elderly siblings talk about how they keep in touch with the deceased sibling's spouse and children. Two-thirds of the respondents in the Moss and Moss (1989) study indicated that the quality of the bond between them and the deceased sibling's family remained the same; whereas the other third reported that the ties became even closer. Only one surviving sibling indicated that the ties became less close.

10

SIBLING INCEST: DISPELLING THE MYTH OF MUTUALITY

Until recently, researchers, social anthropologists, and journalists alike have summarily discounted brother-sister incest as a serious form of sexual abuse. Regularly deemed harmless sex play, sibling incest has even been described as a positive and beneficial experience for both brothers and sisters. The professional consensus is that brother-sister incest is either mutually desired and enjoyable or at least neutral, because, unlike incest involving an adult and a child, sibling incest involves peers. Another operating assumption is that sisters consent to their brothers' sexual overtures and that they are willing participants in developmentally appropriate sex games.

Studies to date probably grossly underestimate the incidence of sibling incest. The shame and embarrassment connected with incest prevent both victims and perpetrators from talking about it. In addition, many adults may have blocked childhood sexual incidents and no longer remember them. A survey of 796 undergraduates of six New England colleges found that 15 percent of the females and 10 percent of the males reported having some type of sexual experience with a sibling.[1] Fondling and touching the genitals were the most common activities in all age categories. Twenty-five percent of the incidents involved force and occurred between siblings who were several years apart in age. Professor of sociology Diana Russell found, in a more recent sample of 930 women from San Francisco who were eighteen and older, that 16 percent reported having had at least one incestuous experience before the age of eighteen. Of these 152 women, 2 percent reported having been abused by a brother. And Russell argues that this figure is lower than it would have been had the women without brothers been excluded from the questions relating to sibling incest.[2] Finally, a study was conducted by Vernon Wiehe. Newspaper and professional association newsletter notices were published asking that individuals who had been physically, emotionally, or sexually abused by a sibling in childhood answer a questionnare. Sixty-seven percent of the respondents said they had been sexually abused.[3] As the issue of sibling incest receives more attention and as researchers begin to focus on what has been, up to now, an undetected problem, the incidence of the abuse will be more accurately estimated.

While there are some cases of sibling incest that are not abusive, that fact has completely overshadowed the numerous experiences that are traumatic, clearly abusive, and often long-term in their negative effects. The burgeoning number of incest survivor self-help groups nationwide and the growing number of incest survivors in therapy attest to the seriousness of the problem. It is encouraging to note that the victims of sibling incest themselves, not the clinicians, are the ones who have broken the silence and begun to dispel the myth of mutuality. For these victims, an experience ignored by society has shaped every aspect of their personal lives.

In many ways, Camille's story reflects the horrors of growing up the victim of a dysfunctional family. Her father was a womanizer who, after staying out all night, would come home and pretend that he'd been there all along. Her mother, deeply in love, put up with him. "I knew she was a very unhappy person," said Camille. "She'd sit alone in the basement and cry. Anytime anything bad happened, I tried to make it better. *I* took care of *her*."

As the youngest of four until another sister was born when she was eleven, Camille looked up to her older brother as a "god." "I was put in my brother's care and told that he'd always be there for me. And I bought it. I was really close to my oldest sister, but the bond between Carl and me was special."

The sexual abuse began when Carl, age eight, put his hands in Camille's panties. Even though she was only a four-year-old, Camille said she was going to tell and ran into the house to find her mother. "I wasn't real clear," Camille said. "I just told her that Carl was trying to hurt me. Even then, I just felt she couldn't handle the truth. I just 'knew' that it was something you didn't tell."

For the next eight years, Carl sexually abused his sister whenever he could. He "felt her up," put pencils in her vagina and broke them, tried to get a dog to have sex with her, urinated on her, and attempted sexual intercourse from the time Camille was ten. The only time she knew as "free" time was when the two were eating together. "He'd be nice as he could be," said Camille. "He wouldn't hurt me then; it was the only safe time."

During this first stage of sexual abuse, Camille was convinced that somehow it was all her fault. Her brother was held in such esteem within the family that Camille assumed

183

she had done something very bad to incur such pain. "I hated myself," she said. "When Carl did something to hurt me, I would burn my hand or something like that. It was painful, but it was something I could control, something he couldn't take from me."

Carl forcibly took his sister's virginity when she was "around eleven." The rape resulted in Camille getting pregnant and Carl aborting the fetus with a hanger. After that, he stopped putting his own body in "there" but put just about anything else—knives, guns, baseball bats, anything he could find. "He'd hold my baby sister and tell me if I didn't do what he asked, he'd hurt her. He used her as a constant threat. I loved my sister more than anyone in the world and would do anything to protect her."

Carl hated fat—something Camille realized during her brief pregnancy. To stop him from abusing her, Camille started putting on weight. Carl didn't like his sister as much when she was heavy, but the abuse did not stop; it just got sicker.

When she turned fourteen, Camille told her older sister. "I said, 'I need your help. He keeps bothering me.' She said, 'What do you mean?' 'He keeps trying to force me to have sex with him.' My sister flipped out and drove away. We've never been close since. She was twenty-one at the time, old enough to understand. I'm not saying she could have stopped him, but she wasn't even there for me. That really hurt."

Even though Carl joined the Army, the abuse continued whenever he was home on leave. One night Carl and some friends taunted Camille as she was drying dishes. One guy in particular kept touching her, and Camille kept telling him to stop. "My brother said, 'You can do what you want with her.' I picked up a meat fork, stabbed the guy in the side, and threatened to call the cops. That stopped the guy and, for all practical purposes, stopped Carl. Yet even today, all these years later, he still tells me how

184

good I look and how I'm the only one who can make him happy."

Camille's first marriage was anything but happy. When Carl came to her apartment and told her not to get married, Camille went right off and married the man. "I had two choices," she said. "I knew both Carl and my former husband were abusive, but I could get away from my husband easier than I could get away from Carl. I married this abusive man who was like another brother." After that marriage disintegrated, Camille met another man, lived with him, and had a son. Only after he held a gun to mother and child and threatened to kill them did Camille go to court to fight for custody. "When I started fighting for my son, I started fighting for me. I decided no one was going to hurt me again."

During the next several years, Camille's weight fluctuated between eighty and two hundred pounds. During one particularly stressful three-month period, she gained a hundred pounds. "Food is so tied in my mind to sex and safety," Camille said. "There are times when I want to lose so much weight I'll disappear; that way, I can't be hurt. And there are other times when the heavier I am, the safer I feel."

A friend concerned about Camille's health "dragged" her to an eating disorders clinic. At the time, Camille was seriously underweight; she gained just enough to "get everyone off my back" and then quit the group. "It was easy for me to convince people that I was okay. I've spent my whole life doing it." And while she's probably read every book on eating disorders, incest, and rape, Camille refuses to join another self-help group or seek individual therapy. "I have a bad problem with doing anything for myself," she said. "If it were you, I'd tell you to get help in a minute. If it were you, I'd probably bring you to a doctor or therapist. But if you took me, I'd probably run away. I need to be in control. I know it's illogical, but that's just the way it is. I don't know how to help myself; it's so foreign."

Camille has never confronted Carl about what happened and still runs into him about once a year. "I don't know how to talk to him; I don't want to see him." As far as her parents are concerned, nothing has changed. Her father still runs around with other women, and her mother continues to suffer. "I'm still her parent," said Camille. "If she has a problem, she calls me. It hasn't changed since I was four." And while her oldest sister acknowledges that Carl is "sick," she will go no further in supporting Camille.

Now almost ten years since the sexual abuse ended, Camille still cannot sleep for more than short spurts. "Whenever I wake up, my first thought is whether Carl is there hurting me. I still get the same feeling. I still feel all of this panic inside." And while she's living with a man who seems to love her very much, Camille puts him through hell. "Weeks go by, and I'm not there for him. He knows about the incest and wants me to go to meetings and make it all better. You know, kiss the sore. But nothing will change what happened to me. I don't now what good it could do. Besides, I don't trust people, anyway."

The dysfunction in Camille's family—a physically absent father and an emotionally absent mother—set the stage for the negative "high accessiblity" of Carl and Camille. In examining twenty-five families of sibling incest, Smith and Israel (1987) found three consistent, distinctive family dynamics: "(1) distant, inaccessible parents; (2) parental stimulation of sexual climate in the home; and (3) family secrets and extramarital affairs."4 When Camille tried to explain why her brother had become so cruel, she mentioned his going to work with his father on the weekends. While with his father, Carl was exposed to "dirty" magazines, girlfriends coming to visit his father, and lunchtime follies when his father and a woman would escape to his truck and make love. "He saw the sick side of life," Camille said. "He was probably mad and frustrated and unable to discuss his feelings. We didn't talk about feelings in our family."

The veil of secrecy in the family, coupled with the parents' inabilty to be "there" for their children, prevented Camille from telling anyone about the abuse she was suffering. "Nobody took me seriously," she said, "and besides, I was the one who took care of my mother. And my father . . . he's the kind who thinks girls ask to be raped." Isolated and devalued, Camille quickly learned to disassociate. "I just wasn't there, if you know what I mean."

To this day, Camille is not "there" when it comes to meeting her own needs. Taking care of others, particularly her son, her "baby" sister, and her mother, is something she does very well. But taking care of herself is a "foreign" concept. "If I'm choking," she said, "I'll wait to get a drink. If I have to go to the bathroom, I'll go in an hour. I have a real bad problem with putting me first in any way."

Camille's low self-esteem has contributed to her feeling that no one, not even the best incest therapist around, can help her regain all that she has lost. She is a member of several self-help groups and reads all of the literature, but she never attends meetings. "I think people should put their ghosts to rest," she said, "yet what happened to me is still there. I can't sleep, I'm untrusting, I have an eating disorder, and I put men through hell. I'd like things to change, but I don't see it happening. I remember being pregnant, the hanger, the pain, the blood, the jellylike fetus, and my brother telling me to clean myself up. Since you can't change that, I don't know what good it would do to try."

The experts say that with early intervention and the cooperation of the perpetrator and the rest of the family, victims of incest can get the help they need. In Camille's case, only part of her family knows about the incest, and they have failed to offer support, let alone the willingness to seek therapy. As for Carl, he did cry once, many years

187

ago, and told Camille he was sorry. Yet his apology was a hollow one, as he continues to tell Camille that she's the only one who can make him happy. The prognosis for Camille getting her life on track is bleak, indeed.

"IT'S JUST SO HARD TO DESCRIBE"

For many victims of sibling incest, the shame and guilt of what happened to them overpower the need to share the secret and to get help. There is a deep-rooted fear that if anyone knew about the incest, they would blame the victim and see her as a "terrible" person. For Angie, it took twenty years and sobering up with the help of Alcoholics Anonymous before she dared to tell anyone about the sexual abuse she suffered at the hands of her brother from the time she was seven until she turned sixteen. "I was crying hysterically," said Angie, "and my AA sponsor said, 'This is bigger than you and me. You are not responsible for what happened; it is not your fault. You need help.' "

Help came from a therapist who specialized in working with survivors of incest and from VOICES (Victims of Incest Can Emerge Survivors). The road Angie traveled on her way to recovery was often treacherous, but it wound its way uphill nonetheless. "Just knowing that I'm not alone—that other women have suffered the same victimization—means a lot."

The support and straightforward information that survivors can find if they reach out for help contrasts sharply with the lack of love and secrecy that enveloped their lives as children. Over and over again, survivors detail family situations in which one or both parents were distant, passive, even withdrawn. "My mother wasn't there for me," said Angie. "And my father came home late every night bombed out of his mind. Unless we were doing something he wanted to do, our relationship was very distant." This distance pushes siblings together and can lead to a younger sibling, usually a sister, idolizing and depending upon an older sibling. "You might say I adored my brother Nick," said Angie. "He was five years older, extremely talented, and my protector. I was his little protégé.

That all changed suddenly when, in the middle of the night, Nick sneaked into the bedroom Angie shared with two other sisters and started feeling her up. "I flipped out and went screaming to my parents. 'He's touching me,' I yelled. My mother jumped out of bed and came running. But Nick was already back in his room, pretending to be asleep. The second time it happened, I ran to my parents again. They told me I was dreaming, to shut up, and go back to bed. I was just a little kid, and they didn't believe me. For the next twenty years, I felt that if anyone knew that secret about me they'd think I was a terrible person."

For many survivors like Angie, the trust they have in an older brother is abused when "suddenly" the brother sneaks into their bedroom in the middle of the night and starts touching them in intimate places when the parents are away. Sibling sexual abuse is rarely a one-time event. And rarely do the young victims fight back. They are scared, confused, and often not aware of what they are doing. For Angie, it seemed as if Nick abused her all the time, but she lost track. "I'd say he molested me at least once a week, but I honestly don't know. I was so scared that it never occurred to me to put up a fight. I was petrified and just wanted it to be over. It's so hard to describe—the revulsion, the hate, the love all mixed in. It was so hard to sort out as a child. I didn't know what the hell was going on, and I had nowhere to turn."

Angie found herself running in circles.

I'd go anywhere with anyone to stay away from my brother. I quit school, convinced that I could never do anything right. I became an alcoholic and used a lot of drugs. I had absolutely no self-worth. None. Then one night when I was sixteen, I got the courage to resist. He came after me that last time, and I kicked him in the face and told him that if he ever came near me again, I'd fucking kill him! That ended the abuse but certainly not the effects of what had happened to me. I think the incest affected every part of my life.

If and when victims of incest do confront the abusive sibling and/or disclose the truth to other members of the family, they can expect any number of reactions ranging from acceptance to denial to complete rejection. Angie confronted Nick before telling anyone else. "It was very empowering for me," she said. "His response was, 'I thought some day you'd be upset about this.' And mine was, 'Upset? That's quite an understatement. If you ever come near me or anyone in my family, I'll tell the entire world what you did to me.' He didn't apologize, and I'm not interested in therapy with him. My anger is too great; it wouldn't be a healing experience for me. I never want to speak to him again."

When Angie told her mother about the incest, she was very upset, apologizing for not having been responsive. But afterward her reaction changed. Through her sisters, Angie has learned that her mother thinks she's "nuts" and is making things up. "Our relationship is very strained. I was operated on for cancer this spring, and my mother came flying up to take care of me, even though I didn't want her here. We tried to talk, but it got to the point where I said I didn't want to continue. I just got too upset."

Angie's other siblings reacted to her "news" with varying responses. The two sisters who had shared the bedroom with her were very supportive. While they both denied knowing anything, Angie suspects that they were abused by the same brother. "But that's just my impression," she said. "They told me their stories about what Nick did to

190

them, but they don't think it was abuse. That's for them to decide." Angie's younger brother doesn't want to talk about it, though he hates Nick and has no relationship with him. One sister, the younger one, is very "embarrassed" by all the incest talk. And another sister is definitely not supportive, angry that Angie is bringing all this up. "She thinks I'm making the family look dirty, that what happened is all in the past."

Even today as a thirty-seven-year-old, Angie suffers the effects of having been sexually abused by her brother. There are members of her immediate family who think she's a troublemaker. It's difficult to say whether she'll ever be able to change their minds (or whether she'll even continue to try). The issue of poor self-esteem still rears its ugly head. And there remains a brother from whom Angie is estranged, who is unwilling to acknowledge the harm he caused his "little" sister, the sister who adored him.

Very often when there is sibling incest, other abuse has gone on within the family. Angie heard that her brother claims to have been abused by their grandmother. ("I somewhat believe it," Angie said, "just because I don't want anyone to disbelieve me.") And Angie suspects that her mother was also abused, though she is not sure by whom. "She acts like me before I got help. She's afraid of everything. She doesn't do anything, doesn't drive . . . nothing." Passed from one generation to the next, incest is an insidious problem with few boundaries, until someone makes a conscious decision to get help and stop the curse.

PASSIVITY AND REPEATED VICTIMIZATION

Children's passive behavior in response to sexual abuse is common for many reasons, including their fear of being hurt, of losing affection and love, of their parents finding out, or of being blamed, as well as their naïveté about what is going on. Yet many children are remarkably assertive in their handling of their abusers. In fact, a considerable percentage of the incestuous experiences end only through the efforts of the victims.[5]

Such was the case with Carrie, who had been sexually abused by her older brother for at least three years. At age eleven, Carrie was hospitalized for eleven months. During her recovery from back surgery, she made plans for what to do when she went home. "Sometime after I got out of the hospital," she said, "my brother did approach me and I said 'No.' I think my fear of getting pregnant was greater than my fear of refusing him. He accepted it. I was shocked, absolutely shocked!" The fact that her brother acquiesced without an argument in no way diminishes the courage it took Carrie to say no and the stress involved in forging her "plan."

It is hardly surprising that incest survivors like Carrie are fearful and that this fear can make them vulnerable to repeated victimization. Carrie was afraid of going through the process of getting in touch with her depressed feelings. She described herself as one who moved between trusting people too much or not at all. She is, she said, a "people pleaser," afraid of offending others. This exaggerated tendency not to offend people could have led to serious trouble one afternoon recently when Carrie was reading by a lake in a secluded area. A group of men who had been drinking suddenly appeared and, worried about offending them, Carrie was slow to leave. Luckily, a car pulled up with people whom the men knew. They started talking, and Carrie took off. Carrie knew that she was in a risky situation, yet her fear of insulting them overrode her sense of personal safety. The study of incest survivors led by Diana Russell (1986) concluded that the incest experience itself can strip away some of the victims' potential ability to protect themselves. The victims feel helpless in the face of potential danger and often jeopardize their own safety.

DEVALUED MEMBERS
OF THE FAMILY

"I would like someday to feel comfortable in my body—like I belong here, like this is mine and I have a right to this space," said Debra, forty-two and a victim of sibling incest. In thinking about her childhood and the dynamics within her family, she realizes that abuse ran rampant. Her mother was verbally abusive, her brother abused Debra physically before the incest began, and the verbal (and possibly physical) abuse between her father and brother and between her parents made every dinner hour an explosive and unpleasant event. According to several experts, abuse within a family—whether it is sexual or not—can set the stage and, in some perverse way, give permission for sexual abuse to a sibling. As Debra said, she didn't realize there was another way; she thought everybody grew up terrified and victimized.

Clinical psychologist Denise Gelinas was the first to point out that people who have been sexually abused within their families are devalued members of the family group. They are often the chosen victim in the first place, and then this sexual abuse further devalues them in the eyes of the family, as well as in their own eyes. "Therefore," said Gelinas, "incest victims usually have very poor self-esteem and don't have many tools for dealing interpersonally with people. They almost always end up with relational imbalances; they don't have fair relationships. Incest victims are exploited a lot, and this exploitation becomes a lifelong pattern, unless they're able to resolve this pattern, for instance, in therapy."[6]

As the devalued member of her family before the incest began, Debra was alone in her unhappiness; there was no one to turn to for support. Even before the sexual abuse began, her older brother Tom played mean tricks on her. He'd put her up on the roof of the chicken house and remove the ladder. Or he'd take the hinges off doors, prop them up, and then laugh with the rest of the family as Debra would go to open one and it would fall on top of her. Her youngest brother, she said, was the "prince" who could do no wrong. He did not marry until he was thirty-seven and, according to Debra, came home every weekend from the time he left for college until his marriage. "He'd come home to Mom," Debra said. "I call that emotional incest." And while the abusive brother Tom lived at home, his position as the oldest brother apparently gave him the "right" to molest his sister, without fear of parental reprisal.

Not surprisingly, Debra did not tell anyone about the sexual abuse. "At that point in my life," she said, "I didn't think I was important enough to make an issue out of it. Besides, I didn't trust anybody."

As Debra got older, she "misplaced" a lot of her anger on other boys. She would lead them on, get them to like her, and then drop them. She married an alcoholic when she was nineteen. And after telling him about the incest, he "browbeat" her with the information. "He constantly called me a whore and convinced me that I was a lost cause. I stayed him for thirteen years and had two children. Only when he became physically abusive to my kids did I find the courage to leave him."

Debra found the courage to break the silence and tell her mother about the incest after remarrying a "very supportive man" who believed her innocence and acknowledged her trauma. Like many family members upon learning of the incest that occurred in their home, Debra's parents flat out denied it. Two weeks later at a family meeting, Debra was presented with a notebook that "included everything I had done wrong since I was eighteen." My husband and I looked at each other, got up, and walked out the door. I've never discussed the incest with my parents again."

Somewhere along the line, Tom "got religion" and called Debra and said that he felt he owed her an apology. When she asked him what for, he said because he had molested her. "I was speechless," Debra said. "I was just so glad to have had it verified." Yet when she hired an attorney to recover treatment costs, Tom's attorney wrote back denying that anything had ever happened and threatening to sue Debra if she ever said a word to anybody. "I have no relationship with him today," she said. "He's crazier than a loon and very, very rich. As far as I'm concerned, he's dead."

POST-TRAUMATIC STRESS DISORDER

In her book *Healing the Incest Wound: Adult Survivors in Therapy,* counseling psychologist Christine Courtois details how many survivors of incest suffer from post-traumatic stress reactions similar to those experienced by victims of war. Though a syndrome popularized after Vietnam, post-traumatic stress disorder has recently been acknowledged by the psychiatric community as a diagnosis that applies to more than those who suffered war trauma. According to Courtois, survivors of incest often experience reactions that alternate between those that are numbing and denying to those that reenact the trauma (like the flashbacks that victims sometimes experience). Over time, these symptoms lead to other problems that include depression, avoidance of intimacy, relational distortions, eating disorders, insomnia, and substance abuse. "Child sexual abuse," writes Courtois, "has been found to affect the victim's personality development and every major life sphere, either at the time of the incest and/or later in life . . . In a clinical sample, the aftereffects are by definition more serious than in the population in general and have become symptoms associated with an array of mental health disturbances."[7]

For some incest victims, part of the disturbance involved their confusion about the change in the abuser's behavior when they were in the bedroom. The silence and more gentle manner of the abuser stood in sharp contrast to their incessant tormenting outside of the bedroom and made the sexual abuse "different" and, in a perverse way, preferable. For an eight-year-old like Cathy, her hatred of her sexually abusive brother was somewhat diluted by what she felt as almost kindness. "As verbally abusive as he was, he never said one word to me in that bedroom," said Cathy. "I was able to see the difference; in that room, there was silence, and I was being treated differently. He was nicer and more gentle, which led to part of my confusion." The subsequent confusion over the kind of person the sibling molestor was and how he really felt made untangling the web of convoluted feelings impossible. Left alone to sort out the mixed messages, Cathy and others ultimately repressed the horror of the abuse, only to have it resurface years later.

For Cathy, her recovery began after listening to a radio talk show that focused on victims of sexual abuse. "I found myself crying and thought that I was a very empathic person. Finally, it came to me that *I'm* an incest survivor, a fact I had repressed for thirty years!"

As a member of an incest survivors' group and through her work with a therapist, Cathy began to realize the many ways in which her secret trauma had affected her. Although she had denied the incest, the abuse had insinuated itself into so many parts of her life. She married someone she didn't love, then became promiscuous after the divorce, going to bed with anyone. While making love with virtual strangers, she would roll over, bury her face into a pillow, and cry inwardly—just as she had done when her brother was molesting her as a child. She has suffered from a low-grade depression, continues to battle a weight problem, and has flashbacks in which she relives what happened to

196

her "like a motion picture." "To this day," she said, "I can still smell my brother's breath."

Her brother is now a millionaire and looked upon by the outside world as a pillar of society. Despite his blanket of protection, Cathy confronted him on her own.

I said to him, "I don't want anything from you, but I remember what you did to me as a child." "What are you talking about?" he asked. I proceeded to tell him how he had tormented me both in and out of the bedroom. And when I finished, he asked, "Are you telling me that you think I had intercourse with a little girl?" I said, "No, I don't think so. I know." He did not deny it or accept it. And at this point, I don't care whether he admits what happened. I know what he did to me. And I don't care if he does or doesn't sleep at night. What matters to me is that I am now able to sleep. I'm on my path!

No matter what form it takes, sibling abuse has been ignored at times because it was viewed as "normal" behavior. "Kids will be kids." They call each other names. They tattle on one another. They sometimes gang up on the "devalued" sibling. They play mean tricks. They can be physically abusive. And, as we've seen all too clearly, siblings can be sexually abusive much more frequently than we ever imagined. The idea that many parents and other adults can excuse such cruel and harmful behavior as the expected effects of sibling rivalry boggles the mind and makes us angry. How nearsighted to conclude that sibling abuse is a normal part of growing up and competing for parental attention. The heart-wrenching tales of sibling incest detailed here and elsewhere alert us to the complexity of the problem and to the multiple causes of such abuse. The role of parents overwhelmed by their own problems and ineffective in their handling of their children, the role of the siblings, and the role of society in encouraging males to dominate and control females all contribute to sibling abuse. If we all recognize the many factors that encourage abusive behavior between siblings, it will help victims, perpetrators, and parents to deal with these factors, stop their abusive behavior, and get professional help if needed.

Lest we assume that all incestuous siblings are older brothers, consider the story of Hal, who was victimized by an older sister from the time he was seven or eight until he reached puberty.

As the youngest of six, Hal grew up in an upper-middle-class family that appeared absolutely "normal." Hal's father was a journalist and a politician, a rigid and extremely demanding man who valued his children according to how well they performed academically. "My grades were bad," said Hal, "and so was my self-esteem." Hal's mother was a homemaker, a "traditional" woman who stayed home while her husband worked. "As the youngest," said Hal, "I was well taken care of. My relationships with my other siblings were affectionate and close."

Hal described his sister Sandy, ten years older, as "stubborn, independent, and assertive." Prior to the abuse, the two enjoyed a warm connection. That changed when, after giving Hal a shower, Sandy dried him off and started fondling him.

> She touched my genitals, I had an erection, and she performed oral sex. I was bewildered but pleased by her interest in me. I thought I was special in her eyes. I think it was enjoyable, although I don't remember that very clearly. There was no sexual release for me.
>
> As I got older, it was hard to admit these feelings, along with the extreme guilt and low self-esteem. I was the only male child in the family, and it was my job to protect the females. I was failing at that job and felt like the traitor in the family. Even though she was older and had initiated

everything, I felt responsible. I knew what I was doing wasn't right, but I didn't refuse.

After Hal started masturbating and had his first ejaculation, he suggested that he and Sandy have sexual intercourse. Sandy was furious. How could he suggest such a thing? "I was extremely disappointed," said Hal, "feeling that I'd been cheated. I was angry, not because she had rejected me, but because I hadn't been able to have any sexual release. At that time, I had no understanding of sexual abuse. That's only come in the last couple of years."

At age twenty-five, Hal told his wife-to-be that he had had a sexual relationship with his sister. "She reacted as if I'd had an accident sometime in the past but that I was doing fine. It was as if nothing had really happened." Hal described himself at that time as hypersexual, promiscuous, very depressed, self-destructive, and a man with very low self-esteem. "I would get depressed for several days, and then I'd snap out of it. I had no idea why. And I would choose high-risk situations sexually and otherwise. I was not leading a healthy life, yet didn't realize the connection between the incest and these effects."

When Hal's eldest son was seven, Hal went into psychoanalysis. It struck me as more than coincidental that Hal began psychoanalysis when his eldest son was seven, the same age at which his sister had first abused him. Although Hal thought at the time that he had started therapy to deal with parenting issues, in retrospect he can see how his cry for help may have been an "anniversary reaction" to the trauma he experienced as a child. And he can see how his therapist danced around the incest issue, focusing instead on the relationship with his parents (not a surprising reaction considering the way many therapists undervalue sibling relationships and accept the myth of mutuality surrounding sibling incest).

Hal tried to confront his sister a few months ago, but she

dismissed him by saying that whatever happened in the past was just a "doctor's game." "All I can do," said Hal, "is try to maintain an equilibrium and give new meanings to intimacy. I need to trust females, to be vulnerable after protecting myself very well all of these years. I became a physician to understand what happened to me from a physical-anatomical point of view. In retrospect, I studied medicine to cure myself. With the help of therapy and the incest survivors group, I'm almost there!"

Older sister/younger brother incest may be similar to mother-son incest. The sister may be insecure with peers or within the family and use her brother for affection, security, and reassurance. Or she may be quite aggressive, possessive, and demanding of her brother sexually and otherwise. In this case, writes Christine Courtois, the brother usually suffers the more severe aftereffects. He may feel shame, guilt, and remorse, as well as great ambivalence toward his sister. His guilt and anxiety may later impede his ability to perform sexually with women in his peer group.[8]

The predominant view of sibling incest has been of mutual sexual exploration among children within the same age range. Seen as a normal occurrence in a child's psychosexual development, sibling incest typically has been dismissed as a harmless activity with few, if any, repercussions. Clearly, such a view is far from reality. Although there are cases in which incest is not abusive—that is, cases in which one sibling is not using power or influence over another younger child for sexual gratification—the painful stories of many incest survivors attest to its potentially harmful and long-lasting effects.

One of the most shocking findings of Russell's incest study is that 16 percent of the women had been sexually abused by a relative before the age of eighteen, and 2.3 percent had been sexually abused by a sibling. If we extrapolate from this 16 percent figure to the population at large, it means that 160,000 women per million in this country have been incestuously abused before the age of eighteen, and 23,000 per million may have been victimized by a sibling. As Russell points out, these figures suggest that "incestuous abuse can no longer be viewed as a problem that involves but a few sick or disturbed sex offenders."[9] Sibling incest is an important social issue because of the intense suffering and sometimes destructive long-term effects that are passed from one generation to the next.

As mentioned, it has been the survivors of sibling incest in most cases, not the clinicians, who have broken the silence. Unfortunately, many therapists like Hal's have skirted the issue or ignored it completely, making disclosure that much more difficult. Time and again, survivors talk about seeking professional help and validation, only to have the issue of sibling incest pushed aside. Many survivors have given up, and only the strongest persevere.

The recent proliferation of self-help groups like VOICES and Survivors of Incest Anonymous has helped fill a much-needed gap; incest survivors can share their experiences with others who have suffered similar pain and humiliation. For many, simply knowing that they are not alone provides the strength to unravel the web of feelings and to put their lives back on track. As with other childhood traumas, the sooner a survivor can get help, the better the chances of making significant progress. Ideally, the survivor will be supported by the entire family, including the abusive sibling, who can admit his (or her) guilt and apologize with conviction. If the family can be reconstructed to protect its members and restrain the acting out of sexual impulses, other therapeutic moves will be effective and wounds can be healed.

As psychologist Marsha Heiman writes in "Untangling Incestuous Bonds: The Treatment of Sibling Incest," "The sibling bond can become an anxiety-ridden and guilt-producing bind when boundaries are crossed and the incest taboo broken . . . As incestuous bonds are untangled, the process becomes one of restoring the sibling relationship so that the family can heal and all of the siblings can move forward in their development—free of pain, confusion, and shame."[10] Although none of the adult sibling sex-abusers in the case histories documented here accepted responsibility and sought therapy, Heiman discusses an adolescent brother who, after months of individual and family counseling, described how he felt. "I'm glad Denise forgives me. I didn't know it then, but I could have lost a sister. The day she said that she didn't have a brother was the first time I knew how much I had hurt her. I couldn't pretend anymore."[11]

11

SIBLINGS IN DISRUPTED FAMILIES

Each year, millions of families are forced to confront the special problems caused by divorce, remarriage, alcoholism, and a host of mental and physical disabilities. Although a great deal of attention has been given to the results of such upheavals in the lives of adults, their effects on the sibling relationship have only recently begun to be explored. Books like Powell and Ogle's *Brothers and Sisters: A Special Part of Exceptional Families* and organizations such as The Sibling and Adult Children's Network, Sibling Information Network, Siblings for Significant Change, SIBS, and SHARE are helping to bridge the gap. Brothers and sisters need the skills to cope with disruptions in their family lives and the facts about where they stand in relation to their parents and to one another. Many siblings feel the stigma of having a mentally ill or physically disabled brother or sister or of having an alcoholic parent or parents who are divorced. The usual sibling stresses, joys, and fears take on added dimensions in a disrupted family, dimensions that need to be addressed if siblings are going to understand their unique feelings and circumstances.

LIVING WITH A DISABLED BROTHER OR SISTER

As is the case with most sibling relationships, growing up with a disabled sibling has both bright and bleak moments. The healthy sibling may, at one time, feel tremendous satisfaction at the smallest accomplishments of the disabled brother or sister. At another time, however, the same child may feel bitter and resentful because of the extra attention given the disabled sibling or because of the caretaking demands placed on him or her. It is helpful to see the effects of a disabled child on the sibling in terms of a continuum, with very positive outcomes at one end and very negative outcomes at the other. It is safe to say that the healthy sibling moves back and forth along the continuum, at times appreciating the benefits of having a special sibling and, at other times, wishing that the disabled sibling were like everyone else.[1]

SHE WAS "EVERYTHING THAT WAS GOOD"

There are people with cerebral palsy who can function in the outside world; Carly was not one of them. When the doctors suggested that Carly's mother put her in an institution because she would always be a "vegetable," her mother told the doctors, "If she's going to be a vegetable, she's going to be *my* vegetable." Although she could sit up, Carly could neither walk nor talk. Her mother did teach her the "rudimentary beginnings of walking" by standing behind her, clasping her arms around her waist, and pushing her feet out, one in front of the other. But Carly could not stand or move on her own.

Whenever anyone suggested Carly was mentally retarded her mother would get extremely angry. She was convinced that Carly could understand and internalize much more than most gave her credit for. "We were always careful about what we said in front of her," her younger sister Jenny explained. "We never talked about her in a negative way because of the chance that she could understand more than she was showing.

"Even though she lived to be almost twenty-one, Carly was totally unspoiled. She was not just a vegetable, even though it sounds like she was. She lit up when anyone came into the room; she loved people. She loved music, too. My sister was everything that was good."

While Jenny was, at times, responsible for Carly's care, she never felt burdened by the responsibility. "Somehow I didn't seem to mind taking care of her," said Jenny. "She needed me. And my mother was very sensitive to *my* needs. She didn't overburden me and hired a babysitter when I was old enough to have my own social life." Jenny recalled going to the beach with Carly and a good friend when she was in sixth grade.

People were staring at Carly like she was some kind of freak. My friend and I just decided to stare at them back. We were on our stomachs, staring them down, and they finally stopped. We thought the whole thing was hysterical; I was eleven then.

I have to say, though, that I went through a time as a teenager when I was a little embarrassed about Carly. There were physical things, like her drooling and her irregular breathing, that I just didn't want to have to explain. It kept me from having friends over. Luckily, I outgrew that.

205

According to Jenny, she and her parents (and, later on, her younger sister) didn't even think about Carly's disability that much. "I'd say we were all pretty well adjusted," she said. "The fact that I grew up with a sib like this from day one made a difference. It was natural to me. Sure, we discussed the fact that she had cerebral palsy to new people who came to the house, but I can't say that, as a family, we discussed her disability at great length. Maybe part of it was that back then our society didn't address issues of the disabled."

As an eighteen-year-old, Jenny had dropped out of college and moved back home. "I was home when Carly died," she said. "I needed to be there. She'd been sick for months and was getting weaker all the time. You assume for a while that people will be with you forever, but I knew she wouldn't live a long life. Still, it was very painful. I still cry when I think about it, and it's been many years."

On the downside, having had a disabled sibling made Jenny's parents overly protective of her. They were strict and sometimes appeared untrusting. "Maybe they were afraid for my life. Maybe they couldn't stand the thought of having another child taken from them." On the positive side, growing up with a disabled sister gave Jenny a "lot of compassion." "I often try to look beyond people's faults," she said. "It's helped me with my relationships with children. I probably decided to become a teacher because of Carly. And I learned patience, having had to exercise a lot of patience with her."

I have more memories of Carly and me than I do of my younger sister. Carly and I were a team; Rita was born when I was seven. I see pictures of us together, but I was closer to Carly. Besides, Rita was the little invader. She took my center stage away; Carly never did that. I never had to be jealous of her. Sure, she received a certain amount of extra attention, but I must have been safe there.

Rita was a different story, and we did not really become close for many years.

Today, I have a friend for life. Rita can tell me to shape up, and I'm going to listen. I'm not going to be offended, and I can do the same with her. I tell her my innermost secrets, things I might not even tell my husband. I think concern for family members brought us together. Blood is thicker than water and more truth than poetry.

Parent-child relationships can significantly affect the way children and adolescents react to growing up with a disabled sibling. If there are open lines of communication between them and if the healthy siblings feel they are being treated fairly, chances are good that their special concerns will be addressed and met. Such was the case with Jenny, whose mother, in particular, made a concerted effort to pay attention to her needs. She never overburdened Jenny with her sister's care and made Jenny feel as important and loved as her disabled sister. "My mother was terrific," said Jenny, "particularly when you consider that there were no support groups at that time. Carly got wonderful care from my mother, and my mother was very sensitive to my needs."

Like many children with disabled siblings, Jenny's feelings ran the gamut from unselfish love and care to embarrassment. She explained that Carly drooled, breathed unevenly, and sometimes blacked out. "Those kinds of things are hard to explain to new people," said Jenny, "and when I was thirteen and attending a new school, I didn't invite friends to my house as often." But her discomfort was short lived and, for the most part, Jenny viewed her sister as a teammate with whom she shared her childhood and adolescence.

Jenny feels she owes her compassion, her patience, and her good relationships with children to having grown up with Carly. "I had to exercise a lot of patience with her," Jenny said. "I can't say I was perfect. There were times

when she would give a look like, 'What have I done wrong?'
And I'd feel like a rat, having expected her to do something
that I knew she couldn't do. But I think she knew I was
really good deep down inside.

"Carly didn't know evil at all. She was totally unspoiled
and just so sweet. She gave us all so much in the short time
that she was with us."

ADULT SIBLINGS OF THE DISABLED

As parents age and can no longer take care of their disabled
child, brothers and sisters are faced with juggling their own
lives and families and the increased responsibilities for their
disabled sibling. Adult siblings must face the realities of
long-term care for the disabled brother or sister and all the
subsequent decisions involving finances, guardianship, and
estate planning. Adult brothers and sisters, who have long
ago left their parents' home and their disabled sibling behind, are called upon to make room for their brother or
sister. This transition can strain the sibling bond or reinforce
the closeness of family and serve as a liberating experience
for all of the siblings.

Cynthia's sister Janie was born with cerebral palsy, but
is able to perform many functions on her own. Still, every
time Janie falls or becomes unsteady, Cynthia plans another
big trip because she knows it might get to the point where
she won't feel comfortable being so far away. "I used to
worry about it a lot more, but now I'm beginning to realize
that I don't have to take care of her—I have to be the one
to *see* that she's taken care of. That took a long time with
a lot of guilty feelings, but I've finally worked that one
through. My father set up financial resources for Janie. It's
my responsiblity to see that the money is handled properly."

Coming to terms with her sister's disability and, more

208

importantly, with her own responsibilities has been a liberating experience for Cynthia and for Janie, too. Like many adult siblings of disabled brothers and sisters, Cynthia struggled to impose her own standards and sensibilities on Janie. She was convinced that Janie was not independent enough, that she needed to expand her horizons beyond the confines of a very limited world. Cynthia's pushing caused no end of problems; Janie rebelled against her sister's aggressive attempts to change her life. Yet, ever so slowly, the dynamics between the two sisters began to change. They started talking about real feelings, including their intense anger toward one another. They started relating to each other as two adults.

The improvement in their relationship and in Janie's sense of independence has been remarkable. People who have known Janie for years can't believe how much she has progressed. She is more outgoing, has developed friendships beyond the family, manages her own checking account, and enjoys a variety of activities outside the home.

Still, there are concerns. Cynthia is reminded that her sister's condition can deteriorate at any moment and that her own freedom will eventually be restricted. Those are the times when she makes new travel plans to use her freedom while she still has it. She must concern herself with her own aging and eventual death as well. Responsibility for overseeing Janie's care will then become her own daughters' obligation. Cynthia is intent on enlisting the next generation of family members to serve as advocates for Janie, relatives who will promote their aunt's interests and help her enjoy a quality life.

The experiences of adult siblings with disabled brothers or sisters vary considerably. Cynthia was one of the lucky ones whose parents planned for her sister's future, by providing her financial security. Cynthia is also lucky to have had a niece with a degree in special education who has been willing to serve as Janie's companion. She has not been burdened with decisions about alternative living arrangements or with finding other competent caregivers. That responsibility may eventually fall on her daughters' shoulders.

Looking back, Cynthia feels she pushed herself to excel because she had a disabled sister. "I put pressure on myself," she said. "Whether my parents encouraged that stance, I don't know." Cynthia also senses that she is less of a feeling person, though she's not sure whether that's more of a result of family or of Janie. "I know that she got far more hugs than I ever did. Early on, I may have resisted the hugs because she was getting them. That was her, and I was going to be different. Now I see my girls and grandchildren giving each other genuine hugs of affection. I can't remember doing that."

Cynthia's negative and positive effects of having a disabled sibling mirror the bulk of research on the relationships between disabled children and their normal siblings. She still feels some resentment because of the extra attention given Janie. And the struggle to find peace within herself vis-à-vis Janie's care has been a long and sometimes difficult one. Yet, like most adult siblings, she has been able to balance the negative effects with all that is good and encouraging about her sister. Cynthia appreciates Janie's sense of humor and is extremely proud of the strides she has made toward independence. In her heart, Cynthia understands that Janie has grown and prospered because of her. There is no greater gift that one sibling can give to another.

CONFRONTING MENTAL ILLNESS

Mental illness knows no class, color, or religion. Neither is it, as we once thought, the curse only of those who suffered terrible childhoods or mixed-up families. Mindstorms

210

of the most terrifying sort can make victims of people from the most caring and supportive families. Helplessly watching someone you love turn into a disturbed stranger is nothing short of wrenching. When you add to that the blame psychiatrists so routinely level at the families of the mentally ill, the experience can become excruciating. Now illnesses such as schizophrenia, manic depression, and unipolar depressions, once thought to be the sad result of cold, loveless mothering, show evidence of being linked to genetics. Knowing the biological origins of mental illness can ease a family's guilt. But no explanation—and no outcome short of full recovery—is likely to ease its pain.[2]

Unlike siblings with a physically disabled brother or sister, siblings with a mentally ill brother or sister often witness the illness develop. Seth described his brother Mel as a "unique" but fairly normal kid. Their relationship as the two youngest brothers of four was a very close and compatible one. The two shared a bedroom and were playmates. The fact that their very different personalities began to emerge during elementary school and that these differences led to physical and verbal battles is not, in itself, a unique situation between siblings. Nor is it unique that Seth, the more physically and socially adept of the two, felt embarrassed by his "funny" brother who never learned to drive, had few, if any, friends, and who constantly annoyed his peers.

What might be considered unusual, or, at least, very sad, was that the boys' parents let their children fend for themselves. They were not "organized" and felt incapable of doing anything to help Mel and of openly discussing their worries and frustrations with the other members of the family. Even after Mel started talking "crazy," even after he pounded his fist through walls and carried on imaginary conversations, his parents pretended nothing was seriously wrong. It took a scene in a restaurant and the intervention of a complete stranger to put Mel in the hospital. During his hospitalization, Mel was diagnosed as schizophrenic. The plan was to move Mel into a residential treatment center where he could get more help and not hurt anybody. But the thought of putting her son in a "crazy house" was too much for Mel's mother, who after much stalling, refused to institutionalize him and took Mel home.

Amidst the chaos, Seth was struggling to carve his own niche in the world. Yet because of all the attention focused on Mel, his successes (and his struggles) were all but ignored. He was a medical student, and nobody seemed to care about him. Feeling ignored (and perhaps unloved), Seth worried about his own mental stability; he was on "shaky" ground. His family was adrift, and he had to paddle faster and faster to stay afloat. "I had to endure shame and the preoccupation of my family with my brother as opposed to me. I became very self-doubting."

Somehow, Seth not only survived but prospered. He became a professor of psychiatry, married, and started a family of his own. Mel's illness influenced his choice to head the in-patient unit at a large hospital and to eventually specialize in the treatment of schizophrenics. He attributes his tolerance for people who are different and his willingness to go beyond the call of duty for other people to his brother. "I don't hold back if I feel someone is in need," he said. "I know that Mel has affected my life in a very big way."

Like other adult siblings, Seth is faced with caretaking decisions as his mother, now in her seventies, ages. Mel is thirty-eight and still living at home. Despite receiving no treatment, he is "substantially better," and he and Seth have gotten much closer over the years. Although he and his two oldest brothers plan to meet soon to discuss caretaking details, Seth has already decided that Mel cannot live with him. His first obligation, he says, is to his wife and children; he has no intention of "subjecting" them to the "chaos" he grew up with. Yet there is no doubt that

Seth will be instrumental in making sure that Mel is well taken care of and that the relative peace and quality of his life will be maintained. "There are a lot of things that can be done for him," said Seth, "and my other brothers and I will do everything we can."

SIBLINGS AND DIVORCE

When parents divorce and go their separate ways, the children most often stay together as a "packaged item." They may shuttle between two households, but they usually shuttle as a group. And while each child experiences his or her parents' divorce differently (boys often have a harder time adjusting than girls), siblings have the opportunity to comfort each other and to make the transition smoother. What little research there is on siblings in divorcing families has focused on how parents can regain control of the children and how the children can help the parents do this. How siblings may serve as resources for one another has been virtually ignored.

One exception is the study conducted by Lee Combrinck-Graham, director of Chicago's Institute for Juvenile Research. Although her study found no differences between families with only one child and families with more than one child in regard to the degree of bitterness or the ease of managing the postseparation adjustment to divorce, it did find that children who had brothers and sisters were healthier, displayed more age-appropriate behavior, and showed better social adjustment than only children. "The point is," said Combrinck-Graham, "that siblings are the constant family relationship. They do get packaged together and they do use each other as resources when their parents divorce."[3]

Not only can siblings help each other; they can make the job of caring for parents and *their* feelings easier. It is not uncommon for one child to take the side of one parent and a second child to take the side of the other. Also not uncommon is switching sides. In this way, both parents are supported, both feel valued. For an only child, the task appears more difficult. "In some ways," said Combrinck-Graham, "an only child has a rotten deal in a divorce, generally because there are tremendous loyalty issues that have to be managed by one person."[4] Having siblings can balance things out and ensure that difficult feelings are shared. This is not to say that all siblings look after one another during a divorce and its aftermath, yet many siblings do find comfort and support from their brothers and sisters.

"My parents' divorce," recalled twenty-four-year-old Candy, "brought my older brother and me incredibly close together."

We were allies for each other. We were both in our early teens when they sat us down and told us they were getting a divorce. It was a major shock—just sort of unreal. Yet after they explained what was going on and what it meant, my brother and I went out together and did whatever we were going to do. I remember that we talked. I immediately said that I didn't think it would be that bad. His reaction was not nearly as positive. I think he was more troubled and wasn't ready to see the bright side. His was probably a more normal reaction than mine.

After my parents separated, my dad was very lonely. I think my dad told my brother that he'd like him to come live with him. My dad really needed him; he was totally alone. My brother sensed that and moved to another state to be with him.

We were separated for a year. That was very hard. It was weird to have my brother leave because I was used to having him around. It was one thing to get used to my dad being gone; it was a whole other matter to have my brother gone. We talked on the phone a lot . . . I remember that.

And then after a year, my mother and I moved to the same city where my brother and dad lived. My brother had paved the way for me at a new school; I felt that he was taking care of me. It was very nice. We still didn't live in the same house, but we would seek each other out. We would have fun together. And we would speculate about mom and dad and how things were going and how we felt about the people they dated and the various situations you come up against because of divorce. We were both open.

I definitely think that divorce is overrated as a problem. I didn't feel torn apart; I was able to make my peace. I totally understood why my parents didn't stay together. And having my brother to talk to really helped. As I said before, we were allies.

There are researchers, such as Judith Wallerstein, who comment on the pervasive sadness and persistent dysfunction in adults who were children of divorced parents. Others in the field, such as E. M. Hetherington and Combrinck-Graham, see divorce as only one event of many that affects a person's adjustment. "Wallerstein thinks of divorce as a crisis that shouldn't go to waste," said Combrinck-Graham. "She's really wringing her hands over it. Hetherington's work shows that some children of divorce do very poorly, but she correlates the many factors that shape a person's ability to function, not just the divorce. My own informal samples show that many children of divorce have grown up and left the divorce and custody bitterness behind."

Increasingly, clinicians are recognizing the important role siblings can play in the adjustment to a divorce. These same clinicians report that most children of divorce meet the challenges of a changing family and get on with their lives. They no longer assume that intervention is needed simply because a family is adjusting to a divorce. As Combrinck-

Graham suggests: "Ask the kids how they are doing, rather than how they are failing. Ask them what kinds of arrangements they've made, what works, and if they have any complaints they think anyone can do something about. Build on the kinds of solutions the children have already put into place. Work from the direction of children influencing parents as well as parents influencing children."[5]

REMARRIAGE AND STEP-SIBLINGS

The fact that parents and children come through a divorce may or may not prepare them for the challenges of remarriage and step-relationsips. The ambiguity and confusion that often surround combined families arise, in many cases, from the fact that remarried families are what Cherlin called an "incomplete institution"—an institution for which there are no agreed-upon typical behaviors and guidelines for solving common problems of family life. How are stepparents different from biological parents? What feelings and responsibilities should they have for their stepchildren? What is a "normal" step-sibling relationship? Is the goal to be just like a biological brother or sister or is it to be more like a friend or a cousin?[6] Without clear guidelines, members of the remarried family struggle to blend all of its members and find workable answers to the almost inevitable problems.

By now, it should come as no surprise that step-siblings, like siblings, have traditionally been overlooked. While fighting among sibling groups in remarried families is frequently cited as a significant family problem, the literature pays almost no attention to the step-sibling subgroup per se, and there is little available literature on therapy with step-siblings. Researchers like Elinor Rosenberg have set out to change that. Her observations on step-siblings—the special issues they face and ways of facilitating smoother transitions as their families are combined—provide important information for family members and clinicians alike.

Rosenberg has delineated the many ways in which step-sibling relationships differ from sibling relationships. Unlike sibling bonds, they are instantaneous; step-siblings have not had the experience of adapting to and accommodating each other over years of individual and family development. In addition, step-siblings lack a shared family history. The customs, values, and styles may differ considerably from one family to the next. Yet they all share the experience of loss; they have all lost their original family and often struggle with feelings about the past. As Rosenberg points out, there are at least three families in every remarried household—his old family, her old family, and the new family. Step-siblings often find it very difficult to compromise to meet the needs of the new family. They wish for their lives to be like they used to be and resent having to change an arrangement with which they were happy or, at least, were accustomed to.

Step-sibling relationships have fluid boundaries. With constantly changing custody and visitation agreements, step-siblings often find themselves moving back and forth between households. "I never know who's going to be sharing my bedroom or who will show up at dinner," complained one eight-year-old. Another complaint among step-siblings is the shift in sibling position, role, and functions. An oldest child may suddenly become a middle child; the "baby" of the family may no longer be the youngest. And certain expectations may no longer carry the same weight. Responsibilities are often redefined, making it difficult for some step-siblings to know exactly what is expected of them.

Abrupt changes in the size of the combined family mean that some step-siblings may have to share a bedroom for the first time or adjust to a new economic situation. Issues of fairness, writes Rosenberg, can be even more sensitive

217

in the step-sibling group. And sexual issues can also cause confusion. Adolescents of the opposite gender may suddenly find themselves living together. Can they be girlfriend and boyfriend? Does the incest taboo (a taboo, as we've seen, that is breached in intact families) apply? Adolescents in remarried families also face a conflict between their need to separate and the need of the combined family to pull together. Just at the time when adolescents are cutting the umbilical cord, they are being asked to recommit themselves to the family.[7]

WORKING IT OUT WITH STEP-SIBLINGS

Step-siblings can make or break a remarried family. If they are intensely conflicted about the new marriage, the step-siblings can collude to sabotage the new relationship. On the other hand, if the new marriage meets the step-siblings' needs, they can work together to support the new union and help to make it last. Step-siblings are a powerful force in the success or failure of remarried families; their influence should be recognized and the unique issues they face should be addressed.

I remember when my son's father was about to remarry. Josh's "new" family would include a stepmother and two stepbrothers, one four years older and one just over a year younger. Josh would not be an only child when he stayed with his "new" family but the middle of three boys.

Every attempt was made to explain the changes that Josh, then five years old, would face as a member of his "new" family. He would be sharing a bedroom with his younger stepbrother whenever he visited (usually twice a week) and would be a participating member of a family with siblings. Josh's opinions on the furnishing of his "new" bedroom were welcomed and he was included in all of the wedding plans. While his stepbrothers were moving from another state, Josh, his dad, and the members of his "new" family spent as much time together as possible before the actual move.

I was excited that Josh would be a part-time sibling. It was doubtful that I would have another child, and I looked forward to his learning to share, negotiate, and compromise with peers in the family. As far as I could tell, Josh was excited as well, particularly about having an older brother to look up to and follow around. The realities of dealing with perceived favoritism, inequalities, and different rules and regulations would come later. At the onset, Josh had two "brothers," not stepbrothers, and that was all that mattered.

Over the years, I watched the ups and downs of step-sibship from afar. As the novelty of the "new" family wore off, the myths of instant love, wicked stepmother, and "step is the same" or "step is less" were confronted with varying degrees of support and success. Yet through it all, Josh insisted on always referring to Danny and Noah as his "brothers"; the step business was completely untenable as far as he was concerned. It didn't seem to matter whether he thought Noah was sometimes a "computer nerd" or that *their* mother bent the rules in their favor or that he didn't always get his father's undivided attention. Knowing that he had two brothers was worth the occasional aggravation he had to face.

Josh's father and stepmother separated more than four years ago; their divorce was finalized just last spring. Despite the feelings of anger and guilt and failure being generated, one incident sticks out. It was the day after the boys had been told about the impending divorce. Danny, then a senior in high school, pulled Josh aside. They talked about their situation and how the breakup would affect their friendship. At the end of the conversation, Danny turned to Josh and said, "No matter what, you will always be my brother." That seemed to be all Josh needed to hear.

Our society requires step-siblings to function without well-developed norms and expectations. That is hard enough when a remarried family begins its journey together. But what happens if and when that new family is dissolved? Do the step-siblings still see each other, even though they no longer live together, either part or all of the time? Where do their loyalties lie—with their biological parent or with the stepparent? Are they still expected to celebrate important occasions together? Until answers to these questions are resolved, step-siblings muddle through their undefined relationship, often playing it loose.

Even though Josh and Noah attend the same school, they rarely spend time together. Danny, a senior in an out-of-state university, is home only for vacations. Josh and he didn't see each other very often this past summer. Still, whenever they did get together, Josh came home and talked about how "grown-up" his older brother was. The changes struck Josh as almost magical; his older brother had become a man. His influence is still felt, and the connection remains. The last I heard, Danny is thinking about law school. And the last time Josh and I had a college talk, he mentioned that he'll probably study law as well.

SIBLINGS IN ALCOHOLIC FAMILIES

There is so much literature on alcoholic families that it seemed the best way to handle this topic would be to recommend books like Whitfield's *Healing the Child Within* and organizations such as Adult Children of Alcoholics. Yet somehow that didn't feel like enough. Unsure of what insights I might add, I set aside this section of the book.

Months later, while scanning Robert Bly's *Iron John*—a book I thought my husband might enjoy—I came upon the author's discussion of the "wound we have that hurts so much we have to dip it in water."[8] And I began thinking about the wounds siblings suffer when their parents abuse alcohol and how that abuse, when turned upon the children as it always is, causes some siblings to rise above the wound and others to get stuck inside it. Of course, neither path heals the wounded child. Children who rise above the wound and appear to be in control—often firstborns—camouflage their problems so well that they fake their way through life until adulthood, when their problems finally make them feel less than human and the lonely, wounded child inside screams for attention. And siblings who get stuck inside the wound—often middle children who begin life with resentful older brothers or sisters and parents who cannot provide enough empathic caretaking—suffer from changeable, moody, depressed personalities.

Children who cover their wounds by, say, doing well in school and being the cheerful ones regularly become the little parents. They perform their duties well but can harbor tremendous resentment toward those siblings in their charge. It is not unusual for them to take out their frustrations on their siblings, sometimes reverting to verbal and/or physical abuse. Yet, when parents wound them by behaving in ways they cannot imagine any parent behaving, the children in alcoholic families do appear to get some support from each other. They come together as victims in the same boat. However, the boat is leaky and can easily capsize. Many adult children of alcoholics report that they are no longer close to their siblings. Growing up, they clung to each other as a means of survival; they were a unit in crisis. Sadly, they never learned the meaning of true intimacy and would rather stay away from those who have become bitter reminders of the past.

"My sense now is that there is this person who is my sister and we have, in some ways, a shared history. But there are all these secrets, and her choice is to maintain the secrets of the family, and my choice is to expose the secrets so I can begin to get well. It would be very emotionally expensive for my sister to reconnect with me."

As a Ph.D. candidate in clinical psychology, Marjorie is very astute about the dysfunction in her family and the many ways in which growing up in an alcoholic and abusive home affected her own development and her relationship with her sister. As the firstborn, Marjorie, like the oldest child in many alcoholic/addictive families, thought she was very close to her mother. She saw her mother as the "good" parent and her father as the ogre. "In reality," said Marjorie, "my mother was the one who abused me much more than my father. Yet I spent all my life trying to win her approval but could never do anything well enough. She always blamed all her misery on my father. After he died, I became the source of her misery. And she sabotaged any possible relationship I might have had with my sister by showing such preferential treatment for her."

Typically, when firstborns in the alcoholic/addictive family start therapy as adults, they recall having been depressed. They may have spent a lifetime trying to run away from these feelings through addictive behaviors themselves. Marjorie described herself as being "process addicted." "For me," she said, "that meant being a workaholic and an overachiever. It was easy to hide my personal failures behind my public succss." Many firstborns learn that they can feel important and special by functioning precociously or fulfilling a helping role.

For much of Marjorie's life, people who chose to be her friends were people who liked her for her caretaking. "They liked me for my generosity," she said, "and for my high tolerance of inappropriate behavior." Yet Marjorie's desire

222

to feel good by taking care of others backfired. Her sister, though dependent on Marjorie, turned on her whenever she could and never developed the capacity to give. Her ex-husband, an alcoholic, abused her help. And her mother, enmeshed in a difficult marriage, took advantage of Marjorie's vulnerabilities and abused her even more than her father.

"I would not consider myself successful in the business of intimate relationships," said Majorie. "I'm not very good at those things. I've got lots and lots of strong friendships with women, but I have only one or two close male friends. And they are like surrogate brothers. Since my recovery, I've gone through many friends. It's part of the process of growth."

In characterizing the younger sibling in the alcoholic/addictive family system, clinical psychologist Rosalie Cruise Jesse described Marjorie's sister Joy to a tee.[9] Joy was raised during the final stages of her father's alcoholism, and her early infancy was marked by her parents' distress and by Marjorie assuming caretaking responsibilities. Marjorie tried to protect her sister from her parents' destructive interactions and from possible abuse. She desperately wanted Joy's affection because none came from her parents. What developed instead was a symbiotic attachment between Joy and her mother, with her mother encouraging rivalry between the two sisters by showing such preferential treatment for the "baby." To this day, Marjorie's mother continues to cling to the dissension she helped create. She's written Marjorie out of her will; all of her vast wealth will go to the younger daughter.

"The war that goes on in the sibling subsystem in alcoholic/addictive families," writes Rosalie Jesse, "is but a reflection of the larger war . . . Parents with disturbed relationships towards each other and ambivalent attitudes towards interpersonal relationships in general tend to create similar disturbances in their children . . . Siblings will often treat each other in accordance with a parent's wishes. To gain favor with a parent, one sibling will war against another without really knowing why."[10]

A DIFFERENT SCENARIO:
IN IT TOGETHER

Jesse reports that many adult children of alcoholics are estranged from their siblings. Adolescence, she writes, often ruptures the sibling bond, a bond that is not repaired during adulthood.[11]

Although there is no doubt that growing up in an alcoholic family creates wars that may never be peacefully ended, there are adult children of alcoholics who share a very supportive and meaningful relationship with their siblings.

The four Martin sisters grew up with an alcoholic mother and father. Now in their twenties and thirties, all of the sisters agree that their parents' drinking drew them closer together. "We were very much a team," said Carol, the oldest of the four sisters. "Nobody wanted to say anything by herself or hide the bottles alone. There was power in numbers. We backed each other up." "In the long haul," said Liz, the youngest, "it brought us closer. Not a day goes by that we don't talk."

Carol described herself as the caretaker, the oldest daughter who felt responsible for making sure that her three younger sisters were okay.

> My mom would go to work during the day and then come home and start drinking right away. So the nighttime was when I would look out for everybody, including my mother. I was the "perfect" daughter, the one who took care, got good grades, did everything right. My next oldest sister Karen was more of a rebel. That was how she got

attention. She resented me for many years because my mom always compared her to me. But we've worked through all of that now and are very close.

Once Carol and Karen left home and their parents had divorced, Liz assumed the caretaking responsibilities. "My mom's drinking got really bad when I was in seventh grade," she said.

That's when she'd drink and fall asleep on the floor. I felt sorry for her then because she was lonely and unhappy. But as I got older and understood enough about her problem, I got angry because she denied that she had a problem. I'd come home with friends, and she'd be passed out on the floor. It was very embarrassing. When I was a sophomore in high school, my dad quit drinking. He got on my mom's case, and that just made her angry. I spent a lot of time trying to make my mom feel better. I grew up quickly, assuming a lot of responsibilities. I remember thinking other girls my age were spoiled.

Liz also remembers how angry Sara used to get at her mother.

She'd say, "You're drunk," go upstairs, slam her bedroom door, and start to cry. Then I'd go and try to calm her down. I was always the peacemaker. In some ways, Sara was the scapegoat of the family. She had a weight problem and was very quiet. She stood in the background and didn't express herself much. And I think my dad treated her differently because of her weight. He was not as physically or emotionally supportive of her as he was with the rest of us. Sara had a lot of jealousy toward all of us. But as we've gotten older, she's losing the weight and getting better, and our relationship improves. I'm there for her; we talk all the time.

Liz was eighteen when her mother died from a stroke caused by her drinking and smoking. "Her death brought

225

us closer together," Liz said. "All we had was each other."
"My mom didn't take care of herself," said Carol.

> She was only fifty-one when she died. I quit smoking the
> night of her wake. And I joined Adult Children of Alco-
> holics about nine months ago. ACOA has been so good for
> me. I've learned so much about myself—the roles I've as-
> sumed and the bad choices I've made. I came very close to
> walking down the aisle with a very sick man. What I used
> to think was normal is so dysfunctional.
>
> All four of us are taking much better care of ourselves.
> Liz has gone to ACOA meetings with me. She never really
> thought she was as affected by our parents' drinking, but
> now she sees how overresponsible she was and how hard
> she's been on herself. Sara has lost 125 pounds and is be-
> ginning to shed a lot of emotional baggage along with the
> weight. And Karen has really cleaned up her act. She's
> pretty much quit drinking altogether and is getting a degree
> in psychology.

Liz was recently engaged to be married. Choosing a maid
of honor from her three sisters was "really hard." "I'm so
close to all of them," said Liz, "but in different ways. Sara
is growing as a person, and I respect that. Karen is very
nurturing. And Carol and I share similar interests; we like
the same things. It wasn't an easy decision, but I've asked
Carol to stand up for me. She is the oldest, and somehow
that seemed like the right choice."

There are deep and complicated emotions surrounding
the experience of growing up in a disrupted family. For
siblings, the disruption can throw their relationship up for
grabs, or it can force brothers and sisters closer together
as they struggle to find a balance in their lives. If parents
are physically or emotionally absent, siblings are in a position to influence one another even more than they other-

wise might be. The way in which brothers and sisters respond to family stress and the methods they choose to cope can cement a supportive, sometime primary, bond or seriously damage the possibilities for a meaningful relationship as children and as adults.

Whether the disruption is caused by divorce, alcoholism, or a sibling's mental or physical disability, a key factor in keeping the family unit together and functioning appears to be communication—communication between parents and their children and between the siblings themselves. Study after study has shown that when siblings feel they are loved, valued, and understood, their chances of adjusting and thriving are enhanced. The significance of parental treatment is clearly evident in disrupted families. The adjustment of normal siblings, for example, often hinges on whether they feel they are treated fairly by the parents relative to their disabled sibling. And in one-parent families, in which the tight-knit relationships heighten the issues, attention must be paid to the individual differences in how children respond to stress.

Siblings in disrupted families need help to balance and juggle the deep emotions they face. Their need for straight answers, fairness, and special attention, if met, can build self-esteem and encourage their psychological and emotional growth. As they grapple with the complexities of contemporary life, siblings depend on the strong family ties fostered during childhood and adolescence to help them over the bumps. Having raised themselves to a large degree, they have developed a real appreciation for their own strengths and for the many ways in which their siblings have helped to define their personalities and to refine their ability to cope. This "sibling debt," if nurtured in adulthood, can help heal old wounds that fester and help siblings get beyond the self-pity that can so often diminish their honest communication with others and with themselves.

12

THE CALL OF KIN:
RECONNECTING WITH SIBLINGS

So many of the adults I interviewed either spoke happily about the recently renewed connection with a sibling or expressed an eager longing to reconnect. Yet for those who described a sibling relationship as either cordial but distant or bitterly severed, the task of strengthening the bond often appeared impossible. To change old patterns—to navigate the relationship differently—felt as dangerous as walking through the mine fields of the past. It can be extremely hard to form a new relationship with an adult sibling we don't really know anymore or never really knew in the first place. And there are few adults who don't believe, deep down, that a sibling got more of something than they did—parental love, advantages, brains, looks. Whether it is true or not doesn't really matter. What counts are the notions about one another that siblings carry with them from childhood, the sibling baggage that can blind them from seeing brothers and sisters as the mature people they've become.

Why bother to forge more meaningful connections with siblings? After all, many adults appear to get along just fine without them. Why take the risk of getting unstuck? The answer is simple: the call of kin. Our basic need to belong to and be part of family demands that we at least try to lay to rest old antagonisms and move on to higher ground. Those who succeed often find that they are more whole, more complete, and bring a clearer, more defined self to other important relationships. Those who cannot or will not give a sibling another chance often find that their unresolved issues resurface and interfere with their life review process and their ultimate sense of inner peace.

While the advantages of sharing a close bond with adult sisters and brothers become more and more apparent with age, the way to go about cementing a meaningful connection is rarely as clear. Childhood labels, parental favoritism (real or perceived), and past disappointments die hard. Despite all good intentions, a sibling's wish to forgive and understand is often greater than his or her ability to do so. Common sense dictates that an important first step in reconnecting hinges upon a willingness to emphasize ways in which the relationship can be more positive (instead of rehashing the past). Also key is seeing oneself on an equal footing with a brother or sister. Of course, equal footing does not translate into seeing a sibling as "the same" or as "a pea from the same pod." Acknowledging and respecting the differences is often a crucial step in coming together again. The act of recognizing the ways in which one is different from a sibling often frees one to appreciate and cherish those traits, attitudes, and beliefs that they hold in common.

A PERSONAL FOOTNOTE

It has been said that brothers and sisters are more ready to consider changing a relationship or working toward such a change than are husbands and wives. Spouses can get a divorce; siblings cannot. It's this difference between a biological bond and a contractual one that increases the chances of the sibling relationship surviving.

As for my brother John and me, we're still redefining our relationship, a challenge made that much more difficult by the thousand miles that separate us. Several years before I decided to write this book, I wrote my brother a letter. I had a gnawing feeling that his poor health at the time stemmed in part from his never having come to terms with my brother Robin's suicide. I wanted him to know that I shared his pain (I had never told him that before) and to describe my own journey of grieving and eventual recovery. It was a heartfelt letter, one I'd hoped would put John and me back in touch. John never answered my letter and when, five months later, I asked him why, he said flatly, "I thought it was silly. I'm not the kind of person who lives in the past." Just like that, John and I were back to square one.

But I'm not one who tolerates unhappy endings well and, a year or so later, I tried again. There was a flurry of activity surrounding third-party political candidates in my area, and I thought John would be interested. I sent him several newspaper clippings, with my comments handwritten in the margins. Almost as an afterthought, I wrote that I'd be visiting our parents for the holidays and how nice it would be to see him. John drove all night to make it to the family holiday dinner on time. I was taken aback by his newfound dedication to family and shocked when he greeted me with a big hug and a "Hello, sis"—a gesture that opened the door to new exchanges between us.

Something had changed; John appeared as ready as I was to reconnect. We took a long walk that weekend, winding our way through the newly developed subdivisions of suburban homes that now encase what used to be our parents' rather isolated and gloriously private abode. As we walked, I began to fear that this enclave of the upper middle class mirrored all that John had railed against for so many years. I was sure he counted me as one of them. Some bad twist of fate had plopped me down right where John felt I belonged. I kept wishing that our walk had taken us through the inner city or down a meandering path in some third-world village. But there I was, a mature adult still enmeshed in my brother's outdated notions of who I was and what I stood for.

In reality, John didn't see me that way at all. The call of family had drawn him home to make his peace. If I hadn't pursued getting our relationship unstuck, *he* would have. For the first time as adults, we spoke honestly about our long-concealed feelings of anger, inferiority, and guilt left over from childhood. For the first time, we told each other that we cared. To be sure, my brother and I are different. He looks at the world through its political and economic institutions; I react to personal relationships. He can work a crowd like a seasoned politician; I'm less comfortable with people I don't know well. Yet underneath some basic differences lie a concern for others and a belief in change.

Since that weekend two years ago, there have been phone calls and shared family visits. I've even begun to put myself in John's shoes and to imagine what it might have felt like to grow up as the third of four children, with number one (me) and number two (Robin) not very anxious to divide up the spoils. (John, you might remember, was just a year and six days younger than Robin.) It couldn't have been easy for either of them, these two young males duking it out for attention and bouncing off of each other as they searched for their unique places. And there I was, a four-year-old tragedienne, wondering how my young life could have been altered so drastically in such a short time. Makings there for some real challenges. And the stage was set two years or so before my sister, Liz, was even born.

To think of all this makes me dizzy. No wonder we each have such bittersweet memories of growing up together. John remembers looking at Liz as Dad's little girl and feeling that she was terribly spoiled because of it. (One of the factors, I suspect, that has kept them apart.) And he remembers Robin as the troublemaker who got a lot of attention as a result. "In that sense," John said, "Robin was a hard act to follow. I think part of my response was to take up the opposite routine. You can't do what the first guy did, so I was much more quiet. Maybe because of that, Mom and Dad decided that I was just fine. But part of *my* perception was that the attention and the love sort of skipped from Robin to Liz."

If John saw my sister as "Dad's little girl" and Robin as "the troublemaker," he linked me to my mother. That made me more traditional and representative of my mother's values and attitudes, stances that John saw as "rather hypocritical" at the time. He apparently didn't notice the years I spent cutting the umbilical cord. Caught up in his notions of the kind of person I must have been, he missed the changes. But I forgive him that because I was just as stuck in my perceptions of him as rigid and terribly judgmental.

Untangling the past and rearranging the pieces have been made a lot easier because both John and I want a better relationship. That's not to say that we're the best of friends yet or that we don't fall back into old habits and feelings. But we like each other and recognize the value of family and of staying close. And unlike years ago when friends of mine were surprised to learn that I even had another brother, people in my life now know all about John. And that's a start.

The past months have been anything but peaceful. A matter of hours after returning home from a working vacation, my then sixteen-year-old child lost control of his father's car, spun off the highway, plowed into a park bench, flipped over, and smashed into a tree. A friend riding with him ended upside down in the back seat and somehow managed to kick his way out of the car without a scratch. Josh wasn't so lucky; he'd broken his back. With time, the doctors said, he'd walk and run and even play baseball again. But first he'd have to endure an eleven-hour operation to fuse a part of his hipbone into his spine, then two weeks in the hospital, followed by several more weeks at home, and six months in a removable brace that ran from his collarbone to his waist.

I cried a lot during the aftermath of Josh's accident—with him, for him, and for me. Riddled with guilt (if only I'd insisted he stay home that night), overcome by sadness and anger and exhaustion, I somehow managed to do all that was required of me. His physical pain was significant; my emotional upheaval harked back to my brother's suicide eleven years before.

I called my sister from the hospital before I called my parents. She would help me with my pain and the unanswered questions more easily than my mother or father could, precisely because she is a sister and *not* a parent. She would have the luxury of emotional distance, which parents rarely manage, certainly not in a crisis involving their oldest daughter and their only grandchild. My sister would remind me how to use my breathing to relax, to inhale through my nose, fill my center with renewed energy, and exhale the spent air through my mouth. She would help me visualize Josh bathed in white light and his broken back healing. My sister's calm sense of direction would focus my energy and concentration, much like the small flower I had taped to the hospital wall as a focal point when I was in labor with Josh.

Once Josh was strong enough to return to school, nothing carried the same weight as before. The freedom from day-to-day caretaking that I'd prayed for while Josh was convalescing was overshadowed by a consuming fear of letting go. How ironic that my six-foot, 210-pound adolescent, in the midst of his quest for independence, had needed me more than he had since he was a baby. And how tricky it became to give him his freedom back. The queasiness in the pit of my stomach felt all too familiar, reminding me of how my sisterly power, influence, and control slipped away as my brother Robin grew up so many years before. Now I was caught again in the battle between the emotional perception that I no longer counted in the life of someone I loved and the intellectual understanding that I'd always matter.

Yet the very fact that I'd been through this push/pull battle before—and that I was able to pinpoint its inception—allowed me to grit my teeth, give Josh the space he needed, and eventually regain my sense of balance. Just knowing that, at another time, I'd survived the battle gave me strength; validating the connection between my feelings toward my brother and toward my son gave me control. And I wondered whether in some karmic sense Robin's spirit and my recognition of what had transpired between us as brother and sister had merged and reverberated at just the "right" moment.

ILLNESS AND THE CALL OF KIN

Empathizing with a sibling who is ill (or in trouble) can help bridge any gap. Despite a strained and distant relationship of fifteen years, Cheryl reacted to the news of her brother David's bout with cancer with concern and the offer of help. Her responding to his need laid the foundation for renewed communication and ultimately led to what is now a very meaningful bond for both of them. Almost any sibling relationship can be improved, if the siblings are willing to put energy into it. Childhood rivalries or adult rifts are left over from a struggle that was very likely the fault of others. If the siblings can see that, it will help them stop feeling guilty or blaming each other the way they used to do.

For Cheryl, it became clear that there was little she could do to change her sister-in-law, who in many ways had caused the rift between David and her. Wisely, she didn't push David to look at things he didn't want to see. With time, he realized how "crazy" and tangled the lines of communication had become and sought professional help. Still, there are problems between the two women, and the best times for Cheryl and David are spent alone or on the phone.

Finding a common ground has encouraged Cheryl and David to talk about their childhood and about the complex relationships between each other and their parents. Although neither of them realized it growing up, their father was an alcoholic. As both Cheryl and David began to get in touch with all the hurt and guilt associated with having a parent who drank too much, they turned to each other for support and validation. They have been able to work on their recovery together, each helping the other through difficult emotional upheavals.

The process of reconnecting is never a direct path but a series of spirals with backward and forward movements. Realizing this helps brothers and sisters anticipate and prepare for what seem to be failures or serious setbacks. Cheryl's first visit to see David and his family after fifteen years was a disaster. Yet Cheryl was ultimately able to accept David's sincere apologies and continue the process of becoming friends again. There is often more than a little courage required of siblings who want to try to make a change in their relationship. Creating new steps to an old dance can challenge even the most accomplished among us, testing our commitment many times. For siblings like Cheryl and David, stumbling along the way made their eventual coming together that much more rewarding.

RECONNECTING WITH AN OLD FRIEND

Only eighteen months apart, Lisbeth and Arnie had what Lisbeth labelled a "pretty intense relationship" during childhood. "We played a lot together and we fought a lot. But even in fighting, we were really good friends. I think we always had a good grasp of each other's feelings without saying very much." As the "good" child, Lisbeth was the responsible and dutiful one; Arnie was the "bright" one who sometimes got away with "murder." "I always felt," said Lisbeth, "that my mother had never really met me. I think she prescribed the kind of people each of us was supposed to be early on. My brother certainly knew me a lot better than she did."

Arnie also felt his mother's overbearing wishes for the kind of person he should be. Just before going to Europe to study on the GI Bill, he told his sister that the "United States is not big enough for Mother and me." That was thirty-four years ago; Arnie has made his permanent home overseas. "I think I saw him one time in a seventeen-year period," said Lisbeth. "I really missed him a lot. At first, I had a strong sense of loss. Then I got used to not having him around and began thinking of him as a distant friend. It's funny, but I never really felt that the lines of communication were closed."

Shortly after Arnie moved to Europe, Lisbeth married. She and her husband had three children. Arnie married an English woman, and that marriage produced four children. The first cousins didn't know one another until recently. "I'd hear how Arnie was doing through my parents," Lisbeth said. "They would tell me all about him and his family. Once in a while, he'd send me a gift. But we really had no contact for all those years."

As her parents' fiftieth wedding anniversay approached, Lisbeth wrote Arnie and asked if he would like to join her in throwing their parents a party. Thrilled with the idea, Arnie flew to the United States to plan the celebration. "We spent most of the time talking and reconnecting and laughing," Lisbeth reported.

> It was funny to see someone I'd been so close to in his middle-age body. Except for the physical changes, I found Arnie the same. Our connection was delightful, and I've often felt that not having spent our early adult years together enhanced our relationship. We could go right back to the way things were with more maturity and without the problems of young families. We hadn't seen each other in all those years, yet both of us had the desire to enjoy the relationship that had been so nice when we were younger.

The friendship between this brother and sister is testimony to the strengths of a special relationship forged in childhood. More than likely separated because of problems caused by their mother, both Lisbeth and Arnie never felt abandoned or hurt by the other. Looking back, Lisbeth found it rather odd that she was never angered by Arnie's lack of direct communication for so many years. She was able to accept the distance between them as strictly geographical and, perhaps, a beneficial distance at that. While other brothers and sisters get caught in the turmoil of family and careers, Lisbeth and Arnie never had to wrangle with those issues between them. They were able to skip early adulthood and come back together with more maturity and few hurts from the past.

Researchers like Stephen Bank are, in general, hopeful about brothers and sisters reconnecting as adults. "I'm optimistic for about two-thirds of the people," he said in an interview. "The other one-third are just stuck, angry, and alienated from life. For them, there is no forgiveness. But I do feel that people like to grow and develop, and that most of them like to be able to put things in perspective."[1]

Because neither Lisbeth nor Arnie had experienced any serious humiliation, horrendous parental favoritism, or grievous physical or sexual injury, they were able to rekindle their friendship, picking up where they had left off. The close relationship they shared as children and adolescents provided the mitigating factor they needed to reconnect after seventeen years of almost no communication. And by initially choosing to spend time together away from their parents, they helped reduce the chance of old roles being reinforced and getting in the way. Bridging the gap between these two siblings was more a matter of being with one another than of starting over again.

BRIDGING THE GAP

When parents die, each child is free to choose whether and how to recognize his or her siblings. Parents can no longer dictate or orchestrate or embitter their children's relationships. For some siblings, this freedom from parental influence releases them to turn away from some or all of their brothers and sisters. But for many others, the need for constancy and continuity is stronger than past differences. For these brothers and sisters, the loss of a parent is hard enough; to lose their siblings would set them adrift without any connection to family. Such a prospect is unthinkable. They will do whatever needs to be done to keep what is left of their family intact. When siblings let go of past rivalries, jealousies, feelings of inferiority, and guilt, they discover ties that are closer and longer lasting than those with other people in their lives. In reconnecting, they come full circle; they return to their roots, to their home.

"Having my brother back in my life feels as if a light has been turned on again," said fraternal twin Angela, whose mother's death and the effect it had on her relationship with her twin was discussed in Chapter Five. "I'm much more fully alive, happier, and feel safer. I feel he likes me again, and that's very healing. I feel more soft; I feel more whole. I can't describe it any other way."

Describing an intimate relationship with a brother or sister doesn't come easily. Precisely because of the shared closeness that is unlike any other, we are often at a loss for words when asked to detail what it means to have a precious friend who is also family. For Angela, the reconnection with her brother made her "whole" again, a concept that encourages us to recognize our disability when a brother or sister is no longer a viable part of our lives. "I think you go around crippled," said Angela, "and sooner or later, it will have its effect."

Angela and Ted circled around each other for some time, as they determined just how close they could get and how much they could share. "Our rebounding," said Angela, "has been a process of reviewing ourselves to each other. And there have been times when I've been very hesitant. I knew there were areas my brother did not want to investigate. I've had to censor myself, but more and more I'm not doing that. And we now tell each other if there's a problem. It's just like with a best girlfriend. And, slowly, the boundaries are widening."

As the boundaries with my siblings widen, I recognize how all of them have had a hand in shaping the person I am, the risks I take, the insecurities I grapple with, the relationships I choose, and all of the right and wrong moves along the way. Their existence, Robin's death, our reconnections as adults have forced me to create new dreams and to open new paths. Without my siblings, I would be a different person—not necessarily better or worse, just different. And now that I am a middle-aged adult poised to greet the second half of my life, my siblings have become even more important. They are a constant; they are family. The comfort of knowing that our bonds will survive despite our differences and that our connection provides each of us with a more accurate picture of ourselves enhances our chances of finding inner peace and satisfaction as we age together.

AUTHOR'S NOTE

M ore than 125 brothers and sisters were interviewed for this book. The initial interviews averaged sixty to ninety minutes, and there were follow-up discussions conducted when needed. Whenever possible, the interviews were done in person; others were conducted on the telephone. I made every effort to talk to siblings across the life span who represented a cross section of ethnic, educational, religious, and socioeconomic backgrounds. However, I do not pretend that the sampling is scientific.

As people heard about this book, they came flocking to me. The flurry of interest underscored the importance of the sibling connection and the need for brothers and sisters (and only children, too) to talk about all facets of their relationships. Because a small number of the siblings I interviewed wished to remain anonymous, I made the decision early on not to use real names, except for those of my own siblings and the Richmond twins. For all of the brothers and sisters who were eager to have their stories and their names published, I am certain you will find yourselves none-theless.

APPENDIX:
SOURCES OF HELP

Rothman-Cole Center for Grief Recovery and Sibling Loss
4513 N. Ashland
Chicago, IL 60640
312-769-3928

The Rothman-Cole Center for Grief Recovery and Sibling Loss
provides individual, group, and family counseling for siblings and
others who are struggling with bereavement. The Center also
offers speakers, educational materials, and bereavement training
workshops. Weekend residential groups held several times a year
attract survivors nationwide.

Sibling Information Network
The A. J. Pappanikou Center
991 Main St.
East Hartford, CT 06108
203-282-7050

An "organization for those interested in the welfare of siblings of handicapped children," the Sibling Information Network was formed to serve as a bridge for sharing ideas, programs, research, or needs regarding siblings and families of persons with handicaps. The network publishes a quarterly newsletter, *Sibling Information Network Newsletter*.

Siblings and Adult Children's Network of the National Alliance for the Mentally Ill
2101 Wilson Blvd.
Suite 302
Arlington, VA 22201
703-524-7600

SAC is a national network established to provide emotional support, education, and resources to brothers and sisters, and sons and daughters of those with mental illness. SAC publishes a quarterly newsletter, *The Bond*.

VOICES in Action Inc.
P.O. Box 148309
Chicago, IL 60614
312-327-1500

VOICES (Victims of Incest Can Emerge Survivors) is a nonprofit international organization of incest and child sexual abuse survivors and pro-survivors dedicated to prevention and recovery through networking, support, and education. As a self-help organization, VOICES offers a new member's kit, bimonthly newsletter, yearly creative anthology, and annual conferences. The organization's Special Interest Groups allow members who share common histories, interests, or lifestyles to correspond confidentially.

NOTES

Introduction

1. Jane H. Pfouts, "The Sibling Relationship: A Forgotten Dimension," *Social Work,* May 1976, pp. 200–3.
2. Michael D. Kahn and Karen Gail Lewis, eds., *Siblings in Therapy* (New York: W. W. Norton, 1988), p. xv.
3. Lynn Atwater, telephone interview with the author, 16 October 1989.
4. Stephen P. Bank and Michael D. Kahn, *The Sibling Bond* (New York: Basic Books, 1982), p. 5.
5. Michael D. Kahn and Karen Gail Lewis, eds., *Siblings in Therapy* (New York: W. W. Norton, 1988), pp. xvii–xviii.
6. Stephen P. Bank, telephone interview with the author, 19 October 1989.
7. Stephen P. Bank and Michael D. Kahn, *The Sibling Bond* (New York: Basic Books, 1982), p. 292.

Prologue

1. Christine Downing, author of *Psyche's Sisters* (San Francisco: Harper & Row, 1988), proposed some of the basic concepts expanded upon here.

Chapter One
Close Encounters of a Special Kind

1. Stephen P. Bank, telephone interview with the author, 19 October 1989.
2. B. N. Adams, "Birth Order: A Critical Review," *Sociometry* 35 (3): 411–39.
3. Douglas Breunlin, interview, 18 December 1989, Chicago, Illinois.
4. Judy Dunn, *Sisters and Brothers: The Developing Child* (Cambridge, Mass.: Harvard University Press, 1985), p. 13.
5. This is not to overlook the important contributions of other women, including Deborah Gold, Frances Fuchs Schachter, Victoria Bedford, Elinor Rosenberg, Helen Koch, Helgola Ross, Toni Falbo, and others.
6. Karen Lewis, telephone interview with the author, 18 October 1989.
7. Deborah Gold, telephone interview with the author, 2 October 1989.
8. Joel Milgram, telephone interview with the author, 10 November 1989.
9. Stephen P. Bank and Michael D. Kahn, *The Sibling Bond* (New York: Basic Books, 1982), p. 12.
10. Michael D. Kahn, telephone interview with the author, 5 November 1989.
11. Gail Sheehy, *Passages* (New York: Bantam Books, 1977), p. 40.

Chapter Two
From Sibling Rivalry to Sibling Genetics: Theories Then and Now

1. Adele Faber and Elaine Mazlish, *Siblings Without Rivalry* (New York: Avon Books, 1987), p. 14.

2. I have drawn biographical details and some interpretation of Freud's sibling rivalry theory from Bank and Kahn's 1980–81 "Freudian Siblings," *Psychoanalytic Review* 67 (Winter): 493–504.

3. Ibid.

4. Christine Downing, *Psyche's Sisters* (San Francisco: Harper & Row, 1988), p. 149.

5. Sigmund Freud, Introductory Lectures on Psychoanalysis S.E., Vol. 15, p. 204.

6. Christine Downing, *Psyche's Sisters* (San Francisco: Harper & Row, 1988), p. 152.

7. Stephen P. Bank and Michael D. Kahn, "Freudian Siblings," *Psychoanalytic Review* 67 (Winter 1980–81): 493–504.

8. Walter Toman, *Family Constellation* (New York: Springer, 1976), p. 5.

9. Stephen P. Bank and Michael D. Kahn, *The Sibling Bond* (New York: Basic Books, 1982), p. 7.

10. Kenneth Woodward and Lydia Denworth, "The Order of Innovation," *Newsweek,* 21 May 1990, p. 76.

11. Sandra Watanabe-Hammond, "Blueprints from the Past: A Character Work Perspective on Siblings and Personality Formation," in *Siblings in Therapy,* ed. Michael D. Kahn and Karen Gail Lewis (New York: W. W. Norton, 1988), p. 356.

12. Clark W. Falconer and Colin A. Ross, "The Tilted Family," in *Siblings in Therapy,* ed. Michael D. Kahn and Karen Gail Lewis (New York: W. W. Norton, 1988), pp. 273–95.

13. Christine Downing, *Psyche's Sisters* (San Francico: Harper & Row, 1988), pp. 21–40.

14. Deborah Gold, telephone interview with the author, 2 October 1989.

15. Karen Lewis, telephone interview with the author, 18 October 1989.

16. Eve Primpas Harriman Welts, "Ethnic Patterns and Sibling Relationships," in *Siblings in Therapy,* ed. Michael D. Kahn and Karen Gail Lewis (New York: W. W. Norton, 1988), pp. 66–91.

17. This and following quotes are from Sandra Scarr, telephone interview with the author, 5 March 1990.

Chapter Three
Growing Up: Childhood and Adolescence

1. Deborah Lowe Vandell, "Baby Sister/Baby Brother: Reactions to the Birth of a Sibling and Patterns of Early Sibling Relations," in *Practical Concerns About Siblings: Bridging the Research-Practice Gap,* ed. Frances Fuchs Schachter and Richard K. Stone (New York: The Haworth Press, 1987), pp. 13–53.

2. Frances Fuchs Schachter, telephone interview with the author, 29 November 1989.

3. Ibid.

4. Stephen P. Bank and Michael D. Kahn, *The Sibling Bond,* (New York: Basic Books, 1982), p. 64.

5. Ibid., p. 64.

Chapter Four
Young Adulthood: Push and Pull

1. Gail Sheehy, *Passages* (New York: Bantam Books, 1977), pp. 120–27.

2. Ibid.

3. Michael D. Kahn and Karen Gail Lewis, eds., *Siblings in Therapy* (New York, W. W. Norton, 1988), p. 339.

4. Karen Gail Lewis, "Symptoms as Sibling Messages," in *Siblings in Therapy,* ed. Michael D. Kahn and Karen Gail Lewis (New York: W. W. Norton, 1988), p. 264.

5. Gail Sheehy, *Passages* (New York: Bantam Books, 1977), pp. 198–216.

6. Joel I. Milgram and Helgola G. Ross, "Important Variables in Adult Sibling Relationships: A Qualitative Study," in *Sibling Relationships: Their Nature and Significance Across the Lifespan,* ed. Michael E. Lamb and Brian Sutton-Smith (Hillsdale, N.J.: Lawrence Erlbaum, 1982), pp. 241, 242.

7. Ibid., p. 241.

Chapter Five
Middle Adulthood: Chance for Renewal

1. Joel I. Milgram and Helgola G. Ross, "Important Variables in Adult Sibling Relationships: A Qualitative Study," in *Sibling Relationships: Their Nature and Significance Across the Lifespan,* ed. Michael E. Lamb and Brian Sutton-Smith (Hillsdale, N.J.: Lawrence Erlbaum, 1982), p. 243.
2. Gail Sheehy, *Passages* (New York: Bantam Books, 1977), p. 426.
3. Ibid., pp. 424, 425.
4. Ibid., pp. 415, 416.

Chapter Six
Siblings in Later Life: Coming Together

1. Gail Sheehy, *Passages* (New York: Bantam Books, 1977), p. 513.
2. Michael D. Kahn and Karen Gail Lewis, eds., *Siblings in Therapy* (New York: W. W. Norton, 1988), p. 415.
3. Paula Smith Avioli, "The Social Support Functions of Siblings in Later Life," *American Behavioral Scientist* 33 (September/October 1989): 52.
4. Victor G. Cicirelli, "Interpersonal Relationships Among Elderly Siblings," in *Siblings in Therapy,* Michael D. Kahn and Karen Gail Lewis, eds. (New York: W. W. Norton, 1988), pp. 447–48.
5. Deborah Gold, "Sibling Relationships in Old Age: A Typology" (Paper presented at the 39th Annual Scientific Meeting of the Gerontological Society of America, Chicago, 19–23 November 1986).
6. Deborah Gold, "Generational Solidarity," American Behavioral Scientist 33 (September/October 1989): 30.

Chapter Seven
Twins and the Meaning of Sibship

1. Nancy L. Segal, telephone interview with the author, 14 December 1989.

2. "How Genes Shape Personality," *U.S. News & World Report,* 13 April 1987, pp. 58–66.
3. Nancy L. Segal, "Cooperation, Competition, and Altruism Within Twin Sets: A Reappraisal," *Ethnology and Sociobiology* 5 (1984): 163–77.
4. Gregg Levoy, "Born Rivals," *Psychology Today,* June 1989, p. 67.
5. Ibid., p. 68.

Chapter Eight
Adult Only Children

1. Toni Falbo, telephone interview with the author, 4 January, 1990.
2. Toni Falbo, ed., *The Single-Child Family* (New York: The Guilford Press, 1984).
3. H. Theodore Groat, Arthur G. Neal, and Jerry W. Wicks, "Without Siblings: The Consequences in Adult Life of Having Been an Only Child," in *The Single-Child Family,* ed. Toni Falbo (New York: The Guilford Press, 1984), pp. 254–56.
4. Ibid., pp. 258–60.
5. Michele Slung, *The Only Child Book* (New York: Ballantine Books, 1989), pp. 25, 30.
6. Denise Polit, "The Only Child in Single-Parent Families," in *The Single-Child Family,* ed. Toni Falbo (New York: The Guilford Press, 1984), p. 205.
7. Ibid., p. 199.
8. Melford E. Spiro, *Children of the Kibbutz: A Study in Child Training and Personality* (New York: Schocken Books, 1965), pp. 68, 138.
9. S. Hawke and D. Knox, *One Child by Choice* (Englewood Cliffs, N.J.: Prentice-Hall, 1977).

Chapter Nine
The Death of a Sibling

1. Helen Rosen, "Prohibitions Against Mourning in Childhood Sibling Loss," *Omega* 15, no. 4 (1984–85): 313.
2. Miriam S. Moss and Sidney Z. Moss, "Death of an Elderly

Sibling," *American Behavioral Scientist* 33 (September/October 1989): 102.

3. Rheba Adolph and Stephen J. Fleming, "Helping Bereaved Adolescents: Needs and Responses," in *Adolescence and Death,* ed. Charles A Corr and Joan N. McNeil (New York: Springer, 1986), p. 113.
4. Charles A. Corr and Joan N. McNeil, eds., *Adolescence and Death* (New York: Springer, 1986), pp. xiii, xiv, and 1.
5. Miram S. Moss and Sidney Z. Moss, "Death of an Elderly Sibling," *American Behavioral Scientist* 33 (September/October 1989): 101.
6. Ibid., p. 103.
7. Ibid.
8. Ibid., p. 102.

Chapter Ten
Sibling Incest: Dispelling the Myth of Mutuality

1. D. Finkelhor, "Sex Among Siblings," *Archives of Sexual Behavior* 10 (1980): 171–94.
2. Diana E. H. Russell, *The Secret Trauma: Incest in the Lives of Girls and Women* (New York: Basic Books, Inc., 1986), pp. 271–72.
3. Vernon R. Wiehe, *Sibling Abuse: Hidden Physical, Emotional, and Sexual Trauma* (Lexington, Mass.: Lexington Books, 1990), p. 51.
4. H. Smith and E. Israel, "Sibling Incest: A Study of the Dynamics of 25 Cases," *Child Abuse & Neglect* 11 (1987): 101–8.
5. Vernon R. Wiehe, *Sibling Abuse: Hidden Physical, Emotional, and Sexual Trauma* (Lexington, Mass.: Lexington Books, 1990), p. 67.
6. Denise Gelinas, telephone interview with the author, 29 November 1989.
7. Christine A. Courtois, *Healing the Incest Wound* (New York: W. W. Norton, 1988), p. 117.
8. Ibid., pp. 78, 79.
9. Diana E. Russell, *The Secret Trauma: Incest in the Lives of*

Girls and Women (New York: Basic Books, Inc., 1986), p. 10.

10. Marsha L. Heiman, "Untangling Incestuous Bonds: The Treatment of Sibling Incest," in *Siblings in Therapy,* ed. Michael D. Kahn and Karen Gail Lewis (New York: W. W. Norton, 1988), p. 165.
11. Ibid., p. 165.

Chapter Eleven
Siblings in Disrupted Families

1. Thomas H. Powell and Peggy Ahrenhold Ogle, *Brothers and Sisters: A Special Part of Exceptional Families* (Baltimore: Paul H. Brookes, 1985), p. 30.
2. Mary Kay Blakely, "A Family Confronts Mental Illness," *Utne Reader,* May/June 1990, p. 50.
3. Lee Combrinck-Graham, interview with the author, October 1989, Chicago.
4. Ibid.
5. Lee Combrinck-Graham, "When Parents Separate or Divorce: The Sibling System," in *Siblings in Therapy,* ed. Michael D. Kahn and Karen Gail Lewis (New York: W. W. Norton, 1988), p. 207.
6. Elinor B. Rosenberg, "Therapy with Siblings in Reorganizing Families," *International Journal of Family Therapy* 2, no. 3, (Fall 1980): 141.
7. Elinor B. Rosenberg and Fady Hajal, "Stepsibling Relationships in Remarried Families," *Social Casework: The Journal of Contemporary Social Work,* May 1985, p. 288.
8. Robert Bly, *Iron John: A Book About Men* (New York: Addison-Wesley, 1990), pp. 33, 34.
9. Rosalie Cruise Jesse, *Children in Recovery: Healing the Parent-Child Relationship in Alcohol/Addictive Families* (New York: W. W. Norton, 1989), p. 100.
10. Ibid., pp. 104–5.
11. Rosalie Cruise Jesse, "Children of Alcoholics: Their Sibling World," in *Siblings in Therapy,* ed. Michael D. Kahn and Karen Gail Lewis (New York: W. W. Norton, 1988), p. 237.

Chapter Twelve
The Call of Kin: Reconnecting with Siblings

1. Stephen Bank, telephone interview with the author, 19 October 1989.

SELECTED BIBLIOGRAPHY

Bank, Stephen, and Michael Kahn. "Freudian Siblings." *The Psychoanalytic Review* 67, No. 4 (Winter 1980–81): 493–504.

Bank, Stephen, and Michael Kahn. *The Sibling Bond.* New York: Basic Books, 1982.

Bedford, Victoria, and Deborah Gold, eds. "Siblings in Later Life: A Neglected Family Relationship." *American Behavioral Scientist* 33, No. 1 (September/October 1989).

Corr, Charles, and Joan McNeil, eds. *Adolescence and Death.* New York: Springer, 1986.

Courtois, Christine. *Healing the Incest Wound: Adult Survivors in Therapy.* New York: W. W. Norton, 1988.

Donnelly, Katherine. *Recovering From the Loss of a Sibling.* New York: Dodd, Mead & Company, 1988.

Downing, Christine. *Psyche's Sisters.* San Francisco: Harper & Row, 1988.

Dunn, Judy. *Sisters and Brothers: The Developing Child.* Cambridge, Mass.: Harvard University Press, 1985.

Dunn, Judy, and Carol Kendrick. *Siblings: Love, Envy, and Un-*

derstanding. Cambridge, Mass.: Harvard University Press, 1982.

Dunn, Judy, and Robert Plomin. *Separate Lives: Why Siblings Are So Different.* New York: Basic Books, 1990.

Faber, Adele, and Elaine Mazlish. *Siblings Without Rivalry: How to Help Your Children Live Together So You Can Live Too.* New York: Avon Books, 1987.

Falbo, Toni, ed. *The Single-Child Family.* New York: The Guilford Press, 1984.

Finkelhor, D. "Sex Among Siblings," *Archives of Sexual Behavior* 10 (1980): 171–94.

Fishel, Elizabeth. *Sisters.* New York: Bantam Books, 1980.

Fissinger, Laura. "Sisters, Brothers—but Strangers." *Redbook,* July 1988, pp. 76, 77, 145–46.

Friedman, Edwin. *Generation to Generation.* New York: The Guilford Press, 1985.

Furman, Wynol, and Duane Buhrmester. "Children's Perceptions of the Qualities of Sibling Relationships." *Child Development* 56 (1985): 448–61.

Gilligan, Carol. *In a Different Voice.* Cambridge, Mass.: Harvard University Press, 1982.

Gleitman, Henry. *Psychology.* New York: W. W. Norton, 1986.

Goetting, Ann. "The Developmental Tasks of Siblingship over the Life Cycle." *Journal of Marriage and the Family* 48 (November 1986): 703–14.

Gold, Deborah. "Sibling Relationships in Old Age: A Typology." Paper presented at the 39th Annual Scientific Meeting of the Gerontological Society of America, Chicago, 19–23 November 1986.

Guest, Judith. *Ordinary People.* New York: Viking Press, 1976.

Ihinger-Tallman, Marilyn. "Perspectives on Change of Custody among Stepsiblings." Paper presented at the National Council on Family Relations, Dallas, Texas, 4–9 November 1985.

Jalongo, Mary Rench, and Melissa Ann Rench. "Sibling Relationships: A Recurrent Developmental and Literary Theme." *Childhood Education* 61 (May/June 1985): 346–51.

Jesse, Rosalie Cruise. *Children in Recovery: Healing the Parent-Child Relationship in Alcohol/Addictive Families.* New York: W. W. Norton, 1989.

Kahn, Michael, and Karen Gail Lewis. *Siblings in Therapy: Life Span and Clinical Issues.* New York: W. W. Norton, 1988.

Kantrowitz, Barbara, and Karen Springen. "All About Twins: Probing the Mysteries of a Double Life." *Newsweek,* 23 November 1987, pp. 58–69.

Keiffer, Elisabeth. "Making Friends in the Family." *Reader's Digest,* January 1988, pp. 77–80.

Kramer, Jeannette. *Family Interfaces: Transgenerational Patterns.* New York: Brunner/Mazel, 1985.

Lamb, Michael, and Brian Sutton-Smith, eds. *Sibling Relationships: Their Nature and Significance Across the Lifespan.* Hillsdale, N.J.: Lawrence Erlbaum Associates, 1982.

Lang, John. "The Gene Factor: How Heredity Shapes Personality." *U.S. News & World Report,* 13 April 1987, pp. 58–66.

Leder, Jane. *Dead Serious: A Book for Teenagers About Teenage Suicide.* New York: Atheneum, 1987.

Lerner, Harriet Goldhor. "Get Yourself Unstuck From Mom: How to Break the Pattern That Is Ruining Your Life." *Working Mother,* December 1986, pp. 64, 66, 68, 72.

McCall, Robert. "Sibling Rivalry Isn't All Bad." *Parents,* December 1985, pp. 88–91.

McGoldrick, Monica, and Randy Gerson. *Genograms in Family Assessment.* New York: W. W. Norton, 1985.

Pfouts, Jane. "The Sibling Relationship: A Forgotten Dimension." *Social Work,* May 1976, pp. 200–3.

Pollak, Otto, and David Hundermark. "Some Unexplored Aspects of the Sibling Experience." *Adolescence* 19, No. 76 (Winter 1984): 869–74.

Poston, Carol, and Karen Lison. *Reclaiming Our Lives: Hope for Adult Survivors of Incest.* Boston: Little, Brown, 1989.

Powell, Thomas, and Peggy Ogle. *Brothers and Sisters: A Special Part of Exceptional Families.* Baltimore: Paul H. Brookes, 1985.

Rosen, Helen. "Prohibitions Against Mourning in Childhood Sibling Loss." *Omega* 15, No. 4 (1984–1985): 307–19.

Rosenberg, Elinor. "Therapy with Siblings in Reorganizing Families." *International Journal of Family Therapy* 2, No. 3 (Fall 1980): 139–50.

Rosenberg, Elinor, and Fady Hajal. "Stepsibling Relationships in Remarried Familes." *Social Casework: The Journal of Contemporary Social Work* 66, No. 5, May 1985, pp. 287–92.

Rubin, Lillian. *Just Friends: The Role of Friendship in Our Lives.* New York: Harper & Row, 1985.

Russell, Diana. *The Secret Trauma: Incest in the Lives of Girls and Women.* New York: Basic Books, 1986.

Schachter, Frances, and Richard Stone. *Practical Concerns about Siblings: Bridging the Research-Practice Gap.* New York: The Haworth Press, 1987.

Schooler, Carmi. "Birth Order Effects: Not Here, Not Now!" *Psychological Bulletin* 78, No. 8 (September 1972): 161–75.

Segal, Nancy. "The Impact of Twin Loss: The Psychological and Social Consequences Facing Singleton Twins." *Twins,* November/December 1989, pp. 21–28.

Segal, Nancy. "The Silent Bonds of Twinship." *Twins,* September/October 1986, pp. 50–51.

Segal, Nancy. "Cooperation, Competition, and Altruism within Twin Sets: A Reappraisal." *Ethology and Sociobiology* 5 (1984): 163–77.

Sheehy, Gail. *Passages.* New York: Bantam, 1977.

Slung, Michele. *The Only Child Book.* New York: Ballantine, 1989.

Spiro, Melford E. *Children of the Kibbutz: A Study in Child Training and Personality.* New York: Schocken Books, 1965.

Stark, Elizabeth. "Beyond Rivalry." *Psychology Today,* April 1988, pp. 61–63.

Toman, Walter. *Family Constellation: Its Effects on Personality and Social Behavior.* New York: Springer, 1961.

Vollmar, Alice. "Together Again." *Friendly Exchange,* Winter 1984, pp. 28–30.

Wiehe, Vernon. *Sibling Abuse: Hidden Physical, Emotional, and Sexual Trauma.* Lexington, Mass.: Lexington Books, 1990.